INDIA IN THE THIRD MILLENNIUM CE

An Inclusive View

Saibal Gupta

CONCEPT PUBLISHING COMPANY PVT. LTD.
NEW DELHI-110059

ISBN-13 : 978-81-8069-884-2

First Published 2012

Published and Printed by

Concept Since 1974

Concept Publishing Company Pvt. Ltd.
A/15-16, Commercial Block, Mohan Garden
New Delhi-110059 (India)
T: 25351460, 25351794, *F*: 091-11-25357109
E: publishing@conceptpub.com, W: www.conceptpub.com
Editorial Office: H-13, Bali Nagar, New Delhi-110 015, India.

Cataloging in Publication Data--*Courtesy:* D.K. Agencies (P) Ltd. <docinfo@dkagencies.com>

Gupta, Saibal, 1937-
India in the third millennium CE : an inclusive view / Saibal Gupta.
p. cm.
Includes bibliographical references and index.
ISBN 9788180698842

1. India—History. 2. India—Politics and government. 3. World history. I. Title.

DDC 954 23

Preface

'It from Bit' is a famous device motto present in the writings of John Archibald Wheeler, the Professor at Princeton University who occupied Einstein's chair, in fields like Plato's cave analogy, structure of physical reality and Upanishads. He is a Vedic scholar. Vedic mind is inclusive mind that tries to grasp all phenomena of creation and the self in one composite picture just as modern physics does, searching for a Theory of Everything that will explain it all. 'It from Bit' is the macrocosmic world of our senses evolving in many dimensions from the microcosmic world, the process not yet understood, where sense is an important part. It is also relevant in understanding human history and society that has to be inclusive in the final analysis or is it? This book is an attempt at inclusive study through time, past, present and future since they are linked, of macro world of kings and nations formed by the micro world of common people, who are the 'bits', as they have toiled, braved, innovated and achieved or suffered to make their own choices and created societies, the 'it'. What drives them to action or to lethargy and despair that reflect on the land they inhabit and make that land great or weak? There is a great deal of randomness, unpredictability and chance. Creation of macrocosmic world from the quantum world of particles is also probabilistic yet it is in the realm of science study. There is one certainty in human history, that it progresses through individual ingenuity. A Galileo or an Einstein cannot be created by royal decree or by an act of parliament or ordained by any Church. It is the right of choice of the individual, the smallest quantum of society, and it is in his freedom of action in creativity that the success of society depends. Kings and politicians who thought people were blind often regretted. People's choice may appear random from a superficial view but it is not. The best political process of governance devised by man so far is the democratic process to maintain the balance of organisation with individual liberty and, though it is not foolproof, it has demonstrated the wisdom of people.

The generation of Indians that straddled the Independence on 15th August, 1947 and who had the benefit of education, whose families had lived through the struggles of the society before freedom with participation in that struggle, however small or remote, and the daily ignominy of living in colonial rule, could not but develop a passion that is India. Whatever their age might have been on that fateful day of 15th August, 1947, when the entire nation amid terrible suffering rejoiced with tears in their eyes, each one of them, with or without conscious knowledge, had a silent vow in their mind born out of the sufferings and values of society in the preceding decades that we shall make our motherland glorious. They felt free as individuals, wherever they might be and whatever their station in life was. We sometimes forget that the prize of freedom is freedom itself.

Unfortunately that euphoria did not last long enough to transform society to an integrated pledge, to overcome age old fragmentation of the Indian society. Fragmentation increased and became an even starker reality in the growth momentum. The pledge is almost forgotten, freedom of individual and their right of choice remain limited and India as a passion is lost to major segments of people at all levels. Fragmentation by religion, caste, wealth, greed of the able, helplessness of the disabled, surrender to corruption both by the haves and have-nots has made the political environment of the country distorted so that individuality has given place to the urgency of belonging to any or everything that holds sway in any region and politics has become a game of capturing the individual by any means.

That minority of Indians, who had the benefit of higher education, of knowing the working of developed democratic society, aware of the importance of individual freedom chose either to escape the mire of commonality in homeland or accepted tamely the death of the individual for the prizes it held for them. But there were others who did not and many became castaways of the socio-political milieu.

This book is a selection of articles written over time of people and society through past and present, that has left indelible imprint on the Indian today, and looking to the future through events that affect individual justice, be that social, political, economic, religious or caste based, producing fragmentation of the individual. The publication year is written below each article and though differing in dates and events they are a celebration of the Indian identity. Some events and statements have been repeated in more than one article but that is only to make them self contained. They are written with hope that as the new millennium progresses those fragmentations, those limitations of the individual will disappear and India, not only on her own heritage but also heritage of mankind, will be reborn to greatness. They are not written with malice for the signs of that rebirth are the guidelines of development. The author is grateful to the journals of original publication for permission to reprint articles, some restored to their original pre-edited forms.

Acknowledgements

As mentioned in the preface, the chapters in this book were previously published by the author in different publications and have been selected for their relevance to the theme of this book. The original publishers have given kind permission for their reproduction. The author expresses gratitude to them. Some articles, edited by them for constraint of space, have been restored to the original. The year of publication is mentioned below each article. The sources are:

The Statesman, Kolkata published from The Statesman House, Kolkata 700 001;

Prabuddha Bharata published by the Advaita Ashram, Rama Krishna Mission, 5 Dehi Entally Road, Kolkata 700 014;

Translations by the Author from his Bengali book *Amar Shomoy* (*My Times*) published by Mitra & Ghosh Publishers Pvt. Ltd, 10 Shyamacharan De Street, Kolkata 700 073, 1997.

Author's lecture in the *National Seminar* (2005) at the Rama Krishna Mission Institute of Culture, Kolkata 700 029

The author is grateful to Shri Samik Bandyopadhyay for tirelessly editing and correcting the manuscript.

Contents

Preface v

Acknowledgements ix

1. **LIVING HERITAGE** 1
   - Bali 3
   - The Magic of Angkor 13
   - Medicine as Adoration 24
   - Jerusalem: Crossroads of History 31
   - Perception 51

2. **FOUNDATION OF SOCIETY** 67
   - Society and Politics in the Perspective of Biosciences 69
   - Conquests of Indian Philosophy 86
   - Religion and Politics in India's History 99

3. **MAKING OF A NATION** 109
   - Rise and Fall of Indian Civilization through the Millennia: 'A Millennium of Darkness' 111
   - Economic Prosperity does not Guarantee Political Stability 118
   - Role of Media and Value Education in Building Society 123

4. **WORKING OF A DEMOCRACY** 131
   - The Price of Democracy 133
   - Middle Class Woes 137

Crisis of Indian Democracy 140
Loksabha Elections 2009 144

5. **MARXISM IN INDIA AND WEST BENGAL** **151**
Too Little and Too Late 153
'De-Industrialization' of West Bengal 157
Communism or Socialist Democracy? 161

6. **GLOBAL ENVIRONMENT : WEST** **165**
The Boat on the Indus 167
The Desert Shrine of Hinglaj 171
Pakistan Today 2003 176
Israel Revisited 179
A Hundred Years of Troubled Iran 185

7. **GLOBAL ENVIRONMENT : NORTH TIBET** **191**
Journey Through Tibet: Nature's Call on the Roof of the World 193
Who Owns the Sixth Dalai Lama? 199

8. **GLOBAL ENVIRONMENT : EAST** **205**
Bengal and Burma 207
Human Faces in Two Chinas of the Nineties : Beijing and Taipei 213
Chinese Expansionism : Why and How 221

9. **THE ROAD AHEAD** **237**
Economic Wars: New Challenges in Multilayered Societies 239
Pains of Industrialization: 'People's Industry' 242
Globalization and The State in Indian Perspective: Think Global, Act Local 247
Politics of Probabilities 253
Thanks for Saving us from Fatka 258

Epilogue **263**

Index 269

LIVING HERITAGE

Bali

Bali is a small island that one can cover in a car in two or three days. Bali is a miniature world with miniature super highways, miniature cities and villages, miniature mountain ranges, jungles, sea beaches and even its miniature volcano. It is like a children's playground. The real Bali is very different from the western pleasure spot at Nusa Dua with its large hotels, beaches with the usual sports, conference rooms, dance halls and all other paraphernalia of a synthetic culture. Talking to people is easy, sometimes in English, sometimes in sign language and sometimes in snatches of Sanskrit because the Vasa Indonesia had as much of its roots in Sanskrit as Indian languages and older people still speak a dialect that sounds familiar to Indian listeners.

Driving north from Nusa Dua, past the international airport at Denpasar the road winds northwest through small cities with clusters of small cottages with a central temple that contains no deity. The courtyards are open, unlocked and there is no alarm at seeing a foreigner, only a little curiosity and a greeting, 'Om, namoh Shivaya', 'Salutation to Lord Shiva', and a smile. There is a small town called Batubulan with many Batik factories, the rich and exquisite cottage industry of Indonesia. The workers are young women, and when I entered the darkened showroom of a batik factory, it was lunch break and the girls were resting. The batiks were exquisite and very expensive, specially the silk ones. The curious girls came around and asked what I wanted. I confessed that I did not want to buy but wanted to talk to them. The girls burst out laughing, pulled me to a seat and said, 'OK, then let us talk.' They asked me my nationality and then, 'Are you a

Hindu?'—and that did it. They sat down around me as if they had found a long lost relative and asked me to stay for the day. They were young, had finished school, and some of them could speak English fairly well. Making Batik is a delicate artwork and woman's job. These girls worked in two shifts and exuded a culture that bore the unmistakable stamp of traditional discipline. I told them they were very pretty and they rolled in laughter and said, 'Oh, come off, the Indian girls are so pretty.' I asked, 'Have you seen many Indian girls?' They said, 'We have seen them in films.' I asked them whether they were married, and they said, 'No.' One of them looked around at the others with a quizzical smile, and said, 'But all of us have one, what do you call it, a boy friend', and burst out laughing. I gave a sigh of great disappointment calling for another peal of laughter. By now we were all great friends. I asked them how they start their day, when they come to the workshop, how they learnt such fine artwork and finally asked, 'Do you offer any prayer or worship before you start work?' One girl replied, 'Yes, we chant a hymn on getting up in the morning and before starting work and then again in the evening when we finish.' I asked her to recite the hymn for me. To my utter amazement it was the Gayatri mantra, discernible in the Balinese pronunciation with excellent phonetics. I thought I would faint.

For some unknown reason more than a millennium back women and non-Brahmins in India were barred from chanting the Gayatri in India.[1] They were not allowed to study the Vedas and Vedanta. Even today very orthodox Hindu fundamentalists hold on to such views. The days have changed. Now there is no bar but in its place has come apathy, even in learned circles, and the notion that it is only history. Hindus debarred the vast majority of their people from the cream of their philosophies and culture and blamed other religions for their downfall. How come that these girls in Bali were chanting the Gayatri? Is it because they got it before the decline of Hinduism in India, which did not touch them because the contact was lost? I asked them, 'How about others, how about your parents and grandparents, the children, the workers, do they also chant?' They replied, 'Everyone does it. Children in schools do it. We have learnt it from our parents and grandparents.' I was transported to ancient India and could barely utter, 'Do you know that we have been related for thousands of years?' They said, 'Yes, we love you. Do stay with us for a day.' I regretted, 'But I do not have the time. I have to go far to see as much as I can of your beautiful country.' They expressed concern like very near and dear ones that I was driving alone on unknown roads. They implored, 'Please drive carefully. The traffic is very bad. Why did you not take a driver?' They said, 'Please do not forget us'—and they came to the gate to bid me farewell. I was transported to another world, another time as I kept on driving. It was a world I had read about but never believed in. It was still there, here and now, and I promised myself, 'I shall never forget, never. How can I? My past is my future!'

I drove on to the ancient temple of Besakih. On the roadside there were stone tablets, walls with scribbled slokas from the Gita, the Ramayana and the Upanishads. The clusters of small cottages with a central temple that contained no deity took on new significance. In ancient days it is said nobody needed to lock their doors. I reached Besakih and walked up the hill, a steep climb. There were small temples in a large hilltop enclosure in which there were altars, but no deity. There was a notice at the entrance that you should enter only if you want to worship. If you want to just appreciate the scenery, go around. It did not say that you had to be Hindu to enter, for God is the same to all. People were sitting on the grass under the open sky in groups in front of each altar. They had a piece of yellow cloth around them and had their heads covered. I sat in one such group. I was in jeans and shirt with cameras hanging around me, sticking out like a sore thumb but nobody objected and nobody took notice. There was a priest in front of the group but he was not delivering any sermon, not chanting anything. Like the rest of the group he was also quiet. Then he rose and from a pitcher poured clean water into everybody's palm in turn, which they drank. The priest came to me, an altogether incongruous presence, with a smile hovering around the corners of his mouth. He poured clear water from the pitcher into my open palm, which I drank, and then he picked up a few grains of wet rice from a plate and pressed them on my temples. The function was over. The congregation rose in silence and slowly dispersed. I understood nothing but my mind was filled with calmness. I started understanding only when I reached the temple at Mengui.

At Mengui as usual everything was open air with small altars and a small pond, surrounded by a low wall. Here I met a priest who spoke fluent English. I asked, 'Where is the deity?' The man pointed to a block of stone in the middle of the courtyard with some etchings on it. I asked again, 'What God is this?' The man said, 'What do you mean by what God? God is only one.' I asked what those etchings were and the man said, 'Those are the marks of the Trinity—Brahma, Vishnu and Maheshwar, or you can say Paramashiva, Sadashiva and Dhyanashiva.' This I understood; you can see the Trinity as different entities or as three different manifestations of the formless Shiva in the Shaivite school evolving from Kashmir Shaivism, another way of emphasizing the unity of God powerfully prevalent in India around the eighth century CE,[2] especially in central and south India. It can be traced way back to antiquity. The sages in antiquity used only one word to describe all this. The word OM has actually three sounds in it, viz. O U M denoting the Trinity of Creation, Sustenance and Destruction, the three faces of Eternity, the three faces of Divinity. If you went back in time and asked a meditating sage of antiquity what it was all about, he would only pronounce OM without spending more words and wasting time. We had forgotten it a long time back and we are still trying to understand it. But how come these people retained it through the millennia? It was all falling into place in my perception without anybody's teaching and I liked it that way. I could also see why communal harmony was stronger in Indonesia than in India and it could keep communal antagonism in leash till it came to be fomented for political reasons. Were the eighth or ninth century then the last period of contact with Hindu India? It seemed to be corroborated by the ruins of the Prambanan temple at Jogjakarta[3] where the main temple is dedicated to Shiva. One of the surrounding smaller shrines contained a statue in relief on stone of Goddess Durga with eight hands, an icon quite prevalent in India around those times in the south, east and central parts of the country, the seafaring areas.[4] The present image of Durga has ten hands. Two centuries after that, by the beginning of the second millennium CE, for some unknown reasons, unknown people clamped down on sea voyages, warning that anybody leaving the shores of India would be marked an outcaste, a code maintained right up to the nineteenth century.

Another interesting episode occurred at Jogjakarta when I went to visit the Buddhist shrine at Borobudur. My guide was a pleasant and erudite Muslim, who had the most improbable nickname of Johnny. It was clear from his conversations that he was very devout and very patriotic. While climbing up the Borobudur hills tier after tier he described all the events of Buddha's life depicted on stone. The carvings became smaller as one approached the top, circumambulating the monument while ascending to the top through the three levels of Buddhist cosmology, namely Kamadhatu (the world of desire), Rupadhatu (the world of forms) and Arupadhatu (the world of formlessness) until at the top there are only Buddha statues in meditation inside lotus bud structures.[5] As my guide explained, it symbolized that as one went higher and higher and approached Nirvana all those facts and ornamentations became irrelevant. But at the top we found a boy and a girl engaged in a love game and openly flirting. The guide became very upset and angry at this act of sacrilege and started scolding them. This incident has stayed in my mind and the guide was quite surprised to receive a hefty tip at the end of the tour.

But the guide did not compromise at Prambanan. This was a restored Hindu temple that contained statues of Hindu gods and goddesses, which were probably not original but replicas put in by the UNESCO during restoration. In any case there was no worship. But it was difficult for Johnny to go inside as a devout Muslim. Probably he would have had no compunction if it were a 'Nirakar' temple dedicated to a formless God as in Besakih. So he asked me to go alone and I understood and respected it. I thought men were like children. They fought bloody wars over symbols—a cross, the crescent of a new moon, a four, eight or ten armed deity—while the Almighty waited patiently for them to grow up some day.

On the last day of my trip, I was driving south in Bali, heading for a place called Tanah Lot. It was a seaside resort built around an old temple on the seashore. The temple stood on a rocky outcrop about a hundred yards from the mainland connected by a bridge of rocky land that remained submerged in high tide. The temple was accessible only in low tide. The temple was dilapidated and was dedicated to Lord Shiva, as most old things in Bali were. It was considered a holy place and also a tourist attraction with several nice restaurants set in the local ambience. I got a little late on the way from taking a wrong turn and reached after dark with a lot of traffic returning. When I reached the large car parking area it was almost empty and the shops were downing their shutters. The restaurants were packed with people, the late diners. I walked down the steps to the edge of water on the land bridge. It was high tide now. The bridge was under water and breakers were coming rushing on the shore. The small temple was silhouetted against the mildly lit horizon. A medium sized tree rose through it. It looked very beautiful. The place was empty. I found an illuminated concrete terrace on the right and on the seaside end of the terrace there was a high concrete platform sustaining a tall pillar in black stone with some etchings on it. A white cloth, loosely wound around the pillar from the top to the bottom, billowed in the breeze. The whole thing looked like a totem pole. I climbed on to the terrace. It was deserted. Another man also sauntered in. He was obviously a local in white T-shirt and trousers and wearing a most improbable white golf cap with red borders. Two ladies sat in the shadows on the parapet on the other side of the terrace.

The man came to me and we greeted each other and started talking. I took an instant liking to him for no apparent reason. He spoke broken English lacing it with Balinese and Sanskrit words. The conversation actually went surprisingly well. The man asked me whether I was an Indian and a Hindu and beyond that did not ask any other personal question. He was more voluble and forthcoming about himself. He said he was a spiritual person. When asked what that meant, he said that he went wherever people were in distress and when called upon to do so. He would go, spend time with them, talk to them and meditate and generally share their sorrow. I asked whether that was his livelihood. He said, 'No. I have a small plot of land up in the north about a hundred kilometers from here. I cultivate it for livelihood. But of course people give me presents when I help them and I gratefully accept. Take for example this dress. It was given to me at the place from where I am coming.' He pointed to his very improbable golfing outfit. 'I went to Java and have just landed from the boat on my way home. One of the ladies sitting over there is my wife. The other lady has recently lost her husband. So I went to her house in Java. She is still suffering, so I have brought her with us. She will spend a few days with us and then go back when she feels better. There is no money involved in this. God has provided enough for me.' He waved generally around him and folded his hands in deference. I felt a little ashamed.

I pointed to the old temple silhouetted against the sky: 'How old is that?' 'Oh, that is probably eight or nine hundred years old but this one'—and he pointed to the stone pillar—'is very recent as you can see.' He said it in a way that meant that age was not important. Age did not necessarily impart truth or grandeur; the important thing was whether it was living and true. I asked what the pillar meant. He said the same thing as the priest at Mengui. It is the trinity fused into one as different aspects of a unitary God or Brahman. 'It all came from you. So you should know. You have really come in search of this, have you not?' I was puzzled. Was it really that? Was I searching for something without knowing what it was? My heart was filled with tranquility and a feeling of purity. I remembered that the people of Bali greeted each other with 'Om, namoh Shivaya' or 'Swastu Asti', meaning respectively 'salutation to Lord Shiva' and 'Peace be with you'. These are two immaculate Sanskrit words of greeting from antiquity. We have lost them a long time back. The girls of Batubulan and the woman in the courtyard residence had greeted me with those words and now this holy man. I also greeted him likewise, being knowledgeable by now.

Meanwhile the man was going on talking, not about scriptures or learned discourses, but ordinary everyday conversation about roads, weather, farming and so on. I became conscious of his conversation when he said, 'Please come with us to our house.' There was real affection and invitation in his voice. I brought out a map and asked where his house was. He pointed to an area close to the sleeping volcano. It was about a hundred miles away. I had to catch the flight early morning and it was a few hours' drive from my hotel. There was no way I could go to the man's house. I told him so. But the man kept on insisting, 'I have a lot to talk to you about, a lot to discuss, a lot to learn. I shall personally escort you wherever you want very early in the morning.' He held my hand and said, 'You do not understand. This meeting of ours is not accidental, not by chance. It has been preordained and prearranged a long time back that you and I shall meet. We have a lot to talk about.' The man's sincerity was not false. I said I genuinely wanted to go, but there was no way. The man was really upset as if the chance of a lifetime was passing by and kept repeating his request. I was surprised but could not fathom his eagerness. When he was convinced that I could not go, he said, 'Well, if you cannot go, let us at least pray together in front of Him', and he pointed to the stone pillar.

Arm in arm we advanced to the altar on which the formless eternity was placed, two individuals separated by thousands of miles of sea, two brothers separated a thousand or two thousand years back, and the teacher was now the student. Everything else will vanish in this world but the Word will remain as one sage had said. The Word will come back again and again and again, from different areas, from everywhere, in different forms. I did not know how to pray or what to pray for. I have never prayed, my only quest has been knowledge. I was now faced with something stupendous. What would I say to Him, praise Him, flatter Him, beg of Him? There was nothing to do except to lay my mind bare to Him, naked. Come and reside here. My partner did not know what the man unknown to him, with whom he was arm in arm, was saying. We stayed like that with bowed heads, hands joined in *pranam*. We straightened after some time. The man held both my hands and looked straight into my eyes, silent. There was a glow in his eyes, his face serene. He was only saying, 'Thank you, thank you' repeatedly. What was he thanking me for?

It seemed that he wanted me to say something. I was silent for most of this encounter, even puzzled. As I looked at the man, beyond him at the symbol of the fused Trinity of Creation, Sustenance and Destruction, at the roaring dark waters of the Pacific Ocean silhouetting the temple of Shiva, infinity, thousands of miles from my home, thousands of years from my roots, something snapped inside me. I freed my right hand and lifted a clenched fist at the sky and recited in Sanskrit the famous verse from the Shwetashwatara Upanishad: 'Hark ye, the sons of the Immortal, I have known Him, the great Being who stands dazzling beyond the darkness; only by knowing Him you can surpass death; there is no other way.' I could actually see the Rishi of the Upanishad standing at the southern tip of India[6] in the same place where thousands of years later sat Swami Vivekananda in meditation, with his beseeching hands spread towards the seas calling on the people of the world. I did not know whether the man understood what I was saying but his face was glowing. He seemed to understand it all, even know it. He again said, 'Thank you', and then went away. We separated and went our different ways without even saying goodbye, as if there was no separation. I did not know his name, his address, he did not ask mine.

1996

References

1. Basham, A L, *The Wonder that was India.* Calcutta/New Delhi: Rupa, 1954.
2. Ibid. Also cf. Ramanujan, A K, *Speaking of Siva.* Reading: Cox and Wyman, 1973.
3. Bernet Kempers, A J, *Ancient Indonesian Art.* Cambridge, Mass: Harvard

University Press, 1959.

4. Basham, op. cit. Also cf. Nihar Ranjan Roy, on *Periplus of Erythrean Sea*, in *Bangalir Itihas* ['History of the Bengali People']. Kolkata: Dey's Publishing, 1949.
5. Bernet Kempers, op. cit.
6. Chatterjee, S C and Datta, D M, *An Introduction to Indian Philosophy*. Kolkata: University of Calcutta Press, 1939.

The Magic of Angkor

It was another time, it was another India. Ocean-going ships then launched from the eastern coasts of India to explore the distant lands of Southeast Asia laden with merchandise, young men seeking fortune, priests and scholars and also soldiers to protect the ships, braving the unstable weather of the region. It started from antiquity going back as far as history can reach. The writings of Periplus, Ptolemy, Plutarch, Pliny, Strabo indicate the presence of a large empire in the eastern part of Bengal by the fourth century BCE known as Gangaridai (Gangarhidi) with its capital at Gange or Gangabandar, which was a large port on the Bay of Bengal at the mouth of the Kumar river.[1] To the west of Gangaridai was the empire of Prasioi (Prachya) situated on the western side of the first downward flow of the Ganga after she comes out of the Rajmahal hills with a seaport at Tamralipta, which still exists as a small town. These two kingdoms were often under one king. But modern scholars seem to agree that the term Gangaridai (Land of the Ganga/People of the city of Gange) was used only by the Greek/Roman/Egyptians to refer to the kingdom of Vanga or Bengal. The valour of the people of Gangaridai has been immortalized by Virgil ('On the doors will I represent in gold and ivory the battle of the Gangaridae and the arms of our victorious Quirinius'—Virgil, *Georgics* (III. 27). The Chinese silk trade, before the discovery of the direct sea route with Southeast Asia and China and the overland route through Central Asia, passed through Northeast

India and through Bengal. The ships from Bengal took the merchandise along the coastal route around the Kanyakumari and brought them to the traders on the west coast, who took them across the Arabian Sea[2] along the coast of Sind and Baluchistan to the mouth of the Persian Gulf. From there it used to go all over Middle East as far as the present Israel, the kingdom of Solomon, and to the Phoenician traders of the Mediterranean. The Indian traders later discovered the direct route across the Arabian Sea to the mouth of the Red Sea and shared this route with the Arabs for centuries.

Similar explorations went to the eastern seas[3] and the mainly coastal trade graduated to ocean-going vessels going to Siam, Malay Peninsula, and Sumatra and then through the Malacca Straits to Java, Bali, Cambodia and Vietnam up to South China. During the Roman Empire the trade in spices from Southeast Asia, silk from China, fine cotton fabric, red pepper and pippali from Bengal,[4] was so prolific that the Roman Drachma became a legal tender in Bengal and still survives in her language as a Bengali asks, 'koto dām?'—how much dām—to ask for what something costs.

After the tenth and eleventh centuries CE the entire sea trade closed down both on the east and the west; the last illustrious passenger to return to Bengal from Sumatra was the Buddhist monk Atisha Dipankar Srijnan in 1027 CE. On the eastern side for unknown reasons a religious injunction came into force banning voyages across the seas and anyone crossing the *kālāpāni,* as the sea came to be called, would lose his caste status.[5] It was so effective that the entire eastern sea trade closed down. It is difficult to know how much this injunction was effective in the south and the west but they also closed down. In the west the traders depended more and more on the Arabs to send their goods and saved the expense of a maritime fleet.[6] In the south the collapse of the Chola and Rashtrakuta empires probably contributed as no big power followed them. All this had deep and lasting effects on the history and culture of India. Today one has to travel to the outposts of Indian civilization to taste the grandeur of the India that was. Their communication with the mainland ceased at various times allowing them to evolve on their own, keeping alive their traditions, culture and way of life unaffected by the changes in their motherland until they also disintegrated or were forgotten. Europeans rediscovered them in modern times. These relics appear like preserved museum pieces of Indian philosophies and cultures of bygone days. The ruin of Angkor is such a museum. For the author it was a pilgrimage.

THE JOURNEY

Cambodia, the land of the Khmers, known as Cambodge in French, Kambuj in old Khmer and Kamboj to us, was renamed as Kampuchea in 1989 and has its capital at Phnom Penh. From the ninth to the fifteenth centuries, the core of the Khmer empire was in the vicinity of Angkor. Ruins of Angkor lie in the province of Siem Reap with its provincial capital at the city of Siem Reap, situated 320 kilometers to the north of Phnom Penh.[7] The area was ravaged in the past decades by civil war and the atrocities and genocide of the Khmer Rouge from which it has not fully recovered. Even today the tourist is warned not to leave the paved road and loiter in the jungle for the risk of landmines. Siem Reap is a small city with an international airport that brings throngs of tourists from all over the world. But there is no direct flight from India. The usual route is to change flight at Bangkok and obtain a visa at Bangkok or on arrival. The local inhabitants rue the fact that there are very few Indian tourists. To them we are rich and better people. One sees big banners across main roads warning tourists that molestation of their children will be punished by imprisonment in the tourists' own countries. This is a warning from the UN to protect the poor population ravaged by the flesh trade in both boys and girls that continues with a high incidence of HIV AIDS.

Coming out of the airport one sees a small sparsely populated city with few main roads and red dusty fields. Apart from a few high-rise new hotels and some shops the rest of the town consists of small houses that are mostly single or two floor wooden houses. The big hotels are expensive but there is a large number of small or medium hotels that are not bad and give good service. These can be booked through Internet and are clean and really cheap. I got a room in one such hotel in a newly built corner of the city and liked it. The hospitality of the people of Southeast Asia is well known and the Cambodians are no exception. I hired a car with a guide for three days at an unbelievably cheap rate. One can get group tour buses but these are mainly European or American groups. I always love to travel alone taking my own time so that my mind can work without being cluttered by unnecessary conversation, allowing me to interact with the local people and come to know the country better. It combines travel with living within my mind. I got an intelligent young man as guide bubbling with stories about each and every site. Whenever necessary he guided me to the safe restaurants, which were large open sheds in the shade of big trees serving tasty and hygienic food. The time was mid-February and it was cool in the shade but very hot in the scorching sun outside. How it will be in summer could be imagined. This was how my pilgrimage started.

BRIEF HISTORY OF THE REGION

The political history of Cambodia and Southeast Asia starts at the beginning of the Christian era and the period from the first to the eighth centuries is known as the proto-historic period. The period before that, the prehistoric period, has yielded scarce data. The presence of cave-dwelling Stone Age people has been registered as early as 6000 BCE in one area. The farming people who domesticated cattle and were organized in small villages appeared after 500 BCE.[8]

The history of this area began in the first century CE when Indian ships appeared, followed some two hundred years later by the Chinese. The earliest site of Oc-Eo in the Mekong Delta from the second century CE has yielded Indian jewellery, Roman coins and Buddhist religious artifacts; the combination indicating the eastern seaboard of India as the source. Indian trade with China through Northeast India to the Bay of Bengal was suffering at this time from the attack of nomadic tribes on the frontier and improved shipbuilding and navigational knowledge pushed Indian ships further eastwards towards China followed closely by the Chinese pushing eastwards. The earliest Chinese records from the third century CE shows the presence of the state of Funan occupying South Cambodia and South Vietnam, which was Indian in culture, Brahminical in religion, with a language from the Mon-Khmer family of languages. The Chinese considered Southeast Asia a land of barbarians and were not interested in settlements. The Chinese from the earliest times were explorers and record keepers of history. The Indians cared little for history and little about exploration except in the line of trade; but brought their socio-religious culture that bonded the small coastal maritime settlements into ports and then into cities followed by states. The Chinese texts and the Sanskrit and Khmer inscriptions describe a mythical origin of Funan from the marriage of an Indian prince of the Chola dynasty or an Indian Brahmin to the daughter of the *naga* king who inhabited the waters and ruled over the soil. Similarly in another inscription from the third century the origin of Champa, a kingdom in Central Vietnam, is traced to the marriage of a prince named Kaudinya who travelled to the land and married Princess Soma, daughter of the *naga* king.[9] The history of this region during this period reads like chapters of Indian history with names of kings and kingdoms like the Champa, the Dvaravati in Thailand, the Pyu in Burma, the Srivijaya and Sailendra in Indonesia fighting with each other. Whether all or even most of these kings were of pure Indian origin is doubtful, as it was common even among known usurpers to take Indian or Sanskrit names to become honourable. The culture was Indian with a mixture of the Vedas, the Upanishads, the Puranas, the Mahabharata and the Ramayana followed by the Mahayana and Theravada Buddhism and all of it mixed with the naturalistic animistic culture of the tribal days. One or other aspect of this mixture predominated, depending on the taste of the king and probably other social or economic factors. Most scholars call this cultural process Indianization rather than Indian colonialism. During the Angkor period from the ninth to the fifteenth centuries all the kings had

Varman as their title and that has continued to the present King of Cambodia who has omitted the word from his used name; but it remains part of his full official name. Angkor is unique in that it has preserved a historic record of this amalgam of cultures along with the political and social history in monument after monument and in extensive galleries of bas-relief carvings with very little destruction in each succeeding epoch that is unparalleled in India or the rest of the world.

TOPOGRAPHY OF ANGKOR

Angkor is situated in a large basin formed by the *Kulen Hills* in the north and the *Tonle Sap Lake* in the south. This plateau is drained by tributaries of the Siem Reap River and intercepted by three hills – *Phnom Bok*, *Phnom Bakheng* and *Phnom Krom*. These hills, sites of the early capitals of Jayavarman II (802-850), Indravarman I (*Hariharalaya at Roluos*, 877-889) and Yasovarman I (889-910), are pure Hindu sites dedicated to Shiva. The total area of Angkor covers 5000 square kilometers.

The *Tonle Sap* is the largest permanent freshwater lake in Southeast Asia. The Tonle Sap River flows from the lake to the Mekong River and Phnom Penh is situated at this confluence. The monsoon rains raise the water level of the lake, and the tides in the Mekong River keep the Tonle Sap River flowing downwards round the year, providing the external waterway for Angkor. It is the main resource for fishing and agriculture in the area. A large population lives in the lake in floating houses fixed to the bottom of the lake with floating vegetable gardens, fisheries inside reed barricades, schools, post office, dispensary, police station, restaurants, one church, wireless stations and mobile markets on boats. A large number of these lake people today are Vietnamese. Most of the important monuments of Angkor and the royal palaces and capital city of Angkor Thom are however situated on the plateau.

Water has always been the most vital resource for the survival of a city. Angkor is an exemplar of efficient water management by rainwater harvesting to supplement the supply from the Siem Reap River, which is rather far, and the Tonle Sap Lake. Vast areas of ground were enclosed by earthen dams called *baray* all around to contain rainwater. The largest one of these measures 8000 by 2100 meters. There are four such *barays* and powerful kings constructed them. In the centre of each *baray* there is an artificial hill on which beautiful ornate temples were constructed approachable by boats in those times. Today most of them are dry with the dams all crumbled except the Indratataka *baray* (built 893 CE) at *Roluos*, where seaplanes used to land during the Cambodian war. There are rainwater reservoirs inside the Angkor Wat.

THE MONUMENTS

It is impossible to describe all the ruins of Angkor in one article. I therefore choose to limit myself to the temple city of Angkor Wat and the capital city of Angkor Thom along with temples of Preah Khan, Ta Prohm and Banteay Srei. Western books describe the derivation of the word Angkor from the Sanskrit *nagara.* This appears fallacious because Angkor Thom is described in our literature as Omkar Dham. Wat means temple and therefore Angkor Wat is Omkar Mandir.

The rationale lies in history. Angkor was established as capital by King Yasovarman I (889-910) and was named Yasodharapura. Angkor was a later name. King Suryavarman II (1113-1150) built the *Angkor Wat* temple but he died before the temple was finished. It was known as Paramavishnuloka[10] and had a large image of Lord Vishnu in the central tower. At Vishnu's feet was embedded a gold urn that contained the ashes of the king. The temple was designed by a Brahmin named Divakarapandita who was reputed to have spiritual powers and was probably the king's guru. Vishnu was removed and replaced by Buddha during the reign of the next significant king Jayavarman VII (1181-1220) who embraced Mahayana Buddhism. In between the two reigns Angkor was defeated and ravaged by the Chams from Vietnam. The Buddhists did not destroy the extensive bas-reliefs on tales from the

Mahabharata, the Ramayana, the Puranas and the king's campaigns, but added a gallery of the Buddha.

The temple became a Buddhist monastery that outlived the empire at Angkor. The Buddha in the central tower is no more and many Buddha statues in the gallery were defaced probably during a short period of Hindu resurgence or more probably by vandals. A large Vishnu statue, which might or might not have been the original one in the central tower, stands in a colonnade on the right side of the *gopura* at the entrance and is still worshipped. A later image of Buddha is also worshipped in the temple. The Vishnu image that is worshipped today was once decapitated but the head was found and reattached and the locals worship it. Western chronicles say that it is a Buddha head on a Vishnu body, but the locals do not think so. The layout of each area of the Angkor Wat was according to the measurements of Hindu architectural and astronomical charts. The temple faces west, something unusual in a Hindu temple. Some westerners offer the explanation that it is actually a mausoleum and faces the setting sun. But a more plausible explanation is that it faces India, the Vishnuloka.[11]

Angkor Wat is an immense monument occupying a rectangular area of 500 acres defined by a laterite enclosure wall, which is surrounded by a moat 200 metres wide and filled with water. The perimeter of the enclosure wall measures 5·5 kilometers. A huge causeway built with sandstone blocks, each measuring 250 metres long and 12 metres wide crosses the moat. The balustrade on the causeway is the body of the snake god Basuki with its multiple heads raised at all the entrances. Even the roofs of the vestibules all around are the coiled body of Basuki. After crossing the causeway over the moat the entrance is through a short flight of stairs to a raised platform, which continues in the form of a cross all the way to the main temple complex with three towers, the Meru Mountains, abode of the gods. The proportion is huge and beautiful. Midway on this inner causeway on two sides are two beautiful ruined buildings that housed the libraries.

Angkor Thom is the capital inner city with palaces from different periods and is encircled by a wall and a moat. There are four gates to enter the city. Over each gateway is a head with four faces pointed in four directions that smile benevolently at the onlooker. This is the head of Avalokiteswara. Inside the large city there are many palaces built by individual kings. There is a large central plaza with a rampart on one side where the king and his retinue sat and watched marching troops or festivals. Jayavarman VII rebuilt the city on the preexistent Yasodharapura and built the rampart, known as the elephant wall because of the rows of elephants on its frontal bas-relief, conquered many countries and ruled over a kingdom extending from Vietnam to Thailand and lower Burma to the borders of the Pagan or Bagan Kingdom of Burma. He built a highway from Phimai in Burma to Angkor.[12]

About 30 minutes' drive from Siem Reap is the beautiful ornate temple of *Banteay Srei* or the 'citadel of women' built in the second half of the tenth century by Rajendravarman II and Jayavarman V. It is an exquisitely ornate temple with a surrounding moat dedicated to Shiva. It has delicately carved panels depicting tales from the Puranas.

Jayavarman VII brought Buddhism but wanted to integrate Hinduism and Buddhism. The elephant wall of Angkor Thom has a bas-relief that shows Buddha sitting on Garuda. Across the plaza there are ruins of twelve small temples that are being rebuilt as Buddha temples but the number and shape indicate that they might have been Shiva temples. At *Preah Khan* he built a temple that has both Buddha and Shiva figures facing each other across a central colonnade. Curiously some Shivalinga bases in the chapels have holes for three lingams, though the lingams have vanished a long time back. Why three shivalingas together, one European tourist asked me. It reminded me of Bali, where Shiva forms a formless trinity in one – the Paramashiva, Sadashiva and Dhyanashiva. It corresponds to the Shaivite schools of India that were strong in the eighth and the ninth centuries. In Bali it is still alive in the temples of Besakih, Mengui and the modern one at Tanah Lot. Interestingly, Jayavarman VII rejected Vishnu, but found Shiva compatible with Buddha, and in Indonesia, a formless Shiva happily coexists with Islam. He probably found

Avalokiteswara and Brahma, the god of sustenance, similar.[13] as both may have four heads. He built a temple to Brahman at *Ta Prohm* that literally means 'Ancestor Brahman'. Thick tree trunks holding and intermingling with stone preserve this temple. It has both Shaivite and Buddhist areas and a dancing hall where Apsaras danced. Indian archaeologists are engaged in preserving this monument after the visit of Prime Minister Vajpayee. Throughout history integration of religions has produced its own enemy, people wanting strife for selfish reasons, and those times were no different. But harmony seemed to have held in Angkor at least till the early fourteenth century when Indravarman III (1295-1307), a follower of Theravada Buddhism, ruled. After that there was a gradual decline. Angkor remained the capital till 1432 though attacked repeatedly. The Khmers gradually shifted towards Phnom Penh leaving Angkor. Mother Nature occupied Angkor and guarded her with giant trees and a dense jungle preserving her unique civilization for posterity.

After three days of continuous walking my legs are aching. I sit in a teashop in the central plaza of Angkor Thom across from the elephant wall. The shopkeeper offers a large glass of very dark tea with lemon and local sugar. It is very sweet but refreshing. The afternoon sun slants into the shop. The shopkeeper's pretty thirteen-year-old daughter comes and sits near me and like all teenagers laughs for no reason, bubbling with curiosity. She asks me where I come from. I look around at the scenery and reply 'from here'. She doubles up with rippling laughter. I ask her name. She replies, 'Sita'. I say, 'My name is Rama. Will you marry me?'—again a peal of laughter. Her mother, busy sorting vegetables, admonishes her across the shop and the adoring father sitting across the table smiles and looks on—a scene from eternity. She asks, 'Will you buy some souvenirs from me?' I reply, 'I can buy you as a souvenir. How much do you cost?' There is laughter all around and the girl runs away to her friends and there is a lot of laughter there. They come and encircle me and I stroke their heads. My mind floats away. I did not conquer this land but it is mine. I won it by love and by sharing. I have given them my heritage and they cherish it and they tell me, 'Rama is ours'. Maybe today Rama is more theirs than mine. I forgot this greatness of mine and became smaller and poorer. I have to win it back for my own survival and growth. I cannot afford to forget my little Sita.

2006

References

1. Roy, Nihar Ranjan, *Bangalir Itihas* ['History of the Bengali People']. Kolkata: Dey's Publishing, 1949.
2. Chatterji, S K, *India and Ethiopia : From the Seventh Century* BC. Kolkata: Asiatic Society, 1968.
3. Roy, op. cit.
4. Barrow, J D, *Theories of Everything*. London: Vintage, 1990.
5. Basham, A L. *The Wonder that was India*. Delhi: Rupa, 1954.
6. Chatterji, op. cit.
7. Rooney, D F, *Angkor*. Hong Kong: Odyssey Publications Ltd., 1994.
8. Ibid.
9. Roy, op. cit.
10. Freeman, Michael and Claude Jacques, *Ancient Angkor*. 1999.
11. Ibid.
12. Ibid.
13. Ramanujan, A K, *Speaking of Siva*. Reading: Cox and Wymans Ltd., 1973.

Medicine as Adoration

'When you have finished your studies, if you want to have a successful life and go to heaven when you die, you must pray every day, when you get up and go to sleep, for the welfare of all beings. Dedicate yourself entirely to helping the sick, even though this be at the cost of your own life. Never harm the sick, not even in thought. Endeavour always to perfect your knowledge. Treat no women except in the presence of their husbands. The physician should observe all the rules of good dress and good conduct. As soon as he is with a patient, he should concern himself in word and thought with nothing but the sufferer's case. He must not speak outside the house of anything that takes place in the patient's house. He must not speak to a patient of his possible death if by so doing he hurts the patient or anyone else. In the sight of the gods you are to pledge yourself to this. May the gods help you if you follow this rule. Otherwise, may the gods be against you.' This is the exhortation of Caraka (Caraka, iii.8.7) with some slight variation in Sushruta (Sushruta, i.10.3).[1] There are minor variations in translation from different sources. It predates the Hippocratic Oath by at least one hundred years and probably more. The Latin version of Hessler (1844) dates Sushruta from 'the heroic age of India the beginning of which is not known but the end of which is marked by the 1000 year BD.'[2]

By conservative estimates Sushruta in written form preceded Buddha by one hundred years. But a single man could not have brought this huge knowledge, from cosmology to embryology, to anatomy and physiology and thence to medicine and surgery, in one lifetime. The compilation at the time of Buddha was therefore the result of several preceding centuries of work. The Rigveda contains a description of amputation followed by replacement by an iron leg. Ayurveda originated around 1000 BCE. There are evidences of the existence of a *Vriddha Sushruta*[3] who predates the present *Sushruta Samhita* in the days of Sushruta Tantra but nothing of that text has survived. Precepts of Ayurveda and Susruta were translated in the known civilized world of Greece, Egypt, Mesopotamia and China. During the Achaemenid Empire in Persia in sixth century BCE there was a regular exchange of knowledge among learned men from different parts of the world.[4] As late as the eleventh century CE *Sushruta Samhita* was translated into Persian and Arabic. The Hammurabi Code of Babylon is concerned almost exclusively with the remuneration and punishment of doctors. The Hippocratic Oath supplements the principles of Sushruta, with an ethics for the remuneration of a physician. Obviously remuneration was not a problem with Sushruta. Knowledge was not an individual's property in ancient India where service was paramount, not its price. This is derived directly from the philosophy of Ayurveda and Sushruta's cosmology that is Vedic in origin with which the book starts. It is well known that Indian philosophies, as opposed to the Semitic theology and religions, are based on a world view of a formless, omnipotent, omnipresent and omniscient consciousness as the cosmic energy behind creation, defining man's position in the universe. 'According to these philosophical concepts, all bodies—material, living, conscious or unconscious—are evolved out of *prakrti* by the subtle influence of *purusa*, the Absolute, or the Primal Self-conscious Principle. The living human body is but a manifestation of these factors, and every component of the human organism, including his mind and sense faculties, is created out of the *tattvas* as evolved out of the prakrti.' The divinity attains its highest manifestation in man. That divinity is therefore intrinsic to everything and every human being, not extrinsic.

This concept is behind the exhortation of Sushruta, that service to man is service to God. 'Above all, the aim of Ayurveda is the attainment of the ultimate truth or salvation by which the human mind realizes the identity of the individual soul with the Universal Soul and can thus rise above unhappiness, pain and mortal destruction.'

The basic concepts of this philosophy have been corroborated by modern science in many areas. But it is necessary to examine what such a life philosophy achieved. Fortunately records exist in medical science of its achievements. The records of achievement in many other areas, such as, mathematics, science, technology, metallurgy etc. are either incomplete or absent because of our reticence to record achievements which could amount to bragging. It is enough to consider only the *Sushruta Samhita.* The work consists of one hundred and twenty chapters compiled in five volumes followed by a sixth volume, known as *Uttaratantra* compiled by Nagarjuna in the third or fourth century BE. Subsequent additions have been made till the eleventh century CE by scholars like Jejjada Acharya, Gayadasa, Bhaskara, Madhava, Brahmadeva, Dallana and Chakrapani Dutta.[5] There are descriptions of seven hundred medicines, three thousand surgical instruments and thousands of disease processes with their symptomatology and treatment—both medical and surgical. Sushruta said, 'Only the union of medicine and surgery constitutes the complete doctor. The doctor who lacks knowledge of one of those branches is like a bird with only one wing.' The entire process of a surgical operation has been divided into three phases—*Purvakarma, Pradhānakarma* and *Paschātkarma*, which correspond to the Preoperative, Operative and Postoperative care of our times.

In *Purvakarma,* apart from preparation of the patient, the preparation of the operation theatre is described; it describes how the room has to be cleaned, with what materials, and then has to be fumigated with the smoke from certain medicinal herbs. The particular area of the patient's body has to be cleaned with certain antiseptic lotions. The patient has to be given a small amount of food before certain operations, such as, on the head, neck and limbs but kept fasting for operations on the abdomen and intestines. The surgeon should once again examine the patient and his records immediately before operation and then clean himself and his hands and prepare himself mentally. With this sort of discipline and application, miraculous advancements were achieved. There are descriptions of almost every type of operation on the body except on the chest. Plastic surgery was used for reconstruction of the nose and ear. Such meticulous operations could not have been done without some form of general anaesthesia. The book *Bhoja-Prabandha* by Pandita Ballala describes an operation on the King of *Bhoj* where a tumour of the brain was removed through a trephine, a hole in the skull. In the description of the operation a drug known as *Sammohini* was used to make him insensible, and after the operation another drug *Sanjivani* was used to bring back his consciousness. The knowledge of such drugs has been lost in antiquity. The meticulous aseptic and antiseptic principles of surgery, described by Sushruta, were discovered in Europe only in the late nineteenth century by Lord Lister. Even the wearing of clean clothes by the surgeon was made mandatory in Europe only in the nineteenth century. Before that the surgeons used to wear the same dirty gown throughout their lives as a sign of their seniority and experience. Mortality even after the simplest operation was naturally high. There was nothing much to choose between Indian and European medicine even in the nineteenth century.

But whereas they continued to progress we remained static from the eleventh century. The idea of serving God through service to man achieved spectacular results over two millennia. Emperor Asoka in his Girnar edict stated that he had created hospitals for both men and animals.[6] A century later, King Duttha Gamani, the Buddhist king of Ceylon, listed among his good deeds the founding of eighteen hospitals for the poor. There was no casteism as far as the practice of medicine was concerned. People from any caste could be a student once he had convinced the teacher of his moral standing and basic learning. Sushruta has detailed curricula for the training of a surgeon, some of which are relevant even today.

In a commentary on Sushruta in a recent book it has been said, 'It is noteworthy that Indian religion and mysticism would permit a system of secular medicine which engaged in sound, rational practice even though not completely free of magical and religious association.' It is tragic that the West has always termed our religion and philosophy as mystical, not understanding their basic practical rationality. The whole underlying philosophy of medicine is neither mystic nor impractical. All activities for the betterment of mankind are a form of adoration of God. Medicine thus has a religious element about it since it brings direct benefit both to the healer and the healed if practised in the spirit of service. This is fundamental to Indian religions, and its realization not only in theory but deep down in one's consciousness and psyche is akin to the realization of God. It is surprising how easily man forgets that and pushes it into the domain of mysticism. It is surprising how easily mankind forgets that their greatest discoveries have been made in the service of humanity. Ancient Indian knowledge developed within this philosophy.

Is the ideal of serving God through service to mankind and thereby realizing God only a mystical Indian theology or is a practical step for the development of humanity itself and really the mother of all religions? Let us examine it from the history of the development of Western medicine.[7] Development of medicine in Europe stagnated after Galen in the second century CE. With all his erudition, Galen brought mysticism into medicine to garner the support of the then Christian Church that snuffed out all quest for knowledge in the subsequent middle and dark ages of Europe. Anything beyond Galen was heresy. Anything that was not in Galen was considered heretic. The Renaissance in Europe freed development in medicine as in other branches of science. What were the influences that brought in the Renaissance in Europe has been the subject of much discussion. But undoubtedly the humanistic rationalism of Greece and the Neoplatonic ideals in Greece, the Middle East and Alexandria were major influences.

At the time of Galileo and Giordano Bruno there was also Andreas

Vesalius in medicine. The King of Spain saved him from the Inquisition. He was convicted for saying that men had exactly the same number of ribs as women and not one less as claimed by the Book of Genesis. Progress continued slowly at first as the humanistic ideals took hold, culminating in fundamental progress in the nineteenth and early twentieth centuries. In the process many people have made great sacrifices, endangered their lives to make new discoveries, sometimes ignoring the mockery and cruelty of society. There are many names like Ambrose Pare (Italy), William Harvey (England), Edward Jenner (England), Ignaz Philippe Semmelweiss (Hungary), Louis Pasteur (France), Rudolph Virchow (Germany), to name but a few. Ambrose Pare is credited with a rich study of Anatomy and surgical techniques; William Harvey with demonstration of blood circulation, Edward Jenner for the vaccine for Small Pox; Ignaz Semmelweiss with demonstration of the cause of sepsis and its prevention in childbirth; Louis Pasteur for demonstration of bacteria as cause of disease and vaccination in preventing them; and Virchow for discovering cellular pathology in disease processes.

Love for humanity was as much a stimulus for progress as love of knowledge. Concern for mothers dying of sepsis made Semmelweiss search for a remedy; he was castigated by society and died a broken man, but he had showed the way.

We are continuing in its momentum. But it is time now to ponder if we are still progressing on the humanistic urges of bygone centuries; or a large portion of the impetus has been taken over by greed. Drug companies invest huge amounts in research not just for the benefit of humanity but to stay ahead in the market. Drugs that enslave and injure man are produced and distributed in a hurry. The richest nations consume the highest amounts of narcotics. Alfred Nobel donated his wealth for the welfare of mankind from a sense of guilt for having invented dynamite. Today there is no such repentance. Research in medicine brings in newer drugs and newer methods that a majority of people cannot avail of. The world is only progressing towards higher discontent. Where is the end? How can we establish our divinity? Is it time to look back at the principles of Ayurveda putting man against the background of something much larger? Einstein had once written, 'The cosmic religious feeling is the strongest and noblest motive for scientific research.' Experience through the ages has shown that this is the only practical principle for the development of socially beneficial research and practice in medicine—an adoration of God through service to humanity. Medicine encompasses many things—philosophy, science, politics, profession and business. But only a spirit of service based on philosophy can really benefit mankind.

2002

References

1. Reich, W T, *Encyclopedia of Bioethics.* Volume 2, New York: The Free Press, 1978.
2. Bhishagratna, K L, *Sushruta Samhita.* Volumes 1 and 2. Varanasi: The Chowkhamba Sanskrit Series, 1963.
3. Ibid.
4. Chatterji, S K, *India and Ethiopia: From the Seventh Century* BC. Kolkata: Asiatic Society, 1968.
5. Bhishagratna, K L. op. cit.
6. Thapar, Romila, *Ashoka and the Decline of the Mauryas.* Delhi: Oxford University Press, 1997.
7. Porter, R, *The Greatest Benefit to Mankind: A Medical History of Humanity from Antiquity to the Present.* London: Harper Collins, 1997.

Jerusalem: Crossroads of History

One day the editor of *Prabuddha Bharata* calls and asks me to write about Jerusalem. 'Why me?' I ask. He says, 'Because you have been there.' I say, 'That was a long time back, actually in 1980, and I do not remember much. I didn't have time to visit all the holy places since I went for a medical conference.' I do not add that I was not interested in religion then. To this he replies, 'Then go again.' This is a shock. I say, 'Are you serious? It will cost a lot of money as the country is very expensive, and I do not know anybody there.' But he is sure and insistent. I am piqued and say, 'Let me see, though I see no possibility of going.' I put the thought behind me. If this is a divine wish then let it be so, that's not my worry.

My daughter and grandchildren are planning to visit me during Durga Puja, and I am eagerly looking forward to that. In the meantime, the Israeli army invades Lebanon. I watch the war on television and cannot help thinking that this is what Sanjaya did in the Mahabharata—a live account of war is a reality now. Yesterday's mythology is today's reality. Has humanity ever achieved anything that it has not dreamt of some time in antiquity? I also tell myself, 'There goes my visit to Israel.'

Eventually, my daughter informs me that they cannot come. I am disappointed. But my son makes an interesting offer: 'Why don't you join us on a trip to Egypt? We've got a cheap pre-season package. You come with us.' 'What a coincidence!' I think, even as I say aloud,

'My journey will depend on whether I can visit Israel as well.' Now it's my son's turn to be surprised—'Why Israel? What for? There is a war going on there.' I smile. 'Do not worry about that. Ask your travel agent to call me.' The travel agent thinks I am mad. 'You want to go to Israel, sir? It is war out there, no visa available. No flight plan will go to Israel and return through an Arab country—the two tours cannot be joined.' I assure him, 'Don't worry, the war will stop, the boundaries will open, the visa will be given. It is still more than a month away.' He keeps coming back with one impossible situation after another and I keep encouraging him. At last I procure e-tickets for each individual flight, the agent makes some circuitous plans, and I get the visa.

I have to show hotel vouchers to get a visa for Israel, but the hotels are full and too expensive, it being the Yom Kippur season. I decide to take a wild chance and send an e-mail to an old assistant, Dr Probal Ghosh, who is now a professor of cardiac surgery in Austria and has an Israeli wife. To my surprise he replies from Israel that he is now located there but sadly will be away during my visit. He introduces me to a senior colleague of his, Professor Joseph B Borman, Emeritus Professor of Cardiothoracic Surgery at Hebrew University Hadassah Medical Center in Jerusalem, who welcomes me with open arms, inviting me to deliver a lecture (which fortunately does not happen) and books a reasonably priced guest-house accommodation for me. Meanwhile, the flight schedule has to be changed, and that means that Probal will also be there during my visit. I am apprehensive that I might get turned away from Israel or Egypt. Israeli security officers at Mumbai airport grill me for an hour as to the real purpose of my visit. I have no lecture material and I say my words are enough material. I cannot say 'religion', and create more confusion, but I keep smiling and am fast and honest with my replies to all questions—each repeated thrice, including the name of Shoshona, Probal's wife. Every article of my baggage is individually screened with special detectors and, still puzzled, they watch me all the way to the plane.

Joe and his wife Ruth (we are already on first name terms) are a deeply religious, liberal, and learned couple. Joe leaves all work and walks with me for two days non-stop through the streets of Jerusalem showing and explaining all the important sites. He has already made detailed plans and prepared notes and maps for me so that we can cover all of Jerusalem in two days. No word of gratitude is enough for them. The third day is free for Probal and Shoshona.

PEERING THROUGH THE HAZE OF TIME

I find the route of my journey significant, backtracking the route Moses took from Thebes (present day Luxor) in Egypt to the Promised Land of Canaan.[1] It was in about 1300 BCE, at Kadesh, that the Egyptians and Hittites fought a terrible battle for control of Canaan; both suffered terrible losses, but both claimed victory. The Egyptian Pharaoh in this war was Rameses II, in whose time Moses led the Israelites out of Egypt. Both armies were exhausted after the battle and left the land of Canaan almost empty, leaving a window of opportunity for the Israelites to populate the land and eventually to build their oldest kingdoms under Saul, David, and Solomon. After Solomon the kingdom was divided into two—Israel and Judea. Jerusalem remained the capital of Judea for 400 years, while Israel had many capitals. The reign of relative peace lasted a few centuries, and then enemies became powerful again, Egypt in the south and Assyria and Babylon in the northeast. In 732 BCE, the Assyrians conquered most of Israel, and in 722 BCE King Sargon II of Assyria captured Samaria—Israel's capital—and exiled the inhabitants, thus sealing the annihilation of Israel. Judea hung on for another 135 years, fragmented by wars and Assyrian occupation, until Babylon, under Nebuchadnezzar II, defeated the Assyrians and conquered Jerusalem in 597 BCE. After two rebellions, Nebuchadnezzar destroyed Jerusalem in 587 BCE, razed Solomon's temple to the ground, and banished the Jews to Babylon and other places. Later, Persia defeated Babylon, and Cyrus II of Persia allowed the Jews to return from Babylon. Some, but not all, did return, and they began to rebuild the temple in 536 BCE, though not to its original grandeur; this was the second temple. Uneasy times continued under Persian and then Greek rule. Alexander conquered the whole area in 333 BCE but did not destroy; and then the Egyptian Ptolemies followed by Syrian Seleucids ruled. Romans occupied the land around 63 BCE, and Herod became king in 37 BCE. He was a strict king and a great builder; he rebuilt Jerusalem and extended and ornamented the temple. The internal squabbles, politics, and revolts continued, with repeated invasion of armies from Rome, until Titus, with 60,000 Roman soldiers, sacked Jerusalem in 70 CE and razed the second temple to the ground. Some stability was achieved during the Byzantine Empire, but then came the Arab, Turk, Mameluk, and Ottoman invasions, punctuated by the Crusades, and finally came the British with the Palestine Mandate. Israel lies in the route of armies from Asia Minor to Egypt and vice versa, and every army on this route has trampled that land. As a result the Jews were scattered until the formation of modern Israel, and strife continues to date.

In the middle of all this, Jesus Christ was born in Judea.[2] According to Coptic tradition, the child Jesus journeyed along this route to Alexandria with Mother Mary and with John the Baptist, and revealed the first miracles initiating the establishment of the Coptic Church in Egypt.[3] This is the holy land for three great traditions, though India is not part of its history except as a distant source of some of the philosophies and material luxuries of the time. Then why have I been sent here? Is it to scour the ground and find my footsteps from a distant past, to be a non-partisan observer amidst all these wars and still be able to feel the divine presence, or prepare to be a protagonist of the future? But I have been here before—in the tenth century BCE carrying silk for Solomon's mother Bathsheba, peacock for Solomon's garden, lapis lazuli and perfumes for Solomon's lover Queen Sheba of Southern Arabia beside the Red Sea where it meets the Indian Ocean! The canvas is too large to grasp or make meaning out of. I can only try my best. Ours is not to reason why.

JERUSALEM

I land at Ben-Gurion Airport at 4 a.m. on 26 September 2006. I go out of the airport, this time uneventfully, and look for a share taxi, *sheyrut* in Hebrew. It is a minibus holding 10–12 passengers with space for luggage at the back. The journey became long as the driver can not resist the temptation of taking in one passenger for Tel Aviv, making the route longer drawing protests from the other passengers. I come back to the reality of the present. About 6.30 in the morning I get dropped in front of my guest house in Jerusalem. I get a small room with a bath. A message from Joe is waiting. I ring him and we decide to meet at 10 a.m., allowing me two hours to doze. I have not slept for 24 hours.

A Panoramic View. Joe comes punctually at 10 and we walk up the hill past an old kibbutz that has now been converted into residential flats and a large public building. This is how most kibbutzim are today, as that particular phase of development of Israel is coming to an end. The old olive trees still skirt the wire-fenced boundary. We walk up to the southern ridge of the deep valley with sloping sides that is Old Jerusalem. The Haas Promenade beside the road affords a fantastic view of the entire old city beyond the Valley of Kidron. Behind us, at the summit, were the old offices of the British administration of Palestine; that area has now been converted to the United Nations enclosure. This area is known as the Hill of Evil Counsel, not because of what they are doing now, but because this was the place where the main Sanhedrin, the supreme Jewish council and court of justice, sentenced Jesus to death. In front of me, far down on the western ridge, a triangular piece of land rising gently upwards, now largely bare, is the old city of David, which could be approached and conquered only from the north. At the bottom of the slope is the Gihon spring that supplied water to the city; it still flows. Originally the spring was outside the wall of David's city. It was later included in the city walls, and the water from the spring flowed into Solomon's Pool and to Siloam Pool further down, protected from invaders. Further up the slope were Solomon's city and the area of the Temple Mount or Mount Moriah, on which stands the golden Dome of the Rock. A little in front of that is the dome of the Al Aqsa mosque. The steeple of the Church of The Holy Sepulchre is close by on the other side. The entire western hill is densely built up. In olden times a shallow central valley ran through; it was filled up with debris from the city and built up. The Arab quarters to the northwest can be easily picked out by their crumbling houses—compared to the Jewish and Christian quarters extending to the eastern ridge. On a higher ridge further away are the modern buildings of the Hebrew University. The panorama is breathtaking, encompassing five thousand years of history of peoples and religions that have shaped much of the world. We turn left on to a wide concrete walkway that goes over the eastern ridge, flanked by flowering trees and following the curvatures of the hill. It goes past the Franciscan convent of Santa Clara, known in English as Saint Clare, co-worker of St Francis of Assisi. I have a deep regard for St Francis, and it would have been nice to see the convent and meet the nuns ... but that was not possible. The walkway is known as Derech Gabriel. At the end it meets Naomi Street, where Joe has his residence. He takes his car out and we continue our journey to the Holocaust Museum.

Holocaust Museum. This is a beautiful architectural creation. It is in the form of a large boat almost hanging in air. Through the centre of the length of the building runs a corridor, which is narrow at one end and gradually widens at the other as it rises up. On both sides are halls depicting the horrors of the Nazi era in large photographs, descriptions, and slides. As one finishes travelling through the halls, one comes out at the raised end open to the sky and light and providing a nice view. It is symbolic of the journey of the Jewish nation. Though I was not told so, I thought that the building was designed as an ark, simulating the ark that was kept in the central sanctum in Solomon's Temple, the ark that has never been found. I forgot to ask about it, as I was numb from sleeplessness and walking. The museum contains pictures and artifacts not only of the Nazi era but also on anti-Semitism in the rest of the West. These latter exhibits are very muted, probably to spare the feelings of present-day friends.

We take a light lunch at the cafeteria and, seeing that I am falling asleep, Joe decides to take me back to the guesthouse. On our way we pass an area called the German colony that has rows of small restaurants. It is close to my place, and Joe advises me to go there at night for dinner as the place becomes festive at night. After catching three hours of sleep, I walk down at night and find the place quite lively with lots of young people eating and chatting. I order lamb chops in kosher style. The crowd is friendly and polite but not overly curious. Modern Israelites are healthy, handsome, and jovial.

Next morning, Joe is unexpectedly busy. I take a taxi to the Jaffa Gate to see the Tower of David and the museum.[4] I get down from the taxi but cannot pay in dollars. A shopkeeper, seeing an Indian, kindly exchanges ten dollars, which pays for the taxi and entrance to the museum. I take a picture of the surroundings and a police officer driving past warns me sternly not to take pictures. The area is notorious for bomb blasts—I get evidence of this after I come out of the museum and Joe catches up with me. A small package is found lying in the middle of the road and a police van rushes in, siren hooting, and in a few seconds the crowded area is empty. Joe says a robot will be released from the van to grab the package. Unfortunately for me, the police see that it is innocuous and drive off, and the robot does not come out.

The Tower Museum depicts the history of Jerusalem from prehistory through all the invasions and different cultures at different periods, with wall carvings, statues, and models of people and buildings. Two exhibits interest me most: the Temple at Herod's time and the Dome of the Rock—the first because it was grand to see the place where Jesus preached and the corridors he walked, and the second because I was not allowed in.

Old City. Leaving the Jaffa Gate, we walk towards Joe's parked car and pass through a rich neighbourhood with opulent apartments and semi-detached houses with private gardens. They are all shuttered and belong to rich non-residents who come during festival times. Jerusalem is a pleasant place to live, with nice weather, wide main roads, and a lot of greenery. We drive to reach one end of the old city and walk in. The old city is a maze of narrow lanes with shops with common walls lining both sides selling all kinds of objects. The Via Dolorosa is one of these lanes. During festival times and holidays the area is packed with people. There are some old residential buildings of proud possessors, and shops of Jews and Arabs and some Christians too. We enter a small shop selling pea pakoras with sauce and hand-made bread. It is delicious. We enter a Jewish shop, with an old man sitting inside. Joe knows him as he had operated on his daughter who now lives in the US with her family. The old man says that though he has roamed the world and done business everywhere, including India, he has never left Jerusalem and this old shop of his family. The shop sells religious memorabilia and other art objects. The old man's son treats us to coffee, Joe speaks to his patient in the USA on phone, and I take pictures of Joe with the patriarch. We enter another shop to recharge the camera battery. It is owned by an Arab, and he deferentially leaves his seat to Joe and goes upstairs for the rapid charger, requesting him to look after the shop. He comes back and while we wait he blames the British for divisions between communities both in Israel and India by their divide and rule policy. Joe is silent. To keep the discussion going I say that a British journalist has recently written that if one could go back and withdraw the Balfour declaration there would be peace. The Arab looks happy, but Joe adds that there would be no Israel then. I quickly add that creation of Israel was necessary for humanity. I should have added that the British also created Transjordan for Palestinian Arabs, where Jewish immigration was explicitly banned. The Arab says that religious wars are continuing and Joe replies that religions should not divide nations. The Arab shakes Joe's hands in seemingly happy agreement and tells me he has seen the Professor often but never talked to him, and he is a nice man. After this mini-summit, as good or bad as the big ones, we part as friends.

Western Wall. A little later we enter a large paved courtyard. One side of the courtyard is the wall of the first temple, which used to be called the Wailing Wall, a name given by outsiders. Today the Israelis call it the Western Wall and they no longer wail. The State of Israel has come of age. In 1980 I saw a deep trench dug all along the wall to find its foundation and people reading prayers or crying behind a protective barricade.The trench is no longer there and the people touch the wall and pray and stick their prayers in written on small pieces of papers in the crevices between the stones, but in the main there is an air of festivity and family party, not sorrow. The men's and women's sections are separated by a low partition. We wear paper skullcaps kept in a bucket for going close to the wall, and I touch and offer *pranāms* at the wall. I feel happy and pass my hands over three thousand years old stones, particularly those with fine grooves along the margins that are of the First Temple. Others are later fillers. Most of the wall is made of these old stones and goes to the bottom of the foundation, as much below as above the ground. The uppermost few layers of small blocks with some cementing material are from the Second Temple. There are orthodox Jewish men with long plaited sideburns hanging out of their black hats. There are also a few children similarly dressed. There are people in black with black hats but no plaited sideburns, and Joe explained they are the conservatives. Most people are dressed in ordinary casual clothes.

Dome of the Rock. Above the wall one can see the golden Dome of the Rock. It was built during the reign of Caliph Abd Al-Malik ibn Marwan and completed in 691 CE.[5] It is not a mosque but a *Mashhad*, a shrine for pilgrims. It is an octagonal structure built in Byzantine style and is a place for meditation. The hill is one of the holiest places in both religions, Judaism and Islam. On the Temple Mount and in front of the Dome is the Al Aqsa Mosque, where prayers are held. In 1980, as far as I can remember, I did not hear the muezzin's call to prayer, and I saw a silent line of Muslims entering the mosque surrounded by armed Israeli guards that are not in evidence today. Joe told me that the prayer call is given now, and I have seen loudspeakers on minarets. The Jewish festival of Yom Kippur, the Day of Atonement, is round the corner and so is Ramadan.

The Prophet Muhammad accepted the fasting of Yom Kippur while he was in Medina and extended it to one month for the Muslims.

Much is common between these two religions. They have the same roots — both originate from Abraham. On that rock God called on Abraham to prove his faith by offering his son Isaac as a burnt offering. Abraham prepared a pyre, laid Isaac on it, and drew a dagger to kill him — when God stayed his hand and declared him as the chosen one. The Prophet Muhammad one night in a dream rode a winged horse from Mecca and reached the rock and from his seat on the horse was lifted to heaven to meet God and received his blessings and command as the chosen one. The story does not end there. The Crusaders camped here when they came to Palestine, and all the Knights Templar churches in Europe have the same octagonal structure as the Dome. The vista is imposing and awe-inspiring, with its long and remarkable history.

After the first major defeat of Byzantine forces to the Arab army in 636 CE, Jerusalem was still holding out, and its ruler Sophronius sent a message to Caliph Umar I in 637 that if he promised to spare the Christian and Jewish inhabitants of Jerusalem, as he did in Damascus in 635, they would surrender. The Caliph accepted the proposal and came to inspect the city to see that his promise was kept. As he was inspecting the Church of the Holy Sepulchre, the muezzin's call to prayer sounded. Rather than pray there itself, he hurried out of the Church — lest his followers, in their enthusiasm, destroy the Church to construct a mosque there — and went on to the open ground outside to face Mecca and perform his prayers. It was there that the Mosque of Umar was built. Today, only a wall separates the two sites; the entrances to the Mosque of Umar and the Church precincts are side by side. Umar I was the first Caliph to take the title of 'Commander of the Faithful'; he died in 644.

Via Dolorosa. We re-enter the maze of streets in the Christian quarter and cross small courtyards and cafés with people sitting and talking, there are impressive houses with common walls. We enter the Via Dolorosa, the route that Christ took carrying the cross. The route is punctuated by fourteen stations, marking the places where the events from Christ's sentencing, through carrying the cross—including places where he fell—to where his crucifixion and burial took place. The last five stations are found within the Church of the Holy Sepulchre itself. Devotees, who walk the route touching the plaques and other objects of remembrance, know these events at every station. We arrive at a place where there is a small barred gate in a wall guarded by a dark man; the passage continues beside it to a courtyard. The gate guards the entrance to the Mosque of Umar, and the passage leads to the small courtyard in front of The Church of the Holy Sepulchre. I ask Joe whether it is possible to enter the mosque; he says no.

Church of the Holy Sepulchre. So we move towards the church, and find its gate in the narrow stone facade ajar. A Muslim family has kept the key to this door for generations. The picture of the present incumbent was published in *Time* a short time back. It was probably a solution to the conflicting claims of Greek, Roman, Armenian, and Coptic churches, each of which controls parts of the present church and conducts services. In any case, the church has been destroyed and rebuilt repeatedly; the last rebuilding was by the Crusaders, and it has been in its present form since 1801. I ask Joe about the Muslim doorkeeper, but he has never heard about him. This church is the site of the crucifixion of Jesus, and of the tomb in which he was buried and from which he resurrected. The site is disputed by some, but recent excavations in the vicinity have shown remnants of what could have been the second North Wall of Jerusalem to the south and east of the church. It is recorded that Jesus was crucified just outside the city wall and that the burial took place in the immediate vicinity. So it is possible that this is the correct site.

We enter through the gate, and right in front of us is a slab of stone supported by wires like a cradle. This is supposed to be the slab of stone on which Christ's body was laid after bringing him down from the cross. I touch the stone and then my forehead—that seems to surprise Joe. I do not know whether he was surprised when I did likewise at the Western Wall, because he was behind me. Within the church we find large, dimly-lit halls with very high domed ceilings, each built as a shrine by different Christian Churches. In the highest-domed central hall is a shrine built as a small chapel with a narrow interior that houses, first, a small quadrangular well with two candles burning on its edge, and then further on, a narrow passage that one has to crawl through; beyond that, in the crypt, is the burial tomb of Christ. In the tomb, a maximum of three people can crouch at a time. The whole place is very dark. The chapel faces the next hall that belongs to the Greek Orthodox Church. I find people taking pictures and decide to try. As I am trying to photograph the interior of the small chapel, a priest gruffly asks me to move on. I am not sure whether I would be allowed to enter, so Joe and I come out of the church. Outside, I think, why not try again? So I ask Joe to wait outside, as he is not interested, and go back inside. There is a queue in front of the chapel with some people holding candles. I don't want to go to the end of the queue and wait a long time and become conspicuous. So I insert myself in the middle of the line, in full view of the priest guarding the entrance. Others do not object. I think that if I am challenged I can say that I treated Mother Teresa, but nobody challenges me. So I enter and do my *pranām* both at the well that was the site of the crucifixion and at the tomb. I feel the satisfaction of a holy mission completed.

THE TUMULT OF HISTORY

Jerusalem occupies a central place in the spiritual and emotive perceptions and aspirations of three of the world's major religions. Each of them looks upon it as the 'holy city', a prototype of heaven on earth. The incessant strife that this city has witnessed is perhaps a reflection of the dogmatic differences between these religions. These dogmas and the history of their development are therefore worthy of dispassionate study, for they also provide insights into how history could have been otherwise, perhaps a little less inharmonious.

The Christians, in the beginning, were persecuted by the Jews, though Jesus got the title of Christ—the anointed one—in fulfillment of Isaiah's prophecy. Romans persecuted them till the fourth century, and in that period and for the next two centuries Christian history is replete with internecine quarrels among different sects and individuals trying to gain ascendancy with denouncements, killings, expulsions, and exiles. The theological debates mainly centred on the nature of Christ—whether human or divine or both—and the nature of Mother Mary. She was most prominent in the Coptic Church, and she still is—for she had gone to Alexandria with the child Jesus. She is painted in dark colours in the very old early Coptic Church in Cairo. Elsewhere in the Christian Church, the female aspect of divinity was downplayed, although many of the early churches were built on 'pagan' sites of mother worship, and in many of them an altar to a Black Madonna can be found where pilgrims pay obeisance. For example, in the great cathedral of Chartres, a black Madonna statue stands atop a fifteen-foot-high pillar, drawing a steady stream of pilgrims. A second Madonna statue exists in the underground crypt next to an ancient and sacred well. The story is that it was a pre-Christian holy site of a mother goddess, and when the Christian missionaries broke down the existing shrine and built the cathedral, they did not or could not destroy the mother goddess, and so accepted her as a 'pre-figuration' of the Virgin Mary. The idea of female divinity was downplayed in the Catholic Church, so as to fully divorce the flesh from the spirit, thus enabling the idea of the Immaculate Conception. Woman as woman was made unholy, making it possible to oust the pagans and the Neo-Platonists. Some of the early paintings of Mary—one of them reputedly painted by St Luke—show her complexion as dark brown. She progressively became white as she went farther north. In the medieval French town of Le Puy there is a high and holy hill that served as a pre-Christian sacred site of a mother goddess, where the worship of the Virgin Mary started at a very early date. On the main altar of the cathedral that was built there, there is a statue of a Black Madonna with child. In the Middle Ages, five popes and fifteen kings came to see her, as did the mother of Joan of Arc, walking all the way from the west of France to pray for her daughter. The cathedral has been renovated many times, but all through, the Black Madonna has stayed.

Sometime in the history of Christianity the Christian armies were given a second cross—the hilt and guard of their swords. They prayed to the God of love, raising their killing swords. The female divinity was further downplayed in the Middle Ages, and virtues like tolerance, acceptance, and creativity atrophied.

Islam was the last Semitic religion to come from the same tree; in its turn it judged the other two. In Islamic doctrine there were five major prophets before Muhammad—Adam, Noah, Abraham, Moses, and Jesus.[6] Islam never considered Jesus as God or Son of God or any part of divinity, but as a prophet like Muhammad, and says that the crucifixion and resurrection never happened. The Christians hated the Jews because a Jew had betrayed Christ, and they hated the Muslims because they summarily dismissed Christ's divinity. Actually, Christians too had not accepted the divinity of Christ till the fourth century; they finally settled for the trinity of the Father, the Son, and the Holy Ghost. So the Muslims accuse them of subverting the One God. The Muslims also hated the Jews for they had betrayed Muhammad's trust.

POLITICS AND SPIRITUALITY

The three Semitic religions share a common root, and have all originated from the sufferings of the poor and downtrodden. But they differ in their ethics, politics, and military strategy, which were connected to religion in both Islam and Christianity until present times—after reason and pragmatism came to prevail over the opposition of the church in Christian nations, but not in Islamic ones. Islam judges other religions, and naturally it also is judged. Sadly, the most audible replies today are coming, not from the humanism and spirituality that exist in Islam, but through fatwas and fundamentalism. One cannot help wondering where God is in all this. God is the destination of all religions. All Semitic religions have produced people of high spiritual attainment, people who feel close to God. All disputes are at the level of theologians, as to who are the true believers of the one God. The Jews have suffered most, having come first. In Medina, Muhammad beheaded six hundred Jews—mostly the rich citizens—

and sold their families as slaves. They were accused of conspiring with the people of Mecca who were opposing the Prophet.

The surprising thing about the Prophet Muhammad is that he succeeded in inserting himself and Islam in the heritage of the Old Testament three thousand years after Abraham, depending on the name of Ishmael, Abraham's child by Hagar, the Egyptian bonded maid of Abraham's wife Sarah, and through his own dream of being lifted to heaven from the horse on Mount Moriah, thus staking his claim on Palestine. Believers say this was a miracle of God, non-believers say it was clever politics. Whichever it was, it is astounding that a tradition could insert a man into a mythological epic after three thousand years! One can only say, inscrutable are the ways of God—and so are those of history and human evolution. Unfortunately, this failed to foster the brotherly feelings that one would expect within a common tradition.

Islam started off by uniting the Arab tribes, and then spread with the sword—this has been common to all Semitic religions including Judaism. Other tribes joined Islam later. The world was tribal when they started, and in large parts it still is. Many of the converts to Islam were oppressed people who found the tenets and practices of Islam liberating.

Rationalism and theology are posterior to the prophetic stage of any religion; they also came to Islam, but seem to have undergone a decline after the early golden centuries of Islamic history. All Semitic religions have laid great importance on dogma and ritual, not understanding them as one of the many pathways to God. Neither has the concept of a supra-denominational God—benevolent to and approachable by all humankind—been endorsed. The Sufi saints of Persia and India,[7] yearning for a personal union with God, found the externalities of law divorced from a personal theology unsatisfactory, and increasingly asserted a way (*tariqah)* and goal (*haqiqah)* alternative to those of the Sharia. Their messages, poetry, and songs helped bridge religious divides by their beauty and universality. In India, both Hindus and Muslims pay homage at the mausolea of Sufi saints. But the role of people like Kabir, Lalan, and many others has been largely inconsequential in the mainstream Islamic social and political culture even in India. Many Sufi saints, like Mazhar Jan-e-Janaan, said that Hindus were *ahlul kitab* (people of the book), thus respecting the Vedas and Vedanta as divine words; but this view did not gain wide acceptance. An individual approach to divinity, deemphasizing the exclusiveness associated with specific religious practices and conceptions of God, is essential if religious divides are to be bridged.

Early Christian sects like the Gnostics, Manicheans, and Nestorians had some special insights into the nature of truth—but were vigorously opposed and subdued. The last two reached many remote areas of Asia. Neo-Platonists were active in Alexandria and Rome in the third and fourth centuries; their philosophy was akin to Advaita Vedanta. Their best known philosopher, Plotinus (205–270), is said to have had a mystic experiences that in Indian philosophical language would qualify as *samādhi.* He led a frugal life in Rome, talking to people and helping those in distress, regardless of their social standing, with total detachment. His last words were to the following effect: 'I am trying to bring back the divine in us to the divine in the All.'

There have been highly evolved spiritual personalities in the Christian tradition—Saint Francis of Assisi was one such—but the foibles and failings of the Church have been equally glaring. The Inquisition of the Middle Ages that virtually hunted down all heresy, real or imagined, and the opposition of the Church to scientific development are cases in point. Even today the Christian Church finds it difficult to come to terms with modern advances in the physical sciences and biology. These modern developments apparently conflict with the concept that God created this world and has a plan for it, an idea that all Semitic religions propound. But the true problem lies with the people trying to work out God's mind.

Dissatisfaction with narrow organized religion with its set ideas, coupled with the new socio-economic and scientific scenario, gradually brought in the secular belief in the primacy of humans, of their intellects and minds. This humanistic trend, set in motion during the

Renaissance, continues unabated. But a 'supra-religious' understanding of human divinity still remains largely foreign to much of humanity.

Jews have had the least chance of doing harm to others after the destruction of their ancient kingdoms, but they have suffered the most, and their cloistered refugee life has repeatedly raised suspicions that they are conspirators against the lands they inhabit. Since their earliest history they have been divided into clans and tribes, and 'conspiring Jews' had almost become a metaphor. Through their long history in Israel and outside in different nations—through wars, occupation, and torture—they had no means to protect themselves, apart from intrigues for or against whomever was ruling. But all this aside, in their countries of adoption, they have produced great men and women in arts and science. They now have a homeland of their own to defend. This task has integrated the different socio-religious factions into nationhood and in a common search for a secular identity.

The Israeli society of today is different from the one I saw in 1980. Israelis have further developed Hebrew for modern use both in general education and science, but most speak English—though not necessarily with an American accent, as I had found in 1980. If they think today that political and military strength are as important, if not more so, than their philosophies, can we blame them? Conflicts in the Middle East have a historical precedent of 'fight to the finish', one way or the other, and this is due to their basis in religion. Is that acceptable in today's shrunken global world? Humankind has to develop and accept secular beliefs, not attacking others or their own weaker sections with age-old divisive religious ethics. Can this be done? On that wisdom depends the hope of humanity.

THE PILGRIM WENDS HIS WAY HOME

I still have one more thing to do: I have not been to any mosque in Israel. So I stand in front of the mosque of Abul Abbas in Alexandria, dressed in my very Indian outfit of white pyjamas and kurta. I ask the Muslims milling around me whether I can go inside. They say I can but at the time of Ramadan it is very crowded and I shall have difficulty.

They are right. I have been to many mosques and enjoyed the serenity inside, but I do not know the rituals of prayer. So I say I can pay my respects from where I am standing, and join my hands in *pranām:* and an unexplained tremor runs through me. I draw immediate attention, and people ask whether I am Indian and of which religion. I say I am a Hindu and consider everybody's God as mine. They say God is one and I nod in agreement, even as I wonder which aspect of God I am acknowledging. God is a multifaceted personality or else the world would not have been so diverse. In this huge, largely empty, universe with no evidence of life near us, so much diversity in nature and life forms exists on this tiny dot of a planet called earth—like a reserve forest, a garden—and we the tinier dots paint God with the colour of our emotions and fight in God's garden!

A man in a spotless white outfit and turban comes forward and says he also is Indian—from Kerala, and is pursuing Islamic studies at Cairo University. He asks my name and what I do. I am lost in my thoughts; so I give him my card unmindfully. 'Oh, you are a doctor,' he says and pockets the card. Later I regret giving my card to a man who did not introduce himself. I was distracted because at the mosque of Abul Abbas they did not cover their heads, and when I asked, they said it was not mandatory, it is not in the scriptures. I have seen many variations of ritual in the same religion from country to country, place to place. I was thinking of Ruth asking me at dinner, 'Don't you believe in rituals?' I replied, 'Yes, of course, but not absolutely.' I was not speaking of philosophy, just on the basis of what I have seen. Ruth almost shouted, 'What! You do not believe in God?' Before I could reply, Joe said gravely, 'Yes, he believes in God.'

WHY?

God cannot be abolished, despite the efforts of atheists and agnostics, for He is connected to the sublime perceptions of humanity proclaimed by the sages of every religion since antiquity. These perceptions are proof of the existence of the indefinable all-pervasive superior consciousness, that consciousness which is the basis of the humanism of Plotinus, St Francis, Kabir, and many others. This whole phenomenon has been given the name God. But religion is inextricably intertwined up with the worldly affairs of humanity! It is probably in the nature of creation that the sublime and the ridiculous must exist side by side. In ordinary times people are calm, wise, and helpful, much like God himself. But come dispute, and religion is used to whip up passion and the devil in people.

I stood thinking, facing the endless western desert of Egypt extending to the horizon and beyond in the blazing midday sun. It is a sea of sand and rock extending beyond the range of vision. I could see the endless universe filled with the same grains of sand. Is it my imagination that collapses these grains into mirages of stars, galaxies, jungles, seas, cities, palaces, and the works of human vanity? Is there nothing but these grains collapsing into the realities of my desires by means of my imagination? But my imagination, my consciousness is also a product of the grains, and those grains must hold the same consciousness as I do. I cannot be a freak in this universe when nothing else is.

My mind is in turmoil, I am lost in thought. Must humanity always grow through violence, war, and bloodshed, and never in peace and tranquility? A voice within seems to whisper—'You could not come to me as a child, you were not ready. You are grown and ready now. Go you into that vast desert, as others have gone before you, naked to your skin, for there is none but you, there is nothing, no tree to lean on, no branches on which to hang your desires that are continually reborn like the waves of the sea, in the little pieces of cloth, little bits of paper stuck into crevices, no shade to sit in, to relax in for comfort. Go not in your name and image lest they make you a saint as an excuse to wallow in their imagined imperfections. You go rushing in a hundred, a thousand, a million names and images. And tell them that the religions I gave over the aeons of time were not meant to serve as shrouds for desires, lusts, ambitions, and vanity. Take those exotic fabrics I gave and wipe off everything they have been stained with and wash them with your tears. They will ask, what shall we do with a

God that does not give us what we desire, no gold, and no fulfilments that please us? Tell them that these were given to clear the darkness of their minds, for them to come to me. Gold I have given them aplenty. They have stashed all that gold in temples and mosques and cathedrals built in my name and in the modern temples of state vaults and they have issued papers instead as wealth—papers with imaginary values they have created; the values that float on the machines they have made of currencies and stocks and bonds made and manipulated by people. My children in the four corners of the earth starve and die, remain ignorant and unable to understand why; the simple people, they do not understand how the tidal waves of values are made and destroyed by the vanities and lusts of humanity and they remain ignorant of the nobility in humanity created from the dust in my image that even I salute, and I cry for them. And they rise up in revolt and kill and destroy, epoch after epoch. How many times have you seen the gold vanish, the papers dwindling to dust cheaper than a cigarette butt, baby's tear, mother's milk, and they never learn? Take away that shroud of religion, reveal Me, and let them see their selves in nakedness before the apocalypse comes, so that they are saved. And they will see.'

2007

References

1. *Tower of David Museum of the History of Jerusalem.* Jerusalem: The Jerusalem Foundation. 1992.
2. *The Bible.*
3. Cannuyer, C, *Coptic Egypt: The Christians of the Nile.* London: Thames and Hudson, 2001.
4. *Tower of David Museum of the History of Jerusalem*, op. cit.
5. Stuart, Desmond ed., *Early Islam.* New York: Time Life Books, 1984.
6. Ibid.
7. *Encyclopedia Britannica.*

Perception

What is perception? Perception is that magic moment, that no-man's land, that fleeting ethereal flight into realization and knowledge. Not knowledge acquired through senses which are the lowest form of knowledge in Plato's epistemology.[1] Is it the suprapersonal rationality of man acting on his object of ideas? Does such a thing exist?

In a roomful of different objects two boys are allowed to enter and stay for a minute. They are then asked to give a list of the objects. The two lists will be different. It is an old Boy Scouts' game known as Kim's game. Why do the perceptions differ? Because two people have two different patterns of perception and those objects which find, so to say, ready familiar sites in their brains are registered easily. If both of them are now asked to write an essay on the room, their essays will also be substantially different. The problem of subject and object and their interrelationships have dominated early Greek and Western philosophy. Ultimately the objective has won. Objectivity and logic have come to be acknowledged as the cornerstone of human reasoning and conception of reality. The process started from Aristotle and was then incorporated into the Semitic religions. It was strongest in the southern part of Byzantium, Alexandria and Spain, which were mainly under Islam, and infusion of these ideas into the rest of Europe through Northern Italy brought about the Renaissance. It is only now that this total reliance on objectivity for an understanding of reality is being questioned as science delves deeper and deeper into the question of Reality in microcosms and macrocosms.

But the doubt should have entered a long time back. Let us take the geometric definition of a point and a line. A point has no length or breadth or height and a line has no breadth, only length. Is it possible to conceive of such things? How can there be anything in space without length or breadth or height? This was only a mathematical assumption and not an objective fact. But on this assumption has been built the most magnificent buildings, cathedrals, mosques and temples. Therefore, such an assumption is useful, utilitarian, but how do we know it is real? Just because an assumption is useful does not mean it is true. Today much of the confidence in science is because it is useful. But the deeper it delves into the Reality of the universe and life, the more tenuous becomes its solid grounds.[2] It may be argued that as science progresses further, all these ambiguities will be resolved just as in the past. But it is becoming obvious that such a solution is not possible without solving the problem of Perception.

Actually this realization came to science quite some time back, let us say in the last century, but was not generally perceived. The pillars of Euclidean geometry and its basic assumptions were challenged at that time. Euclid's fifth postulate, that only one parallel to a given line can be drawn through a given point was shot down by a Hungarian and a Russian, viz. Bolyai and Lobachevski. The German mathematician Riemann shot down Euclid's first postulate that only one line can be drawn between two points. Thus a whole structure of non-Euclidean geometry came into being. This crisis in the foundations of mathematics was attacked by many people, the most notable was Jules Henri Poincare, Professor at the University of Paris in the late nineteenth and early twentieth centuries. Bertrand Russell described him as, 'by general agreement, the most eminent scientific man of his generation.' The details of his mathematical deductions and solutions are beyond the scope of this article and this author, but of greater interest is how he arrived at them and his analysis as embodied in his book *Foundations of Science.* These solutions appeared to him not when he was intensely thinking about the various diverse facts which were contradictory and only pointed to a void. The solutions came to him when he was passing a sleepless, tossing night after drinking black coffee, when he was on a geological expedition and forgotten all about mathematics and the truth came to him by simply looking at a sheer cliff. There are two other similar situations in his life. Then he analyzed the solutions against the background of these situations and decided that the solutions were not merely intuitive. He realized that among the large mass of varied and contradictory objective facts he had actually chosen those which contributed to the greatest harmony of the most. Beyond that there is no fundamental place to go to and the question becomes meaningless. He actually wrote, 'This is a true aesthetic feeling which all mathematicians know but of which the profane are so ignorant as often to be tempted to smile.' He actually hypothesized that this selection of contradictory facts was made by his 'subliminal self.' It was beyond intelligence and beyond intuition. What is this subliminal self? Is it self at its lowest conscious intensity? Is it at that stage that perception becomes acute? Poincare was also one of the few scientists who could foresee the coming of the Theory of Relativity and understood it when it came.

The Theory of Relativity brings us to another great scientist of our times, Albert Einstein, another great stalwart of perception and harmony. His article on 'Science and Religion' is full of these and is an obligatory reading for an inquiring mind. Only a few excerpts can be given here. 'The cosmic religious feeling is the strongest and noblest motive for scientific research', he writes, and again, 'It is very difficult to elucidate this feeling to anyone who is entirely without it.' The cosmic religious feeling must be contributive to the subliminal self of Poincare, where the ego is at its lowest. And this feeling of the subliminal self is very difficult to convey to someone who is driven by ego. Further on, he writes, 'How can Cosmic religious feeling be communicated from one person to another, if it can give rise to no definite notion of a God and no theology? In my view, it is the most important function of Art and Science to awaken the feeling and keep it alive in those who are receptive to it.' Let us take the second sentence first. Why does the scientist write about art? Is it just because he was an amateur violinist of more than average calibre? Imagine listening to Beethoven's Fifth Symphony; or an excellent rendering by Ravishankar or the Raag Bhairon in the voice of Bhimsen Joshi in the darkness of the early hours of the morning. It gives us immense pleasure. Why? There is no objective material gain. What is this pleasure which is beyond self? We are transported immediately to an immense joy, which is beyond self—Suprapersonal. Literature and visual arts offer the same experience. Is it possible to be in this state of joy all one's life? Einstein equates this with the ecstasy of science. What about us, the common people, who are not great composers or great scientists, can we not experience this joy? In the first sentence he says that it has nothing to do with God and theology. It is important to ask here what Einstein means by God, as God has different meanings to different people. Einstein has himself said that he does not believe in a personal God delivering justice and punishment or reward. He believes in Spinoza's God. And what is Spinoza's God? Spinoza denied that the Bible was inspired by God down to the last letter. He was declared a heretic and deserted by his family. He led a lonely life practising his profession of polishing lenses. He identified Nature with God. He said God is All and All is in God. He said that every individual is an expression of something infinitely bigger. Everyone should see himself in the background of this eternity in order to achieve true happiness and contentment. It is our passions, such as lust and ambition that prevent us from achieving it. A Vedantist will say, 'OK, so what else remains, that is God.' The difference is that Spinoza does not say how to become what he asks people to become but Vedanta also shows the way. The God that Einstein cannot believe in is the personal God of Christianity—the extreme dualism of God, his son Jesus and the human sinner. We have known for a long time, a few thousand years, that dualism is for Bhakti, devotion, where man looks at God outside of himself, sometimes with supernatural qualities, ten arms and so on. But for the Jnani, the seeker on the path of knowledge, God is ultimately Advaita, the enlightened self, 'Tat Tvam

Asi'. A Bhakta can also attain enlightenment at the end of his quest when he perceives unity with the object of his love. With Christianity this is the only way possible. Western scientists have always rebelled against this God of dualism, of an external causality, because it does not correspond to their idea of reality and we Indians have been needlessly drawn into this argument forgetting our own heritage. There is no conflict between Vedanta and science. In fact they are complementary and often the Vedanta sets the questions of perception for science. I shall quote at the end a recent letter from John Wheeler, who now occupies the chair of Einstein in Princeton University.

Some of the later day scientists, upto the modern times, have discounted the religiosity of Einstein as his personal opinion, carried over from his childhood upbringing, rather than from his science. Of course there are others who see the point of his cosmic religious worldview. Those who disagree and will not be drawn into a discussion of divinity are really agnostics, not atheists, like Feynman and Penrose. But even they cannot discount Perception for therein lies the instrument for observing the common basic unity and harmony among the large mass of often apparently contradictory facts or objective experiences. For otherwise, how does one explain the emergence of one great physicist or mathematician among many, when the facts are there for all to see? It is that old Kim's game of the boy scouts. That is why the modern day physicist is progressively inclining to the study of that which perceives, viz. the human brain.

In order to conceive the nature of consciousness, the study has been extended even to the perceptive organs of simpler forms of life, like Paramecium, a unicellular organism.[3] What has been realized is that without a knowledge of the nature of Perception, no real knowledge of Reality can be arrived at. Meanwhile the applied sciences and technology continue to be utilitarian, bringing in new powers, new frontiers for exploration of the universe. Something like the point of Euclid. Then why is this quest for Reality? Why do we need it? Because that is the only way man can know himself, himself and the universe he lives in. Otherwise science will only bring in chaos. This does not mean that this quest is utilitarian. There just is no escaping from it because man is made that way. It is fundamental to his psyche and it determines his entire behaviour with himself and the object world. Without this he has no firm ground to stand on, he is always helpless, insecure. This is as innate to man as any other instinct. It can be argued that this is not special in man but a gradual evolution of the insecurity of an amoeba or a paramecium, so that it now grasps the universe. But still the argument remains that this in effect is an enlargement of Perception. It is true that the quest is led and understood by a few Rishis of Physics and Biology as it was led by a handful of Rishis in antiquity. But it affects all of us. An agnostic physicist listens to Beethoven's symphony in rapturous enjoyment and cannot understand why, because he cannot do an algorithmic compression of the music and decide why and how the extra electrons enter his brain.

The question of the brain brings us to the domain of biology. In biology as in physics, man's quest has been progressively towards finding the basic truth, the final common denominator of life. On the way there have been enormous amounts of utilitarian spin-offs in the form of medicine, physiology, environment, bioindustry and even unto the world of fashion. But the main thrust has been to get to the bottom of it all. It started with Darwin's *The Origin of the Species* where a commonality among the tremendous heterogeneity of life forms was first established. From there onwards the quest led to the study of organs, then on to the individual cell, from cell to the molecules which make it and from there to the level of pure energy.

The search for consciousness in the human brain has really intensified in recent years with scientists from all disciplines joining in. The search has led to the ultrastructure of neuron, the cells that the brain is made of. The number of neurons in a brain does not increase after it attains its full growth very early in life. While cells in most other parts of the body are replaced as we grow older, the neuronal cells in the brain are never replaced; so that through our life what we call 'I' is really only our brain since we are really not the same in so far as our other body cells are concerned.

The ultrastructure of the neuron shows the presence of a cytoskeleton consisting of microtubules[4] which are 25 nanometre in diameter on the outside and 14 nanometre in diameter in the inside. Each microtubule is made up of a protein polymer, which constitutes each subunit of the microtubules, which are known as 'tubulin'. Each tubulin is a dimer consisting of two distinctly separate units, viz. alpha-tubulin and beta-tubulin, whose orientation depends on the electric charge or polarity of the dimer. These microtubules occur in all nucleated cells on earth, which means in all cells of the human or animal body up to the level of nucleated unicellular organisms like amoeba or paramecium. In paramecium, the microtubules extend beyond the cell wall as cilia for perceiving the environment and movement. The passage of small molecules through these microtubules and their movement are governed by alterations of electrical polarity inside the microtubules. This is to put it very grossly. The negative charge or the electron is the driving force of all cellular activities of life on earth. This is true from the use of cardiac pacemakers to generation and transmission of nerve impulses.

As we know, the electrons are the most elusive elements of physical reality and cannot be comprehended or visualized individually. Although the cytoskeleton and microtubules are present in all the cells of the human body and govern their biochemical exchanges, they attain their highest development in the neurons. Here they extend from the dendritic or receiving end of the neuron, through the cell and all along its axon to the synaptic cleft, at the junction to the next neuron. That these are somehow connected to consciousness is suggested by the effect of anaesthetic drugs of varying chemical nature which blots out consciousness by their ability to change polarity or electron exchange or quantum coherence, whichever way one looks at it, in the microtubules. This of course, does not explain consciousness or Perception but merely identifies the microtubule as a key player.

Attempts have been made to make computer models of the brain incorporating increasing randomness in their function. Edelman and his colleagues constructed a series of devices known as Darwin I, II, III, IV and so on. These form the basis of artificial intelligence created by man. But these are nowhere near consciousness as Penrose has pointed out that the actual capabilities of even an ant seem to outstrip, by far, anything that has been achieved by standard procedures of artificial intelligence. Cerebral activity or consciousness is non-computable by its very nature and even a quantum computer would not be able to perform the operations required for conscious human understanding. This is pure physics as put forward by Penrose.

How far can one see through science as it is today? One can imagine quantum coherence inside microtubules, a large-scale collective quantum phenomenon, perhaps of the nature of a Bose-Einstein condensate, in a sort of biological superconductor. A small quantum change can produce a cascade, which then collapses into classical neuronal activity. There is of course no guarantee that it will happen every time. It is possible to imagine this small quantum change to be endogenous or through a sense organ or even exogenous through a strong electro-magnetic field. But this quantum-classical collapse or interface in neuronal activity is not understood and even in pure physics the quantum-classical interface is not understood. In brain activity it is more complicated, with the unknown but apparent process of selection at dendritic ends, multiple synapses with different neurons, presence of excitatory and inhibitory nerve impulses and so forth. As Penrose puts it, 'Even if synaptic connections are controlled in some way by coherent quantum-mechanical effect, it is hard to see how one could usefully consider a quantum super position consisting of one neuron firing, and simultaneously not firing.'[5] What would be needed is a new mathematics—a non-computational mathematics. That would be an event as big as the Theory of Relativity and is dependent on Perception. As Penrose himself says, 'The arguments from Godel's Theorem serve to illustrate the deeply mysterious nature of our mathematical perceptions. We do not 'calculate', in order to form these perceptions, but something else is profoundly involved—something that would be impossible without the very conscious awareness, that is, after all, what the world of perception is all about.' On the other hand, John D. Barrow[6] says, 'any limitations of mathematical reasoning, like those uncovered by Godel, are thus not merely limitations on our mental categories but intrinsic properties of reality and hence limitations upon any attempt to understand the ultimate nature of the universe.' So what is it going to be? Shall we perceive Perception?

Both Einstein and Penrose have remarked that the natural laws, which we uncover, have been in existence from long before man has known them and man has certainly not known all of them. Thus, laws of gravitation have existed long before Newton. Nature never disobeys its laws, never acts randomly, and within the boundaries of its own laws, It makes things work so beautifully—from microcosms to macrocosms, from physics to biology. While Einstein calls this cosmic intelligence, Penrose uses a different term, because he is an agnostic. Both agree that the great game of physics is to unravel this intelligence.[7] Advaita Vedanta also says the same thing but only adds that even a single individual can establish his connection to this cosmic intelligence through refining and increasing his sense of perception because he is a part of it or else he will not be in this Universe. And how do we know that Nature is so law abiding and regular? Maybe that is what It wants to appear to our senses. Maybe It has an equal degree of arbitrariness. May be it looks rational when we are looking at it rationally. It collapses into rational reality with our act of observation, not only here and now, but also in the distant reaches of the universe in space and time. That is what the quantum principle states. As Paul Davis says, science may be merely an act of faith. It is also possible that it is completely rational but with a different kind of rationality—the kind that transports us to another world on listening to a Beethoven symphony. How would we know unless we go there? And the great message of the Upanishads is that it is possible to go there.

Since it all boils down to Perception, let us look at Perception itself. A paramecium can perceive its immediate environment and respond to it and even learn from its experience. But its environment certainly does not include the cosmos. The process of evolution can then be seen as an evolution of consciousness at the present end point of which is man whose perception involves his self and the entire cosmos and everything in it. Is it possible that in future there will be another being with a much higher sense of perception seeing beyond what we can see? Scientists and thinkers like Arthur Eddington and Julian Huxley[8] in early twentieth century have ruled out the possibility of another product of evolution in the foreseeable future since man himself is evolving and evolving quite rapidly. Man's consciousness has been evolving very rapidly over the last few centuries. This rapid transformation would not have been possible without a conscious participation in evolution. A definite example is the uncertainty principle and its definite influence on the human thought process in all walks of life in this century.[9] Does that mean that man can voluntarily increase his powers of perception and thereby evolve rapidly in consciousness? Yes, seems to be the obvious answer. If it happens collectively, can it also happen individually? Again, the answer has to be yes, because the collective consists of individuals, and individuals make up the collective. In every age, only a few individuals form the cutting edge of the society and the rest follow suit at a variable gap. Does that mean that an individual can, in his small lifetime, increase his own power of perception to go beyond the limits of what we today call rationality? We are on dangerous ground now, but we have to accept it as possible. A description of a daily ordinary life today would have been called fictitious even one or two centuries back. Even in leading that ordinary life we utilize only a minuscule portion of our cerebral power. By a conscious effort to utilize the dormant areas of the brain can we take our level of perception beyond the time-space constraint within which our laws of causality operate? Its proof has to be beyond the realm of mathematics into the realm of experience. For it is beyond the level of perception that Poincare or Penrose talked about. If theirs is a perception of the greatest harmony of the most, this one must be an even greater sense of the harmony of the universe.

It is not my intention to get into metaphysics but let us judge its probability by our ideas of rationality. Time is intimately connected with human consciousness. We can perceive time flowing.[10] But according to the Theory of Relativity, time and space are interchangeable. We should therefore also perceive space as flowing, but we don't. Einstein must have perceived space as flowing or its possibility in perception as a logical deduction.[11] While on Einstein, let us consider the EPR (Einstein-Podolsky-Rosen) Paradox—the non-locality of two events in space, which are simultaneous and inter-dependant. If non-locality can occur in space, it can also occur in time. Therefore, what is in the future may well be in the past or present. In fact, perfectly logical theories of quantum reality have been put forward on this assumption by Aharonov and Vaidman, Costa de Beauregard and Werbos. After all, there is no such thing as the present—is it this second, this minute, this day or this century? In fact, with our ordinary senses we can never perceive the present. Between the time that a photoflash goes off and we blink, the picture has already been taken. A man who dies in between will never know that his photograph has been taken. So it is with most of our perceptions. It is our perception that gives it the tense, and perceptions vary.

Let us now look at the evidence. Perception is possible with intelligent deductions by a few; after all not everyone becomes Jules Verne or Victor Hugo. However, there are perceptions, which bear no resemblance to contemporary knowledge or experience. Our Puranas are full of such examples, as indeed are some of the old mythologies in other cultures. But only one example will suffice. In the last act of the Mahabharata war, both Arjuna and Aswathhama fired their ultimate weapons in anger and the burning arrows went up into the sky, ready to fall to the earth. The gods were alarmed that creation will be destroyed and asked both of them to control their weapons. Arjuna controlled his weapon but Aswathhama said that he had no control over his weapon. A situation like this did indeed happen in the sixties during the Cuban crisis. America had the capability to destroy its ICBM in flight but Russia with its polar ICBM carrying MIRV and multiple nuclear warheads did not have the capability to destroy them in flight. The story of the Mahabharata could have no bearing on contemporary experience, since 'Arrows once shot do not come back' is a proverb in every culture including ours from very ancient times.

In recent times, two of Swami Vivekananda's written remarks come to mind. He had said that the ancient Sumerian civilization was an extension of the contemporary Indian civilization long before the discovery of Indian teakwood and ancient memorabilia in the ruins of the ancient Sumerian port city of Ur. In 1895 he wrote to Sister Christina that the working class would rise to power in Russia and then in China. He wrote the same thing to Hem Chandra Ghosh in a separate letter. Even Marx thought that the communist revolution could only occur in the industrialized countries like Germany and England and the Bolshevik Party was not even in existence then. There are many such recorded and unrecorded examples.

Is it possible to train the mind to greater Perception? As has been said already, we normally use only a small portion of our brain in our usual life, just as we use only one half of one lung and less than one half of our kidneys. People can train these organs and muscles to become super athletes. Everybody cannot be an Olympic champion, but everybody can go some distance on the way to become a champion, and nobody knows who can ultimately become a champion. Similarly it is possible to exercise with the brain to increase its powers of perception. Voluntary control of the autonomic nervous system is well known and so is conscious withdrawal from the sensory world. There are many people who have seen or heard of such things. But even such will power, power of the conscious mind, faith or conviction is not an end in itself, but only means to an end. Perception can be increased to go beyond time and space. What happens then I do not know, but I would imagine a beauty and harmony beyond imagination. It would seem quite plausible for Valmiki to write the Ramayana before Rama is born because time itself collapses. Plato had called this stage unattainable but Sri Ramakrishna and Advaita Vedanta say that this is attainable—it is an act of faith to pursue it. It is a personal choice whether or not to pursue it—a neoexistentialist choice. But one has to give up some things in its pursuit—restrain the power of the senses, give up lust, ambition, and ego, as Spinoza has demanded. One has to make the mind uncluttered, so that the subliminal self can take over. The pursuit of theoretical physics also calls for a lot of sacrifices. It is much easier to make an invention and earn money, name and fame. One does not know when one starts whether he will reach anywhere in theoretical physics. That is why in the matter of Perception our scriptures say *Nāyamatma Balahinena Labhya*, i.e. the search for the *ātman* is not for the weak. Lots of people fall by the wayside, sannyasin or not. But there is a great deal of beauty even on the way. As Rabindranath Tagore had written, 'my joy is in walking down the path'. There is a great deal of beauty in physics—those who trundle the road do it for joy and beauty. One cannot criticise the other for its act of faith.

I had once accosted my guru Swami Bhuteshananda Maharaj with the question: 'What is the use of all this? We have followed this path for thousands of years but it has only brought us miseries, foreign domination, defeat in every endeavour, unparalleled social and religious exploitation. What is the point of a path so difficult, a goal so unattainable? What have we gained?' He said, 'Nothing. You do not gain a thing. Why are you so interested in all these efforts to know Reality? What do you gain?' I was silent. It is true, an ordinary doctor like me, what did I have to gain? A few days later when we were alone he complained of too much pain in his osteoarthritic knee and said that he found it very difficult to walk. I said, 'But you have to walk. Otherwise it will get even worse.' He smiled, his incomparably benign, sweet smile and said, 'It is then like the quest of the Absolute. You do not gain a thing if you have it, but if you do not have it you lose a lot.'

This is what is known as transmission of Perception. But my original question was wrong. We have not pursued it for thousands of years. Shortly after its revelation in written form the Brahmins captured it and the non-Brahmin castes and women were debarred from its study. It was probably caused by the possibility of material gain from a generally pious society. Because of this wrong use it went into disrepute. Sankaracharya brought it out of darkness but could not give it to the masses. It remained in the hands of the Brahmins. But the urge remained in the masses as is there everywhere in the world. This led to a proliferation of the Bhakti cults with their attendant rituals which the modern mind of rationality so abhors. But it is all the same—it is an act of faith, faith so beautifully displayed in agnostic physicists like Penrose and Feynman. It remained for Sri Ramakrishna and Vivekananda to break all the shackles of superstition and make it available to everybody irrespective of religion, caste, creed, colour, calling, sex, wealth, education, intellect; irrespective of whether one follows *jnan*, *bhakti*, *karma*, *raja*; whether you are a monist or dualist or whether you are a monk or a householder. This is a revolution. Barriers have been broken and what was there for thousands of years has been bequeathed to the entire humanity. It had to be done through the life of one man. That is why Sri Ramakrishna is an Avatara, an incarnation.

In this essay, so far, I have been engaged in an exercise in self-checking trying to gauge whether I have understood, even partially, the new Upanishad of the third millennium.[12] The Upanishads are really a thesis. They start off by saying that what is being sought to be described is beyond description, indescribable. And then they go on to discuss in the light of contemporary scientific and other knowledge, social phenomena etc. to convey the Perception that is not describable. Scientific knowledge was not meagre in antiquity if one reads through the cosmology of the Brhadaranyaka Upanishad, converting the examples to contemporary terms. This new Ramakrishna Upanishad[13] I am talking about is a fitting gift to the third millennium of the Christian era, for it represents the dialectic conflict of the duality of

Christianity and the rationality of science that has directed the tremendous development in science and technology and increased the consciousness of man, on a common ground. It has all got to come together now. Dualism is the creative Force; Advaita is Perception, Presence and Silence. A man who has Perception moves seamlessly from one to the other without conflict.

I shall end this essay with a quote from a letter by Professor John Wheeler. He wrote the letter to a monk of the Ramakrishna Mission of which I have a copy and permission to reproduce. The letter goes thus: 'My wonderful mentor, Niels Bohr, had gone into deep interest into the Upanishads—more, he told me, in the questions than in the answers. I like to think that someone will trace out how the deepest thinking of India made its way to Greece and from there to the philosophy of our times.'

'The Professor at Copenhagen whom Niels Bohr most admired, who was his teacher and subsequent occupant of the House of Honour that Bohr himself was to occupy, was Herald Hoffding. In an evening dialogue between Heisenberg and Bohr at that House of Honour about the uncertainty principle, Hoffding put his finger on the diagram between the double entrance slit and the terminating photographic plate and asked, 'Where can the electron be said to be?' Bohr's reply is immortal: 'To be? To be? To be? What does it mean "to be"?'

'Your wonderful analysis of the great questions inspires us all in the great search that follows the spirit of the Upanishads, of Plato's dialogue and modern science.'

Really, what is it to be? Is it to be or not to be or is it to be and to be and to be and to be? There is no negation here. There is no other way but to be. If one can use a term drawn by Abner Shimony,[14] from Whitehead, in the famous seminar with Penrose, Hawking and Cartwright, viz. there may be a 'protomentality' inherent in every particle of this universe that is asking it to be, asking us to be. The entire physico-chemico-biological evolution of the universe is asking us to be. If there are other universes, other life forms with different chemical compositions, they are still the same. As I sit in wonder in unity with this sea of consciousness and before my mind blows into oblivion and merges in It, the only word I can say is WOW,—or is it OM! This world is neither Illusion nor Reality, as we understand them, but beyond them both.

2000

References

1. *Great Dialogues of Plato.* Translated by W H D Rouse. Harmondsworth: Penguin Books, 1956.
2. Venkataraman, G, *What is Reality.* Hyderabad Universities Press (India) Ltd., 1994.
3. Penrose, Roger, *Shadows of the Mind.* Vintage, 1994.
4. Ibid.
5. Ibid.
6. Barrow, J D, *Theories of Everything.* Vintage, 1990.
7. Einstein, Albert and L Infeld, *The Evolution of Physic.* New York: Touchstone, 1938.
8. Huxley, Julian, *Evolution in Action.* London: Chatto & Windus, 1953.
9. Heisenberg, Werner, *Physics and Philosophy.* New York: Harper & Row, 1962.
10. Hawking, Stephen, *A Brief History of Time.* London and New York: Bantam, 1989.
11. Hawking, Stephen and Roger Penrose, *The Nature of Space and Time.* New Delhi: Oxford University Press, 1997.
12. Chatterjee, S C and D M Datta, *An Introduction to Indian Philosophy.* Calcutta: University of Calcutta Press, 1939.
13. Chatterjee, S C, *Classical Indian Philosophies: Their Synthesis in the Philosophy of Sri Ramakrishna.* Calcutta: University of Calcutta Press, 1985.
14. Penrose, Roger, A Shimony, N Cartwright and Stephen Hawking, *The Large, the Small and the Human Mind.* New Delhi: Foundation Books, 1999.

FOUNDATION OF SOCIETY

Society and Politics in the Perspective of Biosciences

As we look at the society around us the natural question that comes to mind is where we are going. As a country and a society are we progressing? What sort of society are we making for our children and grandchildren? History has taught us that social environment determines what sort of men and women will come out of a society. When we were not independent we knew that without freedom we could not have Rabindranath Tagore's ideal society 'where the mind is without fear, where the head is held high'. So the ideology and parameters of pre-independent India were simple, however arduous the struggle for freedom might have been. What about now? Are we developing towards a society where the right type of human growth can take place? Are we in the right direction to achieve such a society? How do we judge? It is the general social surrounding that determines what sort of people will proliferate in a society. The structure of a society cannot be formed by one or two exceptions but by the mass. What the majority of people think and do and their life pattern as a whole determine the human environment of a society. That cannot be determined only by economic statistics or by political developments in a multiparty democracy. It can only be judged by the direction of social evolution. And that evolution to a successful society in the present day world has to be towards inclusive economic growth with complete social justice, ensuring individual creative freedom and enterprise in every field; i.e. in other words, unleash the creative power of the people. They should not be subservient subjects but partners of the state. These are strong words and their definitions have changed in time and place and been modified by the technological developments of the era but the ideal remains the same for historically judging a society and determining its stability. The development of societies through these apparently contradictory principles of order with freedom is the evolutionary biology of a society. A society behaves like a biological organism. It expands in every direction when the conditions are right and when they are not so, it contracts, trying to go into a shell. This is what happened to us. Through the major part of the last millennium we were continually going into our crooked shell. During this contraction crooked social, cultural, economic and political restrictions come into view. Religious dogmas develop out of such confusion. When that restriction is somehow removed, as in our case with independence, a haphazard expansion pushes every individual to try to grow upwards, out of his immediate surroundings. This is somewhat special in higher mammals and human beings.[1] This serves at the same time as the source of his creativity, freedom of enquiry, thought and consciousness, as also a drive towards domination, exploitation and servitude. Human society cannot behave or be managed like a society of bees or ants. Conflicts and compromises arise and through them there develops a higher consciousness about self, society and environment. If the direction of evolution is towards a higher consciousness of individual freedom with social justice, then that of progress is towards a successful evolution. Or else it would crumble and fail. Economic development is a part of this evolution not its end. There are examples of failed affluent societies in ancient as well as modern times calling for the use of biological sciences as the most important instrument to study them in preference to any other knowledge base.

The biological sciences made rapid revolutionary advances from the end of the eighteenth century. In 1798 Malthus published *An essay on the principles of population.* Within the next 50–60 years Linnaeus,

Wallace and Darwin had made epoch making discoveries and their theories completely revolutionized the thought process of humanity. Darwin's *The Origin of Species* was published in 1859. Shortly before that in 1847 Karl Marx had written his *Communist Manifesto.* In 1848 working class rebellions broke out in England, France and Germany. In 1864 Marx called the First International and in 1876 it failed. Until the First World War Marxism had many definitions and interpretations but after the Bolshevik revolution those centred entirely on the experience of that Revolution and its aftermath in Russia. Darwin died in 1882 and Marx in 1883. The revolutionary progress in life sciences initially helped establish Marxism and it was accepted by Marx himself. It rejected the hereditary and holistic superiority of the aristocrats and the capitalists. It established people's confidence to judge society and its mechanism of exploitation by the scientific analysis that was the greatest contribution of Marxism.

Biological sciences in association with other sciences have progressed rapidly since then. Marxism could not keep pace with it because the kind of freedom of thought and expression that was needed to make it creative was not possible in the Russian State or any other Marxist State thereafter. Within a few decades after the Russian Revolution Marxism started doubting and questioning the advance in knowledge in biological and social sciences because a lot of water had flown through the Volga by that time; the theory of Marxist liberation had by then produced a State with its nationalism and centralized power structure.

Since the beginning of our modern age in the nineteenth century we Indians have been mostly copying others. The time has come for us to trust our capacity for original thought and not try to fit things that do not match our national character and goal. We must now grab the reins of the running horse of history by our own effort. When the primitive man first discovered fire it was an epoch making scientific progress and man has worshipped and used fire for centuries. We use fire today in so many more different ways without the necessity to worship. The epoch making historical contribution of Marxism cannot be belittled, not only in politics but as a philosophical discourse in so many areas. But to worship Marx blindly as godhead and to think that the world has stopped progressing since Marxism-Leninism is sheer stupidity. And the only comparison of Stalinist bigotry in India through the last century can be with the religious bigotry, which has been destroying society. We got the word 'democracy' from Greek antiquity that is almost prehistory. Socrates condemned democracy looking at the democracy of Athens as it was. That democracy has very little resemblance to modern democracy except probably in the allegations of corruption, but it has evolved through human experience through centuries and millennia. Marxism has collapsed in less than a hundred years. Early democracies also collapsed. To understand the reasons, one may find a better explanation in the study of socio-biological evolution and the failure of Marxism to evolve, than in politics.

Evolution of the world started from her birth aeons earlier. The hot globe composed of subatomic particles took thousands of million years by our terrestrial time to cool down. Slowly they formed atoms and molecules and then started the formation of compounds and complex compounds, growing bigger from the small to the complex by chemical process energized by the Sun. Gradually came the first molecules of life, probably five thousand million years back, either by primary growth on earth or by seeding from the space, by comets or other planets like Mars.[2] At first the life forms were unicellular, without any nucleus, as is still seen near deep sea vents in a very hot watery environment. Biological evolution continued from the unicellular to the multicellular and progressively to enormous reptiles, the dinosaurs, which ruled the earth for 135 million years and then became extinct. The first mammals came seven million years back and the first humanoids about four million years back. The first forefathers of modern man, the Cro-Magnon, came about fifteen thousand years back. The known human history of man can be traced back to about five thousand years. The industrial revolution is four hundred years old while modern experimental technological research has developed in the last one hundred and fifty years; the progress in the last fifty to sixty years has surpassed the progress in the preceding three hundred and fifty years. Thus there has been a continuous acceleration in evolution on earth, every phase being faster than the preceding one.[3] The cause of this acceleration is unknown, just as it is not known whether this phenomenon is universal or restricted to the earth or other earth-like planets, if they are in the earth's stage of cosmic evolution.

Let us consider the evolution in the animal kingdom after it separated from the common stem of plants and animals. In our era of climate change and eco-environment we know that both are essential for continuation of life on earth. But how and why did the animals go through evolution? Let us assume that the first DNA molecule, the first and the basic unit of life, was formed somewhere or was injected into the earth from outside. It faced a very hostile environment that could destroy it immediately. It soon developed protection by a cytoplasm and cell wall around it and an internal environment was created to keep it insulated from the external environment but reacting to it for evolution. The DNA material in the cytoplasm gets further organized in a control centre, the nucleus, for further protection, maintaining the internal environment and protection of chromosomes for continuation of life. Thus survival and maintenance of the species is the impetus for evolution. A host of cells is more effective against the external environment, so multicellular organisms evolve and then cells take on specialized jobs to make the organism more effective. Specialized organs to undertake specific functions evolve – like lungs, liver, kidney, heart etc., though these functions existed in a primitive form even in a unicellular organism. Reproduction occurs initially by a simple division of the organism (asexual reproduction), but soon it becomes necessary that the genetic material is enriched and altered by sharing, in order to evolve more easily and adapt better to the changing environment. So there has to be exchange of genetic material within a species, DNA (as chromosome) of one cell has to mix with that of another to produce new cells so that genetic variety may be produced to adapt to the changing external environment. Thus evolution progresses through sexual reproduction and mutation aimed always towards success in Struggle, Survival and Adaptation to an ever changing external environment. The dinosaurs did not have an efficient temperature control centre in their brain to control the internal temperature and perhaps made inefficient adjustments with their bulk and became extinct during the last ice age when the whole world froze. But all reptilians or their precursors, the amphibians, did not perish, the smaller ones developing hibernation as a mode of adaptation to the cold weather. The early mammals originated in later years of the dinosaur era with a temperature regulation centre in the brain and regulatory systems in the body, and they flourished. The less efficient species also continue to survive in the world in their atavistic state and contribute to the biodiversity and biosphere of the world but do not show much facultative development. The cockroaches apparently have survived for millennia. So survivability and reproducibility alone cannot be the direction of evolution as Darwin propounded because many species are more efficient in both these functions than man. Some scientists of course will oppose the idea of a direction in evolution, specially the Marxists, as it may allow a channel for divinity to enter the system.

The evolution in mammals from the early mammals to man is a story of development of the organs—the organs for locomotion and food procurement, digestion, reproduction, hearing, vision, speech, taste, smell and ability to draw inference from hereditary or past experiences. These changes have been rather fast in the evolutionary time scale in different organs. Each organ has had its own evolutionary direction, going into one direction or other, forwards and backwards and some becoming atavistic. Being biped and having freed our hands we have lost the tails but if evolution so demands we can grow tails in a distant future because the rudiments and the computational memory in our genes are still there. Being biped and developing hands, that became wings in flying reptiles and birds, we have compromised our spinal stability and have made our hearts pump blood upwards against gravity. On the positive side it has allowed us to move long distances as in our hunter gatherer stage of development, to do things with our hands and developed our brain. But there are two organs where evolution has been more or less unidirectional so far, viz. the heart and the brain. The primitive heart in fishes is a single-chambered heart, progressively evolving to dual-chambered, three-chambered and four-chambered hearts resulting in the circulation of fully oxygenated blood to the body and most of it to the brain. The brain likewise has undergone more or less a linear evolution. The visual brain is most developed in birds in their small otherwise undeveloped brain, the smelling part in addition to vision in the early mammals still in a small brain; but in man the frontal and prefrontal or thinking and information storage brain has become larger and larger without much reduction of the other areas apart from disuse in modern man. And this increased forebrain and the brain as a whole getting the major portion of fully oxygenated blood pumped by the heart has grown through human evolution from the Ramapithecus to the Cro-Magnon to the modern man without any further major alteration in other organs. And with that has come intelligence and something beyond intelligence—perception of consciousness that is very individual.

As a licence to include consciousness in a discussion of science, I quote Sir Roger Penrose, the famous British theoretical physicist. He wrote in his book *Shadows of the Mind*: '... the arguments from Godel's theorem serve to illustrate the deeply mysterious nature of our mathematical perceptions. We do not just 'calculate' in order to form these perceptions, but something else is profoundly involved—something that would be impossible without the very conscious awareness that is, after all, what the world of perception is all about.'[4] And this is true not only about mathematics and science, but also about music, beauty, love, and the being that we are; and the perception is specialized, individual and unique. A man with acute mathematical perception may or may not love Beethoven's ninth symphony but he will not be able to rationalize either his liking or disliking. The brain has become the nucleus, able to change even the bodily functions, has empowered man to alter his external environment and make choices. Man has become God but unfortunately not all of us. This degree of variation among members of the same species was not there in earlier evolutionary phases.

So has evolution stopped, the end reached? The answer is in the last sentence above that we have become gods but not all of us are or will ever be gods. As the famous biologist Julian Huxley wrote in 1953[5] quoting Whitman, 'It is provided in essence of things that from any fruition of success shall come forth something to make a greater struggle necessary.' Man is a social animal, and human society as a whole is a biological system, and the evolutionary process must continue and that process as in the past stages must continue through thesis, antithesis and synthesis, a Hegelian doctrine. Huxley further wrote, 'But the obverse of struggle is satisfaction and satisfaction in the free enjoyment of one's capacities is another essential thread in human life,' quickly adding, 'Of course, not all fulfillments or all enjoyments are good or right, any more than all biological improvement is progressive.'

What is good and what is right? Feeding human beings to lions was considered good enjoyment at one time but had no evolutionary goodness. Is evolution of the mind a good thing from the evolutionary point of view? Julian Huxley's reply is that by the rules of natural selection 'a high degree of mental activity and mental organization could only have come into being if it was of biological advantage to its possessor.' He has said that the future of the evolutionary process is a 'psychosocial evolution of man'; but his criticism of Marxism—'Thus, for the modern biologist, the dialectical materialism that provides the philosophical basis for Marxist communism is an erroneous survival from days before the principles of evolution were properly understood'—is too dogmatic. Marxists hated Huxley and not unjustifiably because Marxism also evolved from the mind in response to the socioeconomic ills of the time, but the times changed very rapidly through two World Wars and the end of colonialism and the possibilities of change that were there in Marxism were stifled by those who enjoyed power and their followers. Through this time progress continued in biological research and in the understanding of heredity and the genetic code.

Biological evolution occurs through mutation in the hereditary genetic code that is carried inside the nucleus of germ cells, the spermatozoa and the ova. The structure of DNA was deciphered along with the importance of its base sequence in the evolution of life. The mutation occurs for survival in response to a hostile external environment. If that hostility is too great and too rapid for the slow process of mutation to adjust, the organism would die, as it happened with the dinosaurs and many other extinct species. That nucleus for human psychosocial evolution is his brain. The mutation of thought can occur only in a few brains, not a mass. Biological evolution has to occur in a larger population for them to thrive in changed circumstances in preference to the others. Not able to adjust hereditary genetics in their philosophy Stalinist Russia tried to propagate the false scientific data of Lysenko and Michurin's claimed experiments of observing the origin of new genes in chick embryos under certain conditions that were later proved to be false. This is being mentioned just as one example of how facts were being distorted to suit philosophy rather than the other way round. The more serious malady of the death of the individual in Marxist society was exposed by writers like Boris Pasternak and Alexander Solzhenitsyn.

Similarly Livschitz and Khalatnikov of the Russian Academy tried to prove that the universe did not start with the 'Big Bang' as propounded by George Gamow and supported by further research.[6] In spite of its mathematical proof, that it was accepted by the Catholic Church probably put them off. In 1970 they retracted their papers. Political bigotry in an autarchic state forces people in all spheres to play to the power centre and the state to encourage those sciences that support the philosophical existence of the state. This crushes progress of knowledge and adjustment to an evolving world of ideas and brings about collapse of the state. The physical laws and the world of Galileo and Newton rejected the Ptolemaic world supported by the Christian Church and gave birth to the philosophical concepts of determinism; it believed that all phenomena in the world and universe could be solved by deduction if we could know the constants and the laws and their relations. This scientific determinism gave rise to social determinism whose ardent propagator was the French physicist Marquis de Laplace, not a mean scientist by any means. The social determinists believed that once we knew the rules and formulae on which society and history move we should be able to determine what sort of society we want and how to install it. Marxism evolved in that age of social determinism.

But the very year in which the Bolshevik revolution happened in Russia that turned the political world upside down, another silent revolution occurred as Einstein published his General Theory of Relativity. Within a decade Wolfgang Pauli published his Exclusion Principle (1925) and Werner Heisenberg published his Uncertainty Principle (1927) and the era of Quantum Physics came into being. What changes these brought to the firmament of physics, the most fundamental science of all our knowledge, will take long discussions. But in summary, the Theory of Relativity altered the Newtonian conception of the world and its constants and dimensions, interchangeability of matter and energy and theoretically established that there could be infinite dimensions or variables in the universe that we do not know of. Quantum Physics opened up the world of microcosm, smaller and smaller subatomic particles, and their random probabilistic behaviour unexplained by classical physics; these were the basic constituents of the universe but we do not yet know how and why they get together and bring the macrocosmic universe of our senses into reality out of the infinite possibilities. How and why did this universe come into being? The effect of the observer on observation was realized and concepts of reality changed.[7,8] Scientists worked out mathematically correct, apparently impossible postulates that defy classical science and the objectivity of the senses. Objectivity and reproducibility considered fundamental to science and with which science judged all other human knowledge have undergone a sea change. New mathematics came into being. From total adherence to determinism the mind shifted to acceptance of the possibility of simultaneous existence of opposites.

The persons named above were not only scientific researchers but 'Rishis' by our ancient definition and their visions reached much beyond their scientific papers to what it means and the future that all this knowledge indicated. I remember as a college student reading a small book written by Heisenberg on the Uncertainty Principle and sitting for hours staring at the darkness outside. The conversation between Einstein and Rabindranath Tagore[9] remains immortal in the annals of science but cannot be reproduced here as pages will be needed to explain that. Pauli and Heisenberg visited Kolkata mainly to pay homage to Satyendra Nath Bose whose work from an unknown Dhaka University would never have been accepted even for publication as they were revolutionary. He sent his papers to Einstein and out of three papers contained in a single presentation only one, the Bose-Einstein Statistics as it was later called, saw the light of the day in a German science magazine. The other two dealt with fundamentals of Particle Physics that might have won him a Nobel Prize. The postulates of Bose-Einstein statistics have been put to greater use now both in physics and life sciences. The philosophy of scientific progress takes a long time to impact society by slow diffusion and when it does it is a deep impact. It takes much longer for this impact to reach politics and whether it will ever reach depends on what kind of society and politics is in place, a receptive social structure or one that is bigoted not allowing the social base to change to suit its totalitarian political structure. Russia has a rich past in its contribution to fundamental science like deciphering the atomic table, roots of genetics, but there is no contribution of communist Russia in the later progress of basic science in spite of remaining a politically free nation throughout. In the meantime the world was devastated by the World Wars, famines, national wars of liberation from colonial rule and communal divide that is still continuing and many societies are just shut off, breeding terrorism and a lot of other evils. A rigid dogmatic political structure whether based on religion or ideology finds it difficult to change direction as it stifles the society from new ways of thinking and will collapse in the fast evolving world. The famous book *Science in History* by the Marxist British scientist Bernal[10] was a monumental work at its time when first published in 1959, where he traces the development of science in all its branches from its beginning. Today in only 50 years it would be impossible to write such a book (including the edition in 1965) describing all the progress in so many branches of science by one author. At the time of its first publication it was hailed by Marxists as a mark of approval for their scientific social theory but Bernal himself warned of the explosive advancement of science and its problems, the problems that a Marxist society would have to face and true to his prediction could not handle.

The relation of the polity of a Marxist society to the intellectual creative class who can think and innovate in the spheres of culture, fine arts, industry and science including social sciences is rather peculiar. In the growing stage before they come to power they depend on this class to propagate and popularize their ideals.[11] Once Marxism is marketed and put in place the intellectuals are kicked out as they are no longer allowed to question. The internal democracy of Marxism means that both the questions and answers will be provided by the party.[12,13] This is not an original idea of Lenin. It is inherent in Marxism that the intelligentsia is considered a necessary evil and to be monitored. They have to be utilized in running institutions and in undertaking prescribed research on technology and applied sciences but no fundamental thought process about the structure of politics and society must ever be entertained, not even in the fundamental sciences that can raise questions in people's mind. They are controlled by political commissars and above them the leaders. A picture of this frightful arrangement has been vividly painted by Solzhenitsyn in his two books—*The First Circle* and *Cancer Ward*. He wrote that an honest writer in such a society can be like a second government. But Marx himself was the originator of this idea. Hegelian dialectics conceived a central core of consciousness in society that marked the then aristocracy as such a class and Marx brought in dialectical materialism based on the means of production against that class through working class struggle and the prophecy that the working class will create the dialectics of the future. So the educated class became suspect. But the Hegelian 'Hero' need not have belonged to any particular class and could very well be a collective of free thinking people from all classes. Marxist economic theory was incomplete and the production methods changed so fast due to progress of technology that his theory was obsolete before it had even started, did not have the practical time to adjust, and never even wanted. After the fall of the Soviet Union a respectable Communist leader of West Bengal said, 'The remarkable advances of science have made capitalism victorious.' Advancement has been a sad thing for some societies since antiquity, from the discovery of fire, bows and arrows and cannons to the present day and those that follow the same road blindly fall faster.

Another explanation forwarded by some for the fall of the Soviet Union is that because of the hostility of capitalist countries the major investment in Russia had to be in armaments and space research diverting resources from other areas. It may not be entirely unjustified. But in a State-controlled production machinery, whereas production becomes regulated and higher in controlled segments, the same cannot be true in the uncontrolled or less controlled segments because incentive for production is low. The total production in the uncontrolled segment is always higher than the controlled segment in a capitalist or a socialist country. This cannot happen in Marxist economy unless greatly modified and this is what happened in Russian agriculture. Marxist society is therefore a society without free initiatives, and without initiative there can be no development. A new privileged class corners all benefits. SUMMUM JUS, SUMMUM INJURIA, an ideology for justice taken too far converts to injustice. This is the picture of West Bengal today.

So far the past has been analyzed. That analysis is of no value unless it gives a direction to the future and what could happen. If we look at a not too distant future those that are perplexed and depressed by the fall of Marxism in Russia and Eastern Europe and those elated by the victory of capitalism are both wrong. Firstly, the fall of Marxism in Russia does not mean an end of socialist principles—in some form or other socialism is inevitable. It can be predicted on the principles of biological evolution of society alone. The world is becoming smaller through the progress of science and technology, and population is continually increasing with the progress in medical science and biotechnology and other demographic factors of population growth. In the countries where population growth is controlled there is a high proportion of old people. The technology to run away from the world and make colonies outside is far into the future, if ever. Therefore to ensure that production and distribution allow benefits to flow to all segments of the society in world communities there has to be social control on a global scale. But the control should be flexible and as little as possible to allow change and adjustment to variations. Since the pace of social evolution will be variable the process of adjustment has to be rapid and this adjustable socialism will be the formula of the future for human survival and growth. There will be no place for terror in any form. It is possible to grab and hold power through the twin instruments of temptation and terror for some time but not for very long. Secondly, the fall of Marxism is bound to bring unprecedented changes in the structure of capitalism. Between the thesis and antithesis at a stage of world development, if one goes, the other must also change drastically. Apart from philosophy this can be projected from purely economic analysis. For the welfare of all of us it is desirable that the change in capitalism is peaceful but that is not guaranteed as fundamental changes usually come with conflict and turmoil, even armed conflict. That is the truth of dialectic whether for materialism or any other ism.

Against this background of a projected global future, what is the future of our country, how could we prosper? Every society is unique in its development necessities because of different preferences, cultural heritage, collective consciousness and intellect, not to speak of material progress. We are a country of many societies with strong regional identities and have an internal dialectic of different regions with different forms of religious and political bigotry. Regional differences stand in the way of charting out a common developmental roadmap. Lessons from other countries and lessons from our own history should help in the synthesis and integration of a roadmap for different regions that is possible only if there is open governance. The structure of governance in our country that was established by the British has deteriorated by now. The socialism that we dreamt of has been disfigured before the society could be prosperous. Instead of a proper development of capitalism a feudal capitalism is raising its head, and a bankrupt socialism is leaning towards feudal capitalism for survival. In many areas of the country there is very little scope for individual enterprise. Social despair is leading to violent regionalism. What is the way out, where is the ray of hope?

In biological evolution, every species and family has centres of strength and weakness. When the environmental factors are such that they encourage their centres of strength they flourish and if otherwise, they perish. As long as physical strength was more important than mental strength the human race had a tough time. Societies and nations flourish under the conditions of a particular time and devolve at others. Even a few centuries back man could not analyze himself and could not control his environment. Today a society should not depend on luck and circumstances alone but cultivate the sources of strength and be aware of the weaknesses. Where is the source of strength in Indian society? We are not aggressive and contentious like the western civilization or Islamic civilization although the latter can change. We have never stepped beyond our border to attack others, not even to bolster our defensive perimeter, and this has to change. We are not as hard working as the Mongolian races and this is changing. But we have two centres of strength. Firstly it is our long tradition of social goodness and goodwill to live and let live that allowed people of diverse cultures to come to the Indian subcontinent and settle in peace. It became our weakness in the era of aggressive militarism but that phase is hopefully over, but if otherwise it has to be faced inside or outside our borders. The second source of strength has been our creativity, which given the environment has worked wonders in the past and is proving itself today. Even in the present turbulent world the proof of our social goodness is in our daily lives that we lead in spite of a rather weak law enforcement structure.

To increase the space of justice, politics must be responsive to social leadership. Divisive forces fragmenting society reduces individual liberty and enterprise. As it is there is enough fragmentation of our society without adding political fragmentation. Society must be free of terror – not just communal terror but also political and economic terror. Politics must not depend on organizational strength. In a civilized society politics depends on wisdom, not organization. Our democratic constitution is more liberal than that of any other country, with universal adult franchise with no electoral college and no preferential votes. Such a democracy with a large uneducated population can degenerate to mobocracy if wrong political practices are brought into play. That it has held so far is a proof of the essential decency of the people. People, not the politicians, have rejected oppression of a brute majority to enforce its will on others. The people of India have won their first political power through the ballot box after a thousand years and more. They have shown more wisdom than the politicians in exercising that power. When they will be able to exercise that power without fear, obstruction, indoctrination, with individual free judgment whether they are rich or not so rich, villager or rich urbanites, educated or not so educated, the power and creativity that will emanate from this society will conquer the world by its mind alone.

Translated from Bengali. First publication 1992. Reprinted 1998

References

1. Morris, Desmond, *The Human Zoo.* London: Jonathan Cape, 1969.
2. Davies, Paul, *The Origin of Life.* Harmondsworth: Penguin Books, 2003.
3. Huxley, Julian, *Evolution in Action. London.* London: Chatto and Windus, 1953.

4. Penrose, Roger, *Shadows of the Mind*. New York: Vintage, 1994.
5. Huxley, Julian, op. cit.
6. Weinberg, S, *The First 3 Minutes*. Flamingo, 1977.
7. Davies, Paul, op. cit.
8. Venkatraman, G, *What is Reality*. Universities Press (India), 1994
9. Ibid.
10. Bernal, J D, *Science in History*. Harmondsworth: Pelican Books, 1954. Third Edition, 1965.
11. Einstein, A and Infeld, L, *The Evolution of Physics*. New York: Touchstone, 1938.
12. Fedyukin, S, *The Socialist Revolution in Russia and the Intelligentsia*. Moscow: Progress Publishers, 1981.
13. Fedyukin, S, and Eldarova, I K, eds. *Lenin on the Intelligentsia*. Moscow: Progress Publishers, 1983.

Conquests of Indian Philosophy

INDIAN CONQUESTS OF THE MIND

The study of history has traditionally meant study of political history. Only recently in the last two centuries it has included history of mathematics, economics, science, literature, etc. History of philosophy has mainly dealt with western philosophy. That is because like western science it has had a chronological sequence of intellectual development and goes parallel to the religious theosophy of Christianity, sometimes in conflict and sometimes in concurrence. Apart from exceptions like Spinoza and to some extent Kant, western philosophy is philosophy of matter or materialism, culminating in Hegel who inspired Marx. There western philosophy has stopped. Later philosophies like postmodernism, evolutionary biology etc. are not really philosophies but discourses to keep philosophers in business. Christianity has theosophy but no philosophy to link with material philosophy. For Spinoza God did not create the world, He is the world and Jesus preached a religion of reason which valued love higher than all else, both for God and humanity, and the Bible has distorted that. He advised each human being to see himself against the background of an eternity. That is mystical! No wonder he was excommunicated for heresy and rejected by his family and driven to live a lonely life in his shop polishing lenses. Einstein said he could believe in Spinoza's God but not any personal God. Indian philosophies were called mystical until recently by educated men in the West. Advanced psychology also appears mystical to many. Indian philosophies do not deal only with divinity but represent a thought process, which moulds the human mind and society, and its conquest of the human mind is much more difficult to follow. But its impact on human civilization is much deeper and longer lasting than any armed conquest. Like the word 'X' in algebra, God as an unknown quantity helps that process, until He falls in the hands of fundamentalist bigotry usually tempted by women, wealth and power either in this or after life. But fortunately He has also been cultivated by ascetics of all religions throughout human history and they say that He is approachable though not known through the senses.

The early conquests of Indian philosophy are shrouded in antiquity. The Indus and Saraswati valley civilization is the earliest cradle of development of Indian philosophies.[1] The earliest excavated settlement in this Early Harappan civilization is at Kili Ghul Mohammed that has been shown by carbon dating to be earlier than 3000 BCE. This civilization was in contact with the Sumerian port city of Ur with ships sailing from Lothal on the 800 mile voyage along the coast and from there to the whole of Mesopotamia since the rule of the first Sumer dynasty during fourth millennium BCE including a small beautiful temple to a mother goddess at al-Ubayd.[2] Artifacts and inscriptions recording the items brought from the Indus valley have been discovered at the time of Sargon of Akkad, from Larsa during the third Sumerian dynasty and also at Jerusalem at the time of Solomon during the tenth century BCE.[3] At Ur, an inscribed tablet mentions various items brought by sailors, and the list of products shows that they were collected from all over India. Intermediate staging posts have been discovered by Danish excavation teams as recently as the 1950s at Bahrain and other islands. Knowledge was passed through oral transmission before written scripts came into being. The Satapatha Brahmana along with the Brhadaranyaka Upanishad took its written form probably in the seventh century BCE, as names of ruling kings of the time, not only in India but the Middle East and Egypt are mentioned in these texts.[4] Rishi Yagnavalkya, the author of those two treatises and many others of spiritual and practical social value still extant today, lived in unknown antiquity and to whom the knowledge of Brahman, the non-dual unitary divinity was revealed, was the foremost scholar and ascetic of his days. To his ashram resident students came from all over the known world studying science, medicine, astronomy, art, architecture and philosophy along with other practical teachings of the Atharvaveda and carried the knowledge of the Brahman all over the known world through oral instructions. The Achaemenian court at Persepolis during the sixth century BCE was a gathering point of the learned from the known civilized world to hold discourse on all aspects of knowledge, like mathematics, astronomy, medicine, meteorology and seafaring, construction and building, animal husbandry, agriculture and so on and also God. In all these the Indian scholars had a lot to contribute along with inputs in the practical philosophy of life, knowledge and divinity. The power of Vedanta philosophy was supreme at the time. A Brahmin scholar visited Socrates in the fifth century BCE and stayed in his house. It will be fair to assume that he made the journey from Persepolis. A study of Plato's dialogue shows its similarity to Vedanta, especially his dialogue *The Republic* that scholars say was definitely quoted from Socrates.[5] The later revival of Neoplatonism in Alexandria, Mesopotamia and Rome around the second century CE lasted till the fifth century and was even more akin to Vedanta. Plotinus, Porphyry and Hypetia were its prominent philosophers, the last named being a lady, chased and killed by a Christian mob in Alexandria.[6] In the Middle Ages Christianity destroyed their books and banned them, though principles of Neoplatonism were absorbed into Christianity in Rome and into Islam in southern Mesopotamia and Alexandria. Indian connections with Greece were very ancient and a section of Minoan Greeks, known as Kapardins, settled in Vedic India and are mentioned in the Vedas.[7]

The Hyksos or 'Shepherd Kings' of Egypt in the seventeenth century BCE brought the horse to Egypt and the first word for horse in Egyptian language was phonetically very similar to the word for horse in Ancient Tamil.[8] There is later corroboration of this opinion in the Princeton Series on the Middle East and I quote, 'We may assume that the present Dravidian speaking people, of the southern part of the sub-continent of India, extended much further to the north at the beginning of the second millennium BCE.' 'Thus before the coming of the Indo-Europeans, we may assume that Central Asia was occupied by a number of peoples, speaking languages which have disappeared, or of which the last traces are Burushaski and Dravidian speakers.'[9] After 1800 BCE great changes occurred in Mesopotamia, Central Asia and the Indus Valley. Sumerian civilization declined and disappeared in Mesopotamia. In the east there was collapse of the Harappan or Indus Valley culture and in this whole area, including Central Asia, there was severe drought and water shortage and tribes migrated southwards and cities decimated into small villages. This drought, discovered by satellite imagery, lasted till 1600 BCE but its cause is unknown and the Saraswati river, around which the Vedic civilization developed, dried up at this time. The Hyksos were a tribe that migrated from Central Asia to Egypt and the Dravidians migrated southwards inside the Indian Subcontinent as the Saraswati river system dried up. So even intellectual exchange in the known ancient world was much more than what we think today. Is there any evidence that the Vedanta philosophy did leave a permanent mark on humanity? The present day archaeologists and historians fired with a nationalist zeal often make exaggerated claims and the opposition of the antagonists is also often biased by the tradition of colonial scholarship and the Marxist contempt of India. We should leave them and go to pure science for evidence.

The thoughts of Socrates, Plato and Aristotle form the core of Western scientific and rational logic. Advances in fundamental thought in the twentieth century have revealed their closeness to the Vedanta philosophy. It is curious that scientists like Schroedinger, Niels Bohr, Oppenheimer, John Wheeler and many more are erudite Upanishad scholars. Niels Bohr is on record as saying that he goes into the Upanishads to ask the questions if not for their answers. John Wheeler, who is a venerated Professor of Physics at the Princeton University and whose students include scientists like Feynman, occupied the chair that was held by Einstein. He wrote, 'I like to think that someone will trace out how the deepest thinking of India made its way to Greece and from there to the philosophy of our times.' Others have found the thread that we had lost. This is the character of a philosophic conquest.

The next great conquest occurred with the emergence of Buddhism and was mainly eastwards. Buddhism arose basically from the ideals of the Upanishads but rejected the Vedic supremacy. The 'Tat Tvam Asi' or 'Thou Art That' conclusion of the Upanishad meant that everything and everybody is a part of and carried a little bit of the universal divinity. The realization was individual and the supreme goal of life. But in time the path became strewn with many Vedic rituals, which increased the power of the Brahmin priesthood. The Buddha showed the path for the individual with a simple code of ethics that could be practised without the intervention of priesthood, and the caste system became superfluous. This liberated the individual and unleashed a force of purity that took the world by storm. The Buddha established the first order of monks in the world who were celibate and their perfection was attained through many rebirths. Before him ancient Hindu religion had Rishis or very learned men who could choose whether to be celibate or not and celibacy was not an essential prerequisite of gaining knowledge. Over the long period from at least the fourth millennium BCE or earlier, when Vedic knowledge evolved around the Saraswati river, till the time of the Buddha in the sixth century BCE the system degenerated from knowledge to rituals presided over by the Brahmins to deliver credit at a cost to spiritual aspirants mainly to obtain material benefit in this or after life.

Buddhism spread across India and started spreading in Central Asia. The monks went across the frozen heights of the Himalayas, the Pamirs and the Karakorum Pass with nothing but the name of the Buddha and a few scriptures and started settlements. They were followed by merchants. By the time of Emperor Asoka in the third century BCE Buddhist settlements developed in Khotan.[10] From Khotan settlements extended eastwards along the north of the Kun Lun mountain range to the north of Tibet and to the south of the Tien Shan mountain range in the north, around the Taklamakan and Lop Nor deserts, along routes that were later to be known as the 'Silk Route'. The Indian monks, pilgrims and merchants discovered the route two centuries before the Chinese but it did not have that name at the time as silk used to go from China to Europe either through the land route to Bengal or from the first century BCE onwards the sea route to the east coast of India. This was long before the time of Marco Polo. Spreading eastwards north and south of Taklamakan and Lop Nor deserts the settlements reached Tun-Huang (Ptolemy's Throana) at the mouth of the Gansu corridor to China in the north and small settlements like Cherchen in the south, to the north of the Kun Lun Mountains.[11] Archaeological excavations have discovered curious places in the far east southern settlements where both Chinese and Indians lived together with inscriptions in Kharoshti on clay tablets and ancient Chinese written on paper.

The Han emperor Ming-ti of China in the first century CE had a dream of a golden figure floating across his room in a halo of light.[12] The wise men were called and they decided that the emperor had seen the Buddha. The faith had been heard of but not known. An envoy was dispatched to India to bring the teachings of the Buddha and some teachers. They went across the high and dangerous Karakorum Pass that the Buddhist priests had negotiated for centuries to go to Central Asia. Buddhism brought China a new flourish of creativity. A new art form, the Serindian art was born. The silk route for trade between China and Europe and the countries in between came into being. Marco Polo visited China. The trade, prosperity, way of life and philosophy continued for centuries. China remained a Buddhist country for twenty centuries and still is with a gradual resurgence of religion in Communist China. China's ambassador to the USA once made a reference to this special relationship in the following words: 'For twenty centuries, India conquered and dominated China without ever having to send a single soldier . . .' Until modern times in China, Buddhism was the dynamo of intellectual growth, individual enterprise with independent development of science and technology with voluntary search for spiritual enlightenment, for learning and pilgrimage of a higher order that formed the core of relationship with India as long as Buddhism existed in India. They invented paper, gun powder, ice cream; built China's great wall that saved them from Muslim Arab invasion; naval designs that withstood the hurricanes and tornado of the South China Sea; an independent secular bureaucracy that was selected by competitive examination since the time of Confucius; and many innovations of statecraft. The spirituality and practicality of Buddhism made them a great nation.

After Alexander's retreat from India, those of his generals who stayed back in Central Asia and Northwest India established kingdoms; and the eastern portion of this Seleucid Empire, established by Seleucus and centred mainly in Bactria, became the centre of Greco-Indian culture. They embraced Buddhism, and art and culture flourished with close connection to India as Seleucus ceded areas south of Hindukush to the Indian king Chandragupta Maurya.[13] This art form became known as Gandhar art, the name derived from ancient Kandahar. The Buddha had forbidden his followers from making his statue. But that edict was superceded 400 years after his death and the first statue of the Buddha was made in the Greek style wearing Greek sandals in the Gandhar art.

This affinity of the Greek and Indian minds since antiquity is really interesting. From these Greek kingdoms Buddhism spread to the rest of central Asia and around the edges of the Taklamakan desert towards China. As the silk route developed, all countries en route became enormously wealthy and for centuries till the Arab invasion and afterwards, political games were played around capturing trading posts on the silk route. Liberation of the individual led to a great development of intellect. Science, art, medicine, engineering flourished both in India and abroad. Subterranean tunnels were made to bring water from the hills of the Tien Shan range to the Tarim basin far into the desert. The desert became fertile. Human habitations grew deep in the desert with flourishing traditions of art and philosophy. The religious liberalism embraced others who fled from a tyrannical Europe like many sects of Christianity—Gnostics, Nestorians, Manichaeans etc. who found their peaceful refuge in this land. The ancient Indian ideal of God as one and universal and in everything was widely endorsed and realized. The harsh terrain and the violent people who lived in it were pacified. As in China, enterprise developed with surprising innovations. The land was harsh with the desert at the doorstep, with nature's fury in areas close to the desert. So technology evolved to tame the desert, make it green and habitable both for man and God. Temples and Viharas were built. The desired life of a Buddhist is to live in a religious place among like minded people. In India there were sangharams where a householder could lead a religious life expecting *nirvana* in a later birth. Whether one believes in *nirvana* or not this surely was a peaceful life in a peaceful society embedded in a green technology to live at peace with nature. Life was not lazy but peaceful. These temples and Viharas have been dug out of the desert sand after a thousand years by explorers like Sven Hedin, Sir Aurel Stein, Albert von LeCoq, Count Otani and some others.[14] Much of the research in this area was conducted from the Asiatic Society at Calcutta in the good old days. The revelations are surprising. The frescoes and statuettes are of Indian appearance with men and women of surprising beauty and refinement, with women's coiffure as in modern times. Most of the statues were defaced or damaged. Similarly very old Christian churches of extinct sects have been discovered with exquisite art treasures. In fact many of the explorations were for these rare art treasures. Hence the explorers were called foreign devils.

These people and this civilization lasted until the Hun, Mongol and other invaders came from the east and finally Islamic armies from the west. Coming of Islam was particularly devastating, as human figurines were anathema to their religious faith. Temples and monasteries were defaced and destroyed. The desert came back and claimed the land and an entire civilization was buried under the sands, to be discovered after a thousand years. The conquering Islam stopped at the closed gates of China where the only approach was through the Gansu corridor surrounded by vicious desert. This natural land barrier has saved China from intruders through history. Genghiz Khan was the only invader to defeat China. His grandson, the famous king Kublai Khan was the only conqueror to rule over China for nearly 60 years. The Mongol rule was absorbed by Chinese pragmatism as a phase of their own history. Kublai Khan's conquest of Tibet is China's historical claim to annex Tibet. The only other invasion of China was by westerners from the sea in the seventeenth and eighteenth centuries but they could settle only in coastal areas as the central Chinese government and royalty were weak but still one and united. Subsequent history is well known.

But in India no wall was ever built or defences put up across the mountain passes of Hindukush inviting repeated Islamic rampage. The Buddhist Vihara and universities were sacked and the Buddhist population largely converted to Islam. Buddhism in India had become weak by internal decay and laziness. Shankaracharya in the eighth century CE revived Hinduism. He rediscovered the original Upanishad texts and the Vedanta literature that had been destroyed and distorted during the long period of Buddhist culture in India. He recovered the texts, corrected them and wrote extensive commentaries as explanations. He debated with Buddhist Acharyas on the question of the 'Reality' of this world and the path of knowledge and defeated them in debates. Buddhism had undergone considerable metamorphosis by that time. He organized Hindu monastic life into ten principal streams and established four *Maths* or monasteries in four corners of India to maintain the purity of Vedanta philosophy. By the time Islam came two centuries later Buddhism had collapsed but a strong Hinduism strengthened by the philosophical work of Shankaracharya and Ramanuja resisted Islam. The museum at Mathura contains rows and rows of beheaded statues of the Buddha and beheaded statues of Kanishka and other Kushana kings who followed the Mahayana stream of Buddhism that spread to Ceylon and South

East Asia. The first century CE was remarkable for religious developments in India and Central Asia that have influenced the world till our times. Apart from the coming of Christ, the migration of the lost tribes of Israel, the appearance of the first statue of Buddha and the first images of deities of Hinduism, the birth of Mahayana Buddhism (with deities like Tara, the Tantric goddess), birth of Tantra, and China embracing Buddhism happened in the first and second centuries CE.

Over time Islam in India also underwent change. Fusions affected art, architecture, music and dance forms. Sufism came from Iran and flourished in India. The poetry and piety of Sufi saints, like Jelaluddin Rumi, Kabir, Mazhar Jaan-e-Janaan in Kashmir, Lalan Fakir in Bengal and the Dargah of Azmer Sharif drew people from both Hindu and Muslim communities and still do. I had the opportunity to see the Dervish dance to the accompaniment of the music of Rumi in Turkey, the original version and not the filmy one, and its simple beauty, piety and philosophy affected the entire audience comprising all religions. Most of the successful generals of Emperor Akbar were Hindu Rajput kings and he tried to propagate the integrated religion of Din-i-Ilahi. He initiated marriages between Hindu and Muslim royalties, himself marrying the Princess of Jodhpur. He also wrote a poem honouring the Vaishnava saint Sri Chaitanya. This social process continued through Mughal rule under his two immediate successors till the head of Dara Shukoh killed by Aurangzeb's men rolled at the feet of his father Emperor Shah Jahan. Dara was erudite in Vedanta philosophy and liked the religion propounded by his great grandfather. The decline of Mughal power started from Aurangzeb as Hindu rebellions started all over the country. But fusion still continued in pockets such as the Kathak dance based on the Krishna and Radha mythology developed under the Nawab of Oudh who was an ardent dancer himself. Islamic fundamentalism and a ritualistic and divided Hindu society under British colonialism and the colonial policy bent on creating division prevented further fusion at social and political levels. What does the future hold? Will India through a new fusion of culture and philosophy bring about a change that will again work for unification of the world? Will Islam change to the creative culture of Harun-al-Rashid's Baghdad and Iran of the flying carpet days? Or shall we all be extinct in a blood bath in which Islam will be the greatest loser? A philosophy does not develop in a vacuum. It comes with resurgence in every field of human activity and existence, both material and spiritual.

Once I was travelling in Bangladesh from Chattagram to Dhaka by bus. It was during the Puja holidays, which was also the time of Roja or Ramadan. It is a curious coincidence that the Durga Puja, the Navratri, the Ramadan, the Yom Kippur all fall in more or less the same time, probably guided by the agrarian calendar. After we had travelled for about an hour the bus stopped by the roadside and the driver announced that we have a ten minutes stop to do Atas Namaz in a small mosque by the roadside. This is done just before Iftar, the breaking of fast. The young man sitting beside me got up and asked whether I would get down. I had a mind to say yes as my idea of divinity was secular but thought better of it because I was not familiar with the ritual and my presence could be misconstrued as mockery. Those who went to pray returned and the bus started and I dozed off. The same young man woke me up a little later and asked me to make Iftar. A box of food had been supplied to us to break the fast inside the bus. I asked sleepily whether it was already time and he said the prescribed time was 5.26 pm for that day and it was already 5.26 pm. I opened the box and ate some things from it. I do not mind eating anything as long as it did not make me sick and the contents of the box seemed clean and innocuous. I tasted a little bit of everything and closed the box and the boy smiled at me. He had done likewise and we shared the joy of Iftar. I thought by taking that small amount of food I was happily accepted in a country that was mine until fifty years back. But what would have been my fate from my own society and religion by that same action if it were a hundred years back and the country my own? I smiled and went back to sleep. All through this travel roadside restaurants and eating houses were open on both sides eager for customers. Probably the only way to root out extremism of any kind is to make it a financially losing concern.

I cannot resist the temptation to quote part of an article published in the Google website, 'Glimpses of the Octonions and Quaternions History and Today's Applications in Quantum Physics by Kwa´sniewski. A.K.'

OBJECTS CASTING SHADOWS IN THE LOWER DIMENSIONS?

> This Plato's cave idea of shadows is everywhere present in Vedic minded John Archibald Wheeler's writings. Note his famous device motto 'It from Bit'. Wheeler wrote: 'I like to think that someone will trace how the deepest thinking of India made its way to Greece and from there to the philosophy of our times.' 'It is curious that people like Schroedinger, Niels Bohr, Oppenheimer and John Wheeler are Upanishad scholars.' This was another glimpse from the article 'Indian Conquests of the Mind' by Saibal Gupta. (The Statesman.org). The next glimpse is: 'One has the feeling that the thinkers of the East knew it all, and if we could only translate their answers into our language we would have the answers to all our questions.' (Source: *Uncommon Wisdom* by Fritjof Capra, p. 40). Werner Heisenberg should perhaps be also counted an Upanishad scholar. For sure he was Neo-Platonist in thinking and feeling the Quantum Mechanics message. Werner Karl Heisenberg (1901-1976), German theoretical physicist, was one of the leading scientists of the 20th century. Heisenberg spent some time in India as Rabindranath Tagore's guest in 1929. There he got acquainted with Indian philosophy which brought him great comfort for its similarity to modern physics. Anyhow is it not like that with all of them: Wheeler, J. A. and Zurek, W. H. and Schroedinger, Niels Bohr, Oppenheimer and you and me—all we are It from Bit? This was a kind of passionate idea of Feynman at the dusk of his life.

Dr. Kwa'sniewski says as a dissident he was relegated by the Bialystok University authorities from the Institute of Computer

Sciences organized by the author to the Faculty of Physics ul. Lipowa 41, 15 424 Bialystok, Poland. e-mail: kwandr@gmail.com. and I have definite knowledge of Western universities penalizing or demoting scholars or investigators articulating their views on the relevance of Indian philosophical ideas in scientific research on the ground of holding 'mystic' views or losing objectivity unless of course he is of the eminence of Wheeler or Niels Bohr.

References

1. Malik, S C, *Indian Civilization: The Formative Period.* Shimla: Indian Institute of Advanced Study, 1968.
2. Micropedia 12.193.
3. Idem 10.948. Also Malik op. cit.
4. Chatterjee, S K, *India and Ethiopia from the Seventh Century BC.* Calcutta: Asiatic Society, 1968.
5. *Great Dialogues of Plato.* Translated by W H D. Rouse. Harmondsworth: Penguin Books, 1956.
6. Cannuyer, C. *Coptic Egypt: Christians of the Nile.* London: Thames and Hudson 2001.
7. Ibid.
8. Davies, Paul, *Other Worlds.* Harmondsworth: Pelican Books, 1990.
9. Frye, R N, *The Heritage of Central Asia,* ed. Lewis, B and Lowry, H W Princeton: Marcus Weiner Publishers, 1995.
10. Ibid.
11. Hopkirk, P, *Foreign Devils on the Silk Road,* New York: Oxford University Press, 1980.
12. Ibid.
13. Basham, A L, *The Wonder that was India.* New Delhi: Rupa, 1954. Thapar, Romila. *Asoka and the Decline of the Mauryas.* New Delhi: Oxford University Press, 1997. Thapar, Romila. *Early India.* New Delhi:Penguin Books, 2002.
14. Hopkink, P, op. cit.
15. Quoted from Kwásniewski, A K 'Glimpses of the Octonions and Quaternions History and Today's Applications in Quantum Physics', Google, 3 March 2008.

Religion and Politics in India's History

A serious confusion over the relationship of politics and religion hangs over contemporary Indian society. It has led to the rise of fundamentalist forces, casteist forces, intellectual backlash against religion and policies of appeasement which lead nowhere and to the general downgrading of the secular democratic principles of nationhood. It is necessary to examine these within a historical framework since they have been with us throughout history.

The religious ideals of India are basically secular, from its highest philosophies to its basic practices in the communities. What has corrupted this secularism from time to time needs to be studied. A study of the periods of Indian history when it has been on the ascendant will show that they have also been periods of religious and political harmony. Whether it is political and economic stability that has produced religious secularism or *vice versa* is difficult to decide. It will be a fair bet to state that both processes have concurred in different epochs. Attempts at forcible domination of one group by another has always had a disastrous effect on the nation. In the recorded history it was Hinduism and Buddhism at one time and Hinduism and Islam for the last thousand years. Christianity was 'king's religion' in colonial times but there was no forced conversion, something that is raising its ugly head only now. Religious sentiment is important and cannot be wished away. It can be a powerful instrument for both progress and hindrance.

The first empire building and organized politics in India started with Chandragupta Maurya. The architect and theoretician of this first great empire was a Brahmin named Chanakya or Kautilya. Like other Brahmins of his time he was engaged in the study of the scriptures until the invasion of Alexander, when he realized the necessity of empire. So in this case scriptures dictated politics and Chandragupta, a *sudra*, was accepted as the emperor. Chandragupta ultimately embraced Jainism, became a monk, abdicated his throne and died of starvation at Sravana-Belgola but did not alter the secular character of his empire. His son Bindusara followed the same line and extended the empire. Bindusara's son Asoka, an astute and wise king, found Kalinga as an obstacle to his profitable maritime trade with South India and conquered it with a great carnage. The Buddhist scriptures speak of his sudden disgust and conversion to Buddhism but history states that it was a gradual process. He realized that the vast empire, probably the largest in Indian history, could not be ruled with arms alone. Buddhism at that time was a socio-intellectual movement and many religious sects associated with it. He found in the principles of *Dhamma* a philosophy of social responsibility and equality and started propagating it. But he maintained his secularism and gave equal honours to Brahmins and *Sramanas*. His prison had torture chambers and capital punishment was in force. He had an extensive spy network as also a direct control over the army and the civil service. The Third Buddhist Council was held in Asoka's time under the direction of Moggaliputta Tissa and the *Sangha* was rid of all dissidents. The connection of Asoka with this event is uncertain. His power dwindled in the later part of his reign and his last edict written just before or after his death states that he cleaned the *Sangha* of all dissident members. His second chief queen Tissarakkha revolted against his excessive devotion to Buddhism and his successors did not have his ability to keep the reins of power in a single hand and the dynamic pragmatism of his younger days. He did not leave a secular bureaucracy owing allegiance to the state only and his institution of *Dhammamahamatta* boomeranged in later years. The Maurya Empire split into two halves immediately after his death and vanished after 52 years. The eastern half went to the Brahminic kingdom of the Sungas. The western half went to the Greeks, Sakas, Pahlavas and Kusanas in turn, all coming from outside. Kings came and went favouring one religion or the other.[1]

Another Indian empire rose with the Guptas in 320 CE. It was a golden age with religious freedom, political stability, economic affluence and intense creativity. At its pinnacle it lasted for nearly two hundred years but continued on a smaller scale almost till the eighth century. On the eastern fringes of the empire rose the Palas of Bengal in the eighth century. The first king Gopala was elected by the people after a long period of instability and religious persecution.[2] The Palas were secular in outlook though Buddhists themselves, and encouraged and supported literature, scholarship and social justice. King Dharmapala extended his empire as much by diplomacy as by arms. That speaks of a superior culture. The internecine wars among the Palas, the Gurjar-Pratiharas and the Rashtrakutas weakened the political and military power of India and paved the way for Muslim conquest. Even under Muslim rule the basic religious secularism of the Indian people prevailed after the initial Turkish years of war and strife. The best example is Akbar but by no means the only one. He realized the importance of a secular administration, banned forcible conversions and is reputed to have written a poem in praise of Sri Chaitanya apart from forming his secular religious principles in Din-i-Ilahi. Hindu armies won most of the battles for him and his two successors. The rise of fundamentalism under Aurangzeb heralded the disintegration of the Mughal Empire.

There is an interesting parallel between the reigns of Asoka and Akbar. Both were great monarchs interested in religion as a political means of integration. Asoka actively promoted Buddhism after achieving complete control over his vast empire. The reason might have been a genuine love of the ideals of the Buddha backed by a pragmatic decision to bind the empire in a single ethical philosophy without caste distinctions that divided the Hindu society. The early historic Hindu society[3] was bonded in *Puranic* times by mythical stories and holy places of pilgrimage. Siva danced his dance of destruction with the dead body of Sati, his wife, on his shoulder after she had died hearing her husband insulted at her father's house. Vishnu, worried that the world will not last, used his weapon *Sudarshan Chakra* to cut Sati's body into pieces and scattered them all over India. There were fifty-two pieces and they fell scattered in fifty-two places of India. The easternmost was near Guwahati in Assam, the westernmost in Hinglaj in Baluchistan, northernmost in Kashmir, northeast in Nepal and the southernmost in Kanyakumarika. Pilgrims from all over India have thronged to these *Satipiths* since antiquity and still do in ever larger numbers. Thus the boundaries of *Aryavarta* or India were staked out since ancient times and remains intact. The political map of India has continually changed, kings have come and kings have gone but the existence of India as a nation united by religion was never in doubt. Even Muslim or Western conquest did not matter, the Hindu Indian continued to live in his philosophical space. Buddhism also did not matter as Asoka covered the country with the *stupas* and obelisks with the Buddha's edicts engraved on them, sharing many common holy sites. Hindus did not mind much and over time all of these became their holy places too and the Buddha was accepted as a Hindu incarnation of God, an *Avatar*, just as they accepted the first Christian Church outside Israel where St. Thomas landed, as a holy place.

A similar process started with Islam, through conquest of just another religion, because Hinduism itself had many streams of worship. The heterodoxy of Hindu religion could accommodate any religion as her own over a period of time. Interestingly this absorbing power of Hinduism became a problem with both Muslims and Christians during some periods. During the Afghan and Turkic conquest of mainly North India they remained conquerors and imposed authority with their foreign armies and their own bureaucracy. To the Indian kings they were a scourge with a better technology of warfare but to the ordinary Indian they were just another dynasty with another dress and another religion. They would loot the wealth of the temples, carry away the *sivalingas* from Pravas and Somnath, only to be replaced by another *sivalinga* and life went on as before. The invaders, Muslims or Christians, never understood that in the Hindu mind the image of God he worships with devotion is not the God but his image and it does not matter in the end if it is replaced because His ultimate abode is in the heart and mind of the devotee. But in spite of that Hindu society was weakening and contracting under the impact, because their material life was being affected, and they imposed social and religious superstitions seeking to protect individual and family life; in the process society became a closed cocoon stopping creativity and growth. This process had happened repeatedly through the last millennium either in regions or in the country as a whole. Pockets of weakened Hindu kingdoms remained to nurture what remained. The early Sultanates of Delhi remained as colonial powers without integrating much with the sons of the soil and did not flourish either in wealth or prestige. They were replaced one after the other. Akbar was the first Muslim monarch with a difference. His grandfather Babur came from Central Asia from a branch of Mongols with no root to go back to and conquered the Sultanate of Delhi. His father Humayun succeeded Babur to the throne of Delhi but was defeated by a combined Hindu army and thrown out of India. Akbar had to regain that kingdom and retain it, which he soon realized was not possible unless he became an Indian and integrated with the people of the country. He too, like his grandfather, had no place to go back to and he might have been impressed with some of the philosophical tenets of Hindu life and the living culture. So he befriended the Hindu kings, brought learned Hindu men to his inner circle and cabinet and tried to integrate the two religious ideals. Most important of all he did not try to impoverish the Hindus like previous rulers.

What is curious about the reigns of Asoka and Akbar is that these two greatest monarchs of India were similar in their valour, military skills, authority, wisdom and administrative skills and brought about religious unity of the country producing what we would call today a secular society. Asoka embraced Buddhism after being secure on his throne after a fierce fratricidal war to wrench it from his brothers. The Kalinga war was a vicious war that left many dead and left Kalinga desolate. Political pragmatism required to keep the vast empire united, heal the scars of both the wars and correct his own image of Chandasoka, the cruel king, led him to the peaceful secular ethics of Buddhism, more than his own personal devotion to the Buddha. His own devotion increased as he grew older, and led to increasing opposition to his excessive leaning towards Buddhism even within his immediate surroundings, including his family. Immediately after his death the empire was divided into two. Revolt by Pusyamitra Sunga, a Hindu vassal king and general of Asoka, and attack on later Mauryas led to occupation of its eastern half by the Sungas. The western half with its capital at Taxilla was attacked continuously by the Greeks and Central Asian tribes. A Hindu backlash, a strongly centralized administration controlled personally by the king, absence of a secular bureaucracy selected without favour dedicated to the nation and not to a king, absence of nationalism and a sense of national identity of the people, economic downturn specially in the remote less fertile provinces have all been blamed by different researchers for the surprisingly fast collapse of the Maurya empire. Reading through them one cannot help thinking that all these factors played their part. Hindu backlash was definitely there though how strong it was in affluent and cultured urban centres like Magadh where Buddhist learning prevailed and in remote areas where Hindu religious culture prevailed at this time is not known, though there was a definite division in later centuries.[4]

A similar Muslim backlash raised its head after the liberal era of Akbar but not immediately. Akbar's death was followed by three fratricidal wars of succession among brothers, one putting Jehangir on throne, the next Shah Jehan and the third Aurangzeb. The Hindu kingdoms empowered under Akbar were reluctant participants in all of them. The final backlash was at the accession of Aurangzeb that was followed by punitive taxation and social ostracism of the Hindus.[5]

The decline of the Mughal empire started at Aurangzeb's time and accelerated after his death as Hindu rebellion spread across India and foreign colonialism started on Indian soil taking advantage of the political instability of internal wars, just as it had happened at the beginning of the Muslim invasion.

Such a rapid fall from a pinnacle of history in two completely different phases of Indian history is worrying and needs to be studied afresh as we are developing as a nation. In both there was a factor of religious backlash, mild to start with after Asoka and slowly developing after the reign of Akbar—one community aggrieved at the larger social and political space being occupied by the other. In both situations there was economic downturn due to the burden of a large empire and social and geographical divides. In both there was absence of a secular bureaucracy and army dedicated to the nation and increasing distance of the people from the ruling elite. In both there was absence of consciousness and pride in India as a nation. Overriding nationalist pride can overcome even social exploitation of the aristocracy as was seen at the time of the French Revolution when many nations attacked France and were repulsed even in the midst of social disarray during the revolution. At the time of Jehangir at the peak of Mughal power Hindu businessmen from the western coast of India brought the British admiral to the Mughal court for recognition as their saviour after the British had defeated the Portuguese fleet at Kalikat. Neither the Emperor nor the Hindu traders had anything of the pride required to spend money to develop a navy of their own in the face of foreign competition, instead of playing lackeys to a foreign power. A secular bureaucracy chosen without favouritism through competitive examination and dedicated to serve the nation and not the king since the time of Confucius has maintained China's freedom through the vicissitudes of history. Buddhism and Taoism in China have never meddled in politics and vice versa even to the present time. As long as Europe was busy with the religious wars of the Crusades it remained in the dark middle ages. There are many examples like these from the history of other countries, but India has never had the integrated binding of a sovereign proud nation.

In order to flourish as an independent sovereign nation the nation is the first priority, without indulging in religion which has to be left to the people and religion in its turn should not meddle in politics. A bureaucracy selected through competitive examination from the entire society without favours remains responsible only to the nation, and not to any political entity occupying power at any time; and ought to enforce rule of law with the help of an independent judiciary. The armed forces should bear the responsibility of defending the nation and remain subservient to the civil leadership for that task. The ruling political entity must be sensitive to public opinion and the distress of the people at multiple levels through the participatory mobilization of a multilayered social leadership and not through its agents. Is it not possible to build such an India? Many of the instruments were installed in British India, and most have been enshrined in our Constitution; they must not be corrupted for narrow short term political gains.

Is there a concurrence of this type of politics and leadership in our religious heritage because the importance of religion in national life cannot be denied? I can speak only of Hindu religion not having much knowledge of secular Islamic scholarship on society and politics and it is up to them to respond to this. There is a book in Vedanta lineage known as *Ashtavakra Samhita*[6] that is a dialogue between Sage Ashtavakra and King Janaka. This is a lesson in non-dualist Advaita Vedanta addressed to kings and rulers of a nation. Human beings with perception of the non-dualist formless divinity or *Brahman* or unitary God of the Vedas develop a mental attitude to the material world that gives them the realization that the whole world with all its parts are but different manifestations of the infinite divinity that suffuses this universe. This gives them a kinship to that world as parts of their own self. It is the highest tenet of Hindu philosophy and attained by few. In the book King Janaka expounds to the sage Ashtavakra how he administers his kingdom and lives the material life and duties of a king with knowledge and perception of the non-dual unitary divinity in the non-dualist world with total non-attachment, devoid of personal desires and undertakes decisions and actions that are necessary for the welfare of the kingdom and the society. Thus he is a *Rajarshi*, both a *Raja* and a *Rishi* or sage at the same time, who are the best kings and rulers according to the Hindu tradition. It has to be noted that the ideal is of a *Rishi* mentally and intellectually with the decisiveness of action of a *Raja* – not a religious king but a pious king. A *Rishi* is a *jnani*, a seeker of God in the path of knowledge, a *yogi*, a follower of *Brahman*. Such a king does not promote any particular religion of his subjects but is respectful and impartial to all, nor does he try to develop a new religion. He is calm and pious and loving in his knowledge of the ultimate unitary nature of divinity but respects people's need of a personal God and rituals, of which there are many in Hindu religion itself, not to speak of other religions. He cannot have that personality unless he has deep piety born out of the knowledge and perception of the non-dual formless omnipresent universal divinity. All religions and cultures know it but not as consciously as it is propounded in the Vedanta. The book is a description of a king with emotional detachment and impartiality but with universal love and decisiveness in action to do his duty or *karma* of protecting and enriching the nation and society as a caretaker. This Hindu ideal of governance of nation is difficult to attain in total perfection but gives a roadmap.

I have a dream, that is only personal, that problems like those associated with Babri Masjid will one day be solved in a manner that sends proper signals to the world. Our country has brilliant architects who can design a sublime structure, not promoted by the politicians but by the people themselves, where Hindus and Muslims can worship, maintaining their independent traditions and customs. Such a temple-mosque constructed deliberately and jointly will be the edifice of a future India.

1998-99

References

1. Thapar, Romila, *Asoka and the Decline of the Mauryas.* Delhi: Oxford University Press, 1997. Basham, A L, *The Wonder that was India.* Delhi: Rupa & Co., 1954.
2. Basham, A L, op. cit; Roy, Nihar Ranjan. *Bangalir Itihas* [History of the Bengali People]. Kolkata: Dey's Publishing, 1949.
3. Beteille, A, *Society and Politics of India.* (London School of Economics Monograph on Social Anthropology), Delhi: Oxford University Press, 1992.
4. Roy. *Bangalir Itihas,* op. cit; Thapar, Romila. *Asoka and the Decline of the Mauryas,* op. cit. and *Early India.* Harmondsworth, Penguin, 2002.
5. Basham, A L, *The wonder that was India.* op. cit.
6. *Ashtavakra Samhita.* Translated and annotated by Swami Nityaswarupananda, Calcutta: Advaita Ashram.

MAKING OF A NATION

Rise and Fall of Indian Civilization through the Millennia: 'A Millennium of Darkness'

A millennium is ending and a new one is beginning. Recorded Indian history dates back over four millennia and its origins are shrouded in the misty dawn of mankind with a light of revelation shining here and there. It may have something to do with the fact that ancient India or rather much of it got detached from the mass of Africa and migrated northeast to attach itself to the bottom of the Asian landmass about 65 million years ago, about the same time that the dinosaurs became extinct.

The records of the earliest of these four millennia, i.e. the second millennium BCE are also vague though recent researches are shedding more light on its extent, outlines and culture – a civilization extending probably to Central Asia and Mesopotamia.[1] Such evidences are based on recently discovered archaeological evidence of Pre-Harappan settlements around the Caspian Sea and evidences of links and similarities between Pre-Harappan Indus and Gangetic cultures and those of Central Asia and Mesopotamia. Swami Vivekananda once stated that the ancient Sumerian civilization was a colony of Pre-Aryan India. Though such assumptions were probably intuitive in nature, in later years remnants of Indian teak wood dating from the fourth millennium BCE were found in Ur, the ancient Sumerian port city where Indian ships from Lothal and other ports in the vicinity made regular trips. After going through the Persian Gulf and the

Gulf of Aqaba the ships used to dock at Ur beside the Euphrates River. On the huge Ziggurat at Ur, built during the Third Dynasty (2200 – 2100 BCE), was the shrine of the moon god Nanna, the god of the sea tides and sailors. Even the ancient Greek culture was a dark men's culture that white Greeks migrating from the north took over later.[2] Around 1800 to 1600 BCE this civilization encompassing the known world underwent a slow decay extinguishing itself in Mesopotamia and Central Asia. Whereas it became extinct in these regions, the proto-Dravidian (Kassites, Caspian or *Kasva*) speakers migrated southwards to the Indian mainland while the major bulk of later Burushaski speakers migrated towards Iran and Babylon. As they retreated into the Indian mainland, the process of cultural fusion slowly spread southwards into central India. The theory of a sudden or repeated Aryan invasion destroying the Pre-Harappan and Harappan culture, which was so close to the heart of some European scholars of the eighteenth and nineteenth centuries and was propagated extensively through the school curricula without any material evidence in its favour, is almost rejected today as there is no evidence of such a source of massive hordes of Aryans from a particular area of Central Asia. What has been found till now is a small culture, known as the Andronovo culture in the region of the Caspian sea which comes closest to the description of the Aryans.[3] But they were neither hordes nor world conquerors like the Mongol hordes in a later millennium. What happened was a gradual process of southward migration of a mixed proto-Indian Dravidian (?) culture extending to the Caspian Sea mingling with Harappan culture and diffused southwards with the migration of population. Much of its content was pre-Aryan, like probably the asceticism of Indian culture. This view has been supported by recent work combining anthropology with archaeological data confirmed by carbon dating.[4] As a result, by the beginning of the next millennium, that is the millennium before the birth of Christ, a grand civilization took shape in India, particularly in north and central India, which was by no means entirely Aryan, even if a separate Aryan race existed.

Philological similarity in language among different tribes migrating in different directions from Central Asia has shown[5] that a stray word like 'htr' –a beast of burden, a draught animal, a horse – found in ancient Egypt in the seventeenth century BCE for the first time when foreign invaders from Asia, the Hyksos or 'Shepherd Kings' of Egypt, first came to Egypt and brought with them the horse, suggests a connexion with the common Indian word for 'horse'. We have to assume here a pre-Aryan Dravidian borrowing into later Sanskrit, 'ghutra', horse; whence we have Tamil 'kutirai', Kannada 'kudare', primitive Telugu 'gudra' or 'gutra' leading to current Telugu 'gurramu' and later Indo-Aryan 'ghota', 'ghota-ka', whence new Indo-Aryan 'ghoda' which has ousted the genuine Aryan (Indo-European) word 'asva'. The word for elephant also went from the Old Tamil to the rest of the world. Thus the ancient Indian civilization is not an Aryan gift but pre-Aryan in origin and might have migrated to Central Asia around the Caspian Sea in which Aryan tribes have been gradually assimilated and a new synthesis emerged, whereas in its outposts in Central Asia and Mesopotamia it has been largely replaced. The Aryan theory, as is now clear, was propagated by European colonialists who wanted to give an intellectual and historical justification for their conquest as a second beneficial Aryan invasion. It is one of the jokes of history that after receiving the same 'Aryan Treatment' at the hands of Hitler they started looking askance at the Aryan theory in the new psychological environment.

The picture becomes clearer from 700 BCE onwards which roughly is the time of the compilation of the *Satapatha Brahmana* containing references to contemporary historical people and events. This is followed successively by the advent of the Buddha, the invasion of Alexander, the formation of the first Indian empire under the Mauryas, the ascent of Asoka, establishment of Buddhist Greek states in Central Asia, the beginning of the spread of Buddhism into the entire known civilized world, mainly eastwards. The first millennium BCE is therefore the epoch of a grand Indian civilization taking shape and expanding to the rest of the world.

The process continues into the first millennium CE with further expansion of both Buddhist and Hindu Indian civilizations into South East Asia, Central Asia and China. The remains and the grand stories of the Central Asian civilization were unearthed and discovered in the nineteenth century by explorers like Sven Hedin, Aurel Stein and others, a work which in a large measure was directed from Calcutta. In this millennium the entire hostile region of Central Asia was pacified and settled with a great upsurge in trade, commerce and culture around the great silk routes. Expansion also occurred in other areas and Buddha statues of this period have been found as far away as in Lake Malaren near Stockholm in Sweden. There was an upsurge in art, architecture, science, mathematics, astronomy, medicine and in every branch of human endeavour which is still handed down to us as our cultural roots.

Cultural decay started towards the end of the first millennium CE. Two things happened separated by two hundred years—the beginning of the Hindu revival under Shankaracharya and Muslim invasion eastwards into Central Asia and India. The beginning of the second millennium CE, the end of which we are seeing today, is marked by a gradual and inexorable Muslim conquest of India and Hindu protectionist orthodoxy pulling down its shutters like a worm under attack. Barring stray episodes this was the general pattern. The result was that Buddhism vanished entirely from Central Asia and India, the process ending at China, who shut her doors. The intellectual life of India was paralysed behind the bolted doors of a Hindu orthodoxy under attack and a Muslim culture which always looked westwards at its roots of origin for mental, intellectual and spiritual succour. From the Hindu point of view the protectionist orthodoxy revived by the valorization of their spiritual supremacy by Shankaracharya and Ramanuja saved Hinduism from total destruction.[6] Limited fusion and development occurred in art, architecture and music but it stopped there. Efforts by Muslim liberals for greater fusion and developments were repeatedly undermined by Muslim orthodoxy still bent on conquering and converting or later to maintain a separate identity linked westwards and denying to be Indian. In many ways the Muslim orthodoxy remained more orthodox than in many progressive Islamic countries. No new progress occurred in science and technology and knowledge in general and in developing an open and gracious society, based on justice, in spite of the presence of a great deal of wealth in the country. As a result, the entire second millennium has been a period of great torture for the common man, paralyzing the ideas of creativity and justice, and as a matter of fact many portions of the country reverted back to primitive life. As we know now, many of the so called primitive tribal areas today were the seats of great culture in a multilateral society. The degeneration of India was compounded by the rise of civilization in Europe many of whose founding principles and philosophies were influenced by ancient India, as in the teachings of Socrates and Plato.

This millennium marks the total loss of self esteem by Indians both Hindus and then Muslims. Looking westwards did not save the Muslims, a thing that has to be remembered by Indian Muslims today. Into this morass and cauldron of Indian degeneration came the new aggressive European civilization imbued with the moral legitimacy of an aggressive Christianity. Christianity reached India before it reached Europe, but this second wave of aggressive Christianity was totally different with its ideas of conquer and convert just as the Muslims had started out to do. Writings and sermons from the missionaries and the missionary related works in the eighteenth and nineteenth centuries remind one of Christian barbarity perpetrated on the shores and lands of Africa. In the case of India it probably acted as one poison killing another and the side shows of intellectual liberalism, development of language and printing, activity of organizations like the Asiatic Society and a great many scholars opting to work under the Church or the East India Company but pursuing their own intellectual enquiry gradually won greater ground and a great many hearts.[7] A great Indian rebirth started under this canopy of European liberalism, scarcely noticed by the conquerors at first. This rebirth, though stimulated by European liberalism, was wholly Indian in its content. Aping a culture does not produce a new culture but a new synthesis does. The sparks for welding this new synthesis were wholly Indian and based in antiquity. For example, one such major spark came from a poor priest of the Kali temple of Dakshineswar, viz. Ramakrishna Paramahansa, whose standards in a span of one hundred years now fly in five continents, in countries as diverse as Russia and Argentina, Brazil and Japan, and whose monks come from all major religions and countries of the world, preaching unity of religions and the teachings of Vedanta as interpreted in the context of contemporary society. Hinduism provides the proof that a great culture is never supplanted or destroyed but modified.

Closer at hand, in the Indian milieu, revival of Hindu liberalism and free enquiry has been naturally paralleled by the rise of Hindu orthodoxy. Similarly, Muslim liberalism has been paralleled by the growth of Muslim orthodoxy. This is where we stand today, at the great divide. What is in store for us in the third millennium CE? An optimist would see that the intellectual basis for the ascent in the first millennium CE was laid at the end of the first millennium BCE. The clash of orthodoxy and paralysis of humanity in this great country of ours in the second millennium CE started towards the end of the first millennium CE. The basis of our present development spearheading our march into the third millennium CE is the revival of liberalist ideas and the freedom of the mind throughout the Indian society which has already been laid at the end of the second millennium from the nineteenth century CE – by Hindus, Muslims and Christians alike. In spite of the tussles and clashes of today, one can foresee the birth of the third wave of a world conquering Indian culture, which has never conquered by arms but by the brain and the heart. Let us leave behind the darkness of the second millennium and march towards the dawn of the third with the head held high. After all Indian civilization has the tradition and the capacity to rise from its ashes.

1998-99

References

1. Frye, R N, *The Heritage of Central Asia,* ed. Lewis, B and Lowry, H W. Princeton: Marcus Wiener Publishers, 1995.
2. Bernal, Martin, *Black Athena: The Afroasiatic Roots of Classical Civilization, Volume 1: The Fabrication of Ancient Greece, 1785–1985.* London: Vintage, 1995.
3. Frye, op. cit.
4. Malik, S C, *Indian Civilization: The Formative Period.* Shimla.: Indian Institute of Advanced Study, 1968.
5. Chatterji, S K, *India and Ethiopia from the Seventh Century BC.* Calcutta: Asiatic Society, 1968.
6. Beteille, A, *Society and Politics in India.* New Delhi: Oxford University Press, 1992.
7. Ibid.

Economic Prosperity does not Guarantee Political Stability

Political Stability Depends on Global Strategy Devoid of Clichés

In our present euphoria over our economic recovery one may be called a cynic for pondering whether economic affluence guarantees political stability in the historical context of India, but the question is pertinent.

Economic prosperity is nothing new in the Indian subcontinent but for the last three centuries, whatever might have been the structure of production and distribution in each epoch. We have had very little internal political stability barring the days of the three empires—Maurya, Gupta and Mughal. As for external political security we have had eight foreign invasions in the preceding two and a half millennia—the Greeks, the Kushanas, the Sakas, the Huns, the Turks, the Afghans, the Mughals and lastly the British. The first seven came through the northwest frontier. The Greeks came only to Punjab and later ceded most of their Indian territory to the Mauryas. The Kushanas conquered northern India and ruled until their base in Central Asia was lost. The Sakas and after them the White Huns were resisted by the powerful Gupta empire, as they came in waves for two centuries. When they broke through after the death of Skandagupta, as the empire weakened due to internal intrigues,[1] they were also too weak to make a difference and their second king Mihirakula fled to Kashmir.

Plausibly the resistance given by the Gupta Empire to them diverted the fury of Central Asian nomadic tribes to Europe.

The Turks came initially for looting. Later Muhammad Gharry defeated Prithviraj Chauhan and established the Delhi Sultanate starting off the Islamic epoch of India. Muhammad Gharry died soon after and his kingdom in Afghanistan vanished but the one in Delhi continued. In this epoch another major foreign invasion was averted as Chengiz Khan's hordes passed close to North India and Iltutmis or Altamas, the Sultan of Delhi, paid an enormous tribute. But in 1398 another Mongol invader, Taimur attacked and sacked Delhi destroying the Turkish power in India, which survived in the Deccan as the Sultanate of Bahmani. Afghan kings occupied the throne of Delhi ineffectually for a short while until Ibrahim Lodi was defeated by Babur, a fifth generation descendant of Taimur.

All this is schoolboy history but they have a pattern of similarity. All the invasions, including the last one from Britain from a different frontier, did not succeed in their first attempts. They retreated and waited, harassing the defenders with probing attacks and subversion, along with espionage to find weaknesses and betrayers and they always found some. Even Babur followed this technique against Ibrahim Lodi. Babur was a sensitive man, a poet, but when it came to statecraft he was unrelenting. And in the interlude of wars Indians will allow trade across the border and on the mountain passes with people crossing over, because business must go on even if the enemy's agents are crossing over. We never went on hot pursuit of the enemy. Prithviraj wanted to go after his victory in 1091 CE but did not have the means and did not get help from other kings. One year later he was defeated followed by massacre. Vijaynagar did not follow up after defeating the Bahmanis more than once but lost the last battle through an undercover commando action and were destroyed. Are we still continuing our foreign politics in the same tradition?

European strategists like Clausewitz,[2] and till the present day have thought that the best place to fight a war was on the enemy's soil, but we never went out of our boundaries. Only the Maurya Empire protected the northwest frontier with vassal states. The next people to do so were the British who fought and lost two Afghan wars. Then they befriended the Afghans as they realized that the Afghans were not the main enemies; it were the Russians who were trying to reach India through Persia and Afghanistan. Throughout history, barring exceptions, we lacked in strategy, weapons, firepower, diplomacy, cohesion, cunning and a will to fight. We do not know what a nation at war means though war is today looming over Asia.

We never thought of India as a nation until now. It was a conglomerate of kingdoms fighting against each other.[3] The people did not care who the king was apart from a few who hovered around the throne for favour and betrayed when it suited them. The leaders of trade and commerce who were the financial powers behind the throne often refused support to the king in critical times and even betrayed, let alone support an expedition. Kings may come and kings may go but money, they thought, will be there forever. Europe was also a conglomerate of kingdoms with each one of them nurturing a strong nationalism that however did not prevent them from joining hands when needed.

Indian kings were no better. They would conquer their neighbour's land and put it to waste. Prithviraj himself defeated the Chandellas and left villages in ruins. The Turkish invasion overran India weakened by constant fighting among three powerful kingdoms – the Palas, the Rashtrakutas and the Pratiharas. The same thing happened with the Maratha forces of the Peshwa, Bhonsle, Sindhia and Holkar when the British were occupying India. Curiously this political blindness was a legacy from Muslim India. Rich traders on the west coast took refuge under the Portuguese and then the British to protect their sea trade and introduced them to Emperor Jehangir. But neither they nor the Emperor developed a navy. The sea was not a threatened frontier to them, only a means to make money even when marauding navies were looting India. The origin of such blindness can be traced primarily to a selfish greed of wealth and power. The Marathas were the same race but they had greater distrust for their own kind than the foreigner.

When I see their progeny in power today I feel uneasy because that legacy of blindness has not ceased.

China lying far to the east always had a global strategy and was vigilant even about their western frontier of treacherous desert and high mountains. They sent repeated expeditions to survey and police these lands outside their borders at the time, in addition to building the Great Wall so that Genghis Khan was the only invader in history who could reach the Chinese heartland. Others from the Hsiung-nu in antiquity to the western powers only groped at the periphery for short times. We never even had a map of Afghanistan and Central Asia in spite of having a prolific trade.

All this can happen again because our mindset has not changed much but the world has changed. We have many frontiers today, and the techniques of invasion are also many. We are becoming rich, the rich being few, and that makes enemies. We are proud of our democracy that needs a lot of money to run and increases the twin dangers of corruption and subversion. We are a military power but not strong enough in a global sense. We have a nuclear arsenal but we are not an accepted nuclear power and politically not strong enough to use it even if necessary. There are pressures and it is uncertain which way global politics will turn and how our internal politics would react. We have to have clear goals and a global strategy devoid of clichés and emotions, a game we have never played. The riches of our land and our brains have attracted invaders but have never given us strong political stability for any length of time and this has bedevilled our intellect, initiatives and way of life and our freedom.

To survive and develop in this world we must be staunch nationalists and rationalists in spite of differences and individual or collective frustrations and need a reduction in our individual levels of greed. We have the opportunity but do we have the will? We have the brains but do we have the brawn?

2006

References

1. Basham, A L, *The Wonder that was India.* New Delhi: Rupa, 1954.
2. Clausewitz, Carl von, *On War.* Tr. Graham, Trubner, 1893.
3. Basham, op. cit.

Role of Media and Value Education in Building Society

A nation is not just a geographical boundary but is a philosophical and biological entity. The people in a nation are accustomed to think, act and follow a lifestyle automatically often without a theoretical and intellectual cognition of the values they are following. This is the common man's sense of value and it is the one sense that ultimately determines the history of the nation. Any change in the environment, whether political, economic, commercial, and technological or in any other manner, is recognized or reacted upon through this intuitive process and cultural heritage. Alterations in some of the values inherent in that sense occur in keeping with the traditions of the society. Here the society really acts like a biological organism for its survival or proliferation, enrichment and expansion. When the change is hostile it acts for its survival and when the change is congenial for growth it proliferates and enriches itself. This has been seen again and again in the history of India and many other nations with a long history. Every nation reacts to such situations in its own accustomed ways and therein lies its true sense of values and source of strength or weakness.

India, throughout history, has been a successful nation commercially, intellectually and culturally. Political failure and subjugation by foreign power has been our bane, preventing continuous and sustained growth in other fields. During each such epoch we have reacted by folding up into a cocoon and survived by somehow weathering the storm. Restrictive values sprang up during these periods ensnaring the society in the name of religion and curtailing individual liberties. Thus sea voyage was totally banned in a successful and dynamic seafaring nation and surprisingly the moratorium was successful and total. A country that had developed sublime and dynamic religio-philosophies and propagated them boldly to the world through ambassadors who braved expeditions to alien countries and cultures and seeded their ideas for global transmission folded down with religious injunctions when faced with a hostile, alien, conquering culture. Thus each epoch has created a different set of values in the name of the same religion creating utter confusion.

I have referred to Professor John Wheeler elsewhere in this book. He occupied the chair in Princeton University that was once occupied by Einstein, and guided students like Richard Feynman and some other Nobel Laureates. He wrote a personal letter to a monk of the Ramakrishna Order that I have reproduced earlier in this book. We know that historically the thoughts of Socrates and Plato and in a later age that of the Neo-Platonists were profoundly influenced by the Upanishads. I think we can see the influence of the ideals of the Upanishads on the western history after the Renaissance when seeded with these ideas from the Near East men and women plunged into the unknown both physically and intellectually, facing personal danger without any regard to the material comforts of a settled life. Intellectually they challenged the dogmatic ideas of the Christian Church and physically they risked the wars they believed in, and altered and enriched the history of humanity. They are in a state of pause now as they are questioning more and more the materialistic and deterministic basis of a mechanical universe. All this could not have been possible without an underlying sensation of the impermanence and futility of material life in this world. This is seen again and again in the lives of the western disciples of Vivekananda who accepted him and sat at his feet before his own countrymen appreciated him.

We Indians are in an epoch of expansion of a free India after a thousand years of darkness and poised to take on a globalized world that has grown smaller through technology largely developed in the west with more intimate people to people contact than ever dreamt of in the past. We, the present older generation, are fortunate to have seen its beginning that the younger generation have not. We have seen the self-confidence and the self-respect that were generated in this sleeping country through the teachings of our deepest and ancient thoughts by people like Raja Rammohun Roy, Sri Ramakrishna, Vivekananda, Aurobindo, Rabindranath Tagore and people like them from different parts of the country, so that men and women plunged into the freedom struggle discarding the safety of their material lives. Freedom has brought a sea change in our society, in our political, social and economic lives. The change has been very rapid and it seems that we were not prepared for it. A vast impoverished country with diverse cultures, languages and economic disparities was given a democratic structure that was essential. But the people were not ready for the responsibility of freedom given to them, a freedom that is not present in many other nations in the developing world. This was unavoidable. Responsibility cannot be developed unless it is given. Due to this rapid change the social fabric is being torn apart or at least severely strained by three opposing philosophical forces—the rank capitalist materialism of the West, the anti-religious bias of the Marxists and some western liberals of the immediate preceding era and our traditional social and religious ethics. Politics is making the situation complicated with its corrupting influence pulling and distorting one or the other or all of the three main emotional tendencies to gain political support. This unstable situation can be stabilized only by the evolution of an ethical basis for our society if we are to survive as a nation. And in any society that ethical basis has to evolve from the traditional value sense in order to be stable. Are the fundamental roots of our traditional sense of values dynamic enough to face the challenges and demands of the present day world? Therein lies the answer whether they can evolve and flourish in the world of the future.

Let us examine the value system that drives the young generation of today. They are more assertive, dynamic go getters than the laid back past generations. That is a value addition and in keeping with the roots of our culture that we had forgotten for a thousand years. The youth of today are progressively revolting against any restriction to personal freedom and individual choice. Individual freedom has to be tempered with collective responsibility whether in the familial, social or national life. The relationship of the individual and the society has been complicated in all ages and all societies. The social ethics of our last few centuries is neither healthy nor acceptable today. We have endured an abject slavery of the individual, suppressing all initiative and enterprise. But in the fundamental roots of our traditional wisdom there has been a balance and harmony allowing men to live with enterprise in harmony with thir environment – both nature and people. Swami Saradananda has written in his book *Sri Sri Ramakrishna Lilaprasanga* that although Sri Ramakrishna was an *advaiti* he instructed most of his disciples, both monastic and householder, on the principles of *vishistadvaita.* The philosophy of *vishistadvaita* unifies nature and people in a unitary perception of God that inculcates in the mind a vision of the world beyond differences of race, culture and religion where, devoid of egotism, enterprise and dedication can converge to give a direction to the society. This is a philosophy that instills a sense of values and ethical principles to establish a harmony in the material domain that is so necessary today.

In the field of administration and management the edicts of the *Bhagavad Gita* have been recognized the world over and also in the management institutes in our country. Dr. Subir Chowdhury, former Director of the Indian Institute of Management at Kolkata recently said in a lecture that when he had gone to England to do his Ph.D. under a Professor he found him reading the *Gita* when he first met him. The Professor remarked that it was not necessary to come all the way to the West to learn management when the wisdom existed in the knowledge of his own country.

Another aspect of individual freedom that is getting hold of the young generation under the influence of the western media and our media too is sensuous freedom. This is becoming a social problem in many parts of the country, often with an overtone of violence. The anti-religious segments of the intelligentsia are also stimulating it. The good thing is that the educated achievers in our society seem immune to this, laughing it off as a joke. But it has had serious effects on the more numerous 'not so educated'. Why has education been neglected so much in our country? It almost seems that politicians across all ideological lines do not like a large educated population who would ask embarrassing questions and will not be amenable to empty slogans and the vote machinery. Notwithstanding all the hurdles put by politics to restrict the freedom of education by slogan shouting, India has a large young population educated with liberal education who are the hope for the future of our country. Politicians have started shouting again to ban English and computer education—a move started at one time by Marxists in Bengal with disastrous effect on society. Harmonizing sensuous pleasure with responsibility to the individual and society had been a norm in our traditional culture. Our rich traditions in music, dance and painting owe their distinctive quality to this perfect balance of sensuousness and self-control within the well defined parameters of aesthetic sensibility. Commercialization of sensual pleasure to augment desire through films, advertisements and other media for higher financial profits dominates the western society and is disastrous for a poor society like ours where most desires remain unfulfilled. On a world scale the uncontrolled and unfulfilled desire of some societies has been the cause of wars, revolts and terrorism as the gulf between rich and poor widens. Do we want the world to go up in smoke pursuing uncontrolled competitive desires or do we have the resource and responsibility as an ancient culture to the world and to ourselves as well? Does not the media, particularly the Indian media, also have that responsibility?

Our society is fast converting to a money-oriented society. For all our hallowed ideals we are a very greedy people and have actually always been so in a general sense though with very marked exceptions. Our political history for many centuries is replete with stories of bribery and treachery. The political scenario since independence has taken it to unprecedented proportions so that it has percolated to the grassroots of the society. Corruption exists in high places in most democratic societies but the total corruption of the population in India has reached a magnitude that threatens the security and integrity of the country. Here the media are trying to play a role within its limitations but are helpless as the rule of law is being undermined at every point. The British earned respect in India by establishing the rule of law. That was a colonial era and there were deficiencies. But we are subverting even that since independence and the problem is becoming so enormous that the law enforcing agencies are becoming inadequate. As a result our political structure is failing and the political arena has become a haven for criminals, middlemen and all sorts of brokers. The people are helpless and frustrated and are sliding into corrupt and unethical activities that are sometimes considered as cleverness. If this continues any further the society will break down or people will take law into their own hands and the red lights are already flashing. Our traditional philosophical concept of a *rajarshi* to rule the country, the idea of philosopher king adopted by Plato, which was followed only marginally after independence, is not in sight today because the political culture itself prevents the rise of such persons to power. Vivekananda had said that religion could not be pursued in an empty belly. If he had been alive today he would have probably said that religion would be laughed at in a committee of thieves. The makers of our Constitution might not have foreseen this. Today in the absence of a unified religious or civil code, the media alone can uphold and promote an honest environment.

One has to ask what should be the basis of ethics and what role media can play in it. By the media we mean not only print or electronic media. Music and art are powerful media. Our nation was inspired by music and arts in our freedom struggle. Even before that, folk music by people like Lalan Fakir, Mukunda Das and others made people conscious of social injustices and imparted an ethical sensibility to the society. In more recent times the IPTA projected the humanist values and concerns inherent in classical Marxism. Today we seem to be in a void and most of the music being churned out is exotic dance music or love songs. That is because we are on a limbo. A large section of the people believes that ethics should be secular. The fall of Marxism has exposed the hollowness of secular ethics in countries that had embraced Marxism. Those who espouse secular ethics dare not comment on Islam, Christianity and Sikhism, the three major religions of India who have followed their own religious ethics through difficult times and of course need to be investigated. The only target of the secularists is the Hindu religion, the most broad based religion. Some people find it confusing because it is the most liberal religion that, through the philosophies developed over millennia, has provided perception of God to people of many different emotions, beliefs, and intellectual tendencies.

Even today the Ramakrishna Mission has monks belonging to every religion. Many people even in Kolkata, the city where its headquarters is, do not know this. There are other religious movements who are broad based in their work in foreign countries. It is time that the media refuse to publish uninformed and derogatory articles against Hindu philosophies and take care not to undermine the ethical basis of the major segment of the population. They do it for profit because some political party is promoting a particular brand image of Hinduism and others are opposing it and there are benefits to be gained by supporting one or the other. Both these segments are doing harm to people and to the Hindu ethos. But on the other hand as desperation and social depression grow with the absence of ethics in society, progressively larger crowds are thronging the temples of India than in political processions. It is time that politics leave religion to act on its own to build the ethical basis of society with the help of the media, without which a rule of law cannot be enforced.

2005

WORKING OF A DEMOCRACY

The Price of Democracy

In Plato's dialogue *The Republic*, Socrates denounces the democratic state as a lower form of government where the poor people revolt against an oligarchic state producing the lawlessness of a liberty which degenerates to licence.[1] People get tired of this anarchy and appoint a strong man to restore order and, unperceived, tyranny is established. The prediction has come true in the history of many nations. On the other hand Winston Churchill's remark that 'democracy is not the best form of government but all the others are so much worse' has come true so far in the history of British democracy. Where then is the truth?

The concepts of democracy have changed since the days of Socrates mainly through the evolution of British democracy and its modifications in other countries so that the structure of democracy now differs from country to country. But the fear of democracy degenerating into mobocracy and oligarchy, has remained real. It happened at the time of the French Revolution. Such fear had once influenced the French Constitution and subsequently the American Constitution. The British do not have a Constitution but depend on the history of evolution of democratic institutions and practices over centuries as precedents and are guided by pragmatism.

Democracy is actually an oligarchy by consent. But the consent by whom and how remains the moot question. Consent by a limited franchise tends to be more oligarchic as it was in the Athens of

Socrates. The executive arm has to be oligarchic to some extent but is controlled by the legal framework of the society and by the people who constitute the electorate. A powerful fourth element added in the last century has been the media serving as a channel of communication between the oligarchy at the top and the people at large. Therefore, democracy, in order to be successful, must function well at the deeper participating levels of the society and in its three controlling arms. Development of oligarchy and tyranny at these levels is bound to corrupt the whole system and bring it down. There is a real danger of that happening in our country.

Let us first look at the electorate. The fathers of our Constitution took an unprecedented bold step in introducing universal adult suffrage right from the beginning, which has come only gradually in other democracies. They had faith in the wisdom of the Indian masses irrespective of education and economic status; people have by and large kept that faith through many vicissitudes. There was no other way to bring succour to the oppressed classes. But has the system that has subsequently evolved over the last half century allowed their wisdom a fair play? The answer is a definite No. The ruling junta of every political party tries to subvert the will of the people. This is done through money, through threats, through frank tyranny and by inciting the basest instincts in the populace. Socrates said that this is the characteristic of the 'oligarchic man' with uncontrolled love of power and money.

Let us then look at the mode of construction of leadership in our country. Socrates opined that only 'the philosophic man or woman who has escaped the fetters and darkness of the physical world of the senses and obtained the freedom and dazzling radiance of the world of mind' and thus is unselfish and nonpartisan, is fit to rule a state. This dream can only be realized by a 'philosopher-king, an unlikely combination perhaps, but not an impossible one.' This has also been our ancient thinking. On the contrary our politicians today, belonging to all political parties, act and declare openly that politics is a game of grabbing power by any means. Obviously a golden mean has to be reached between the utopia of Socrates and the reality of today. Barring exceptions, British democracy has been able to find such men through centuries but we are yet to learn. One look at the people fighting the elections shows the character of the Indian polity. It is because rising in rank within a political party is often through chicanery and corruption or through dynastic succession. All of them are as bad and retrogressive as the next. There are exceptions, but often to preserve the clean image of one leader the parties use a thousand ruffians. The most potent way to get votes is to adopt a carrot and stick policy of temptation and terror. Even educated moneyed people are not immune to these methods and are only too vulnerable to temptations.

Money power is essential in every democracy, a fact that is not condoned but tolerated within reason. The difference in our country is that most of this money is unclean and this has corrupted the society to the grassroots level producing an unhealthy society where the good never wins. The squabbles inside any party are more severe today than the sham ideological squabbles among parties that are projected outside. Parallels are often drawn with the USA but the proportion of election money to national wealth is far less in the USA than in India. The average cost of fighting a Lok Sabha seat is officially around rupees fifty lakhs for each candidate and in important seats it is many times more. The importance of the candidate determines his own contribution. Even if the party bears most of it, one's capacity to raise money for the party becomes a prime consideration to rise to leadership. Therefore a politician has to have a substantial source of money, either personal or mostly collected. The scars of money are also visible in the governance of the USA and the highest executives have sometimes played up to different cartels promising undue favours. This oligarchy has sometimes forced decisions harmful to their own country and others as well. But the scars in our system and our society are deeper. Murders have become commonplace and easy, and the legal infrastructure is breaking down. When people lose faith in the legal structure of a society, the society crumbles and democracy becomes mobocracy. The only hope and protection in our society is that people have shown more wisdom than the politicians.

It has been said that continuous vigil is the price of freedom. Continuous vigil is also the price of democracy and this vigil has to come from the top. It needs minds that can see far into the future beyond the rabbles of the present and their narrow self-interest.

2004

Reference

1. Rouse, W H D, tr. *Great Dialogues of Plato.* Harmondsworth: Penguin Books, 1956.

Middle Class Woes

Political parties in India often play their games close to the danger zones of society. It is like dribbling close to the sidelines in a football game. If you are through you win. If not, the ball goes out but nobody loses. But in the political games that all political parties play it is society that loses and loses very badly. The large silent majority who suffer do not even understand the game. A small minority at the top understands but they are themselves the players. That leaves the educated middle class who understand but are incapable of doing anything. They do not have their unions and they do not have the CII. But they can sway the votes. That is important but then elections come only once in five years. Both the extreme right and the extreme left in the political history of the world have despised the middle class. Both Lenin and Hitler hated the middle class. In a democracy shades of such opinions persist and surface from time to time both from the right and the left plunging the country into crisis.

The latest such game has been played by the dominant party at the centre. Having won a precarious power after years of struggle they planned to make good and buy insurances for the future. The most important insurance for holding on to power in a democratic society is money where power does not come out of the barrels of guns but out of bags of money. Having a precarious hold on power and not sure of a second term in office they had to make hay in a short time. Faced with a huge internal debt the obvious course for the government was to rob the middle classes because they are the beneficiaries of much of this internal debt. Moreover the middle class has no united voice and no power base and come election time a strategy can be worked out. So against the run of the economy a total tax holiday on dividends was given. Experts who usually act as hired goons of the government churned out a lot of learned talk on globalization and free economy. The middle class went mad to earn dividends. But they were afraid of the sharks of the share market and were unable to play the game. The private mutual funds are unsafe but there is a government-sponsored mutual fund, the Unit Trust, and this class, in spite of everything, trusts the government. For three years they poured in money, even their life's savings into this fund. After three years the honeymoon is over and their money gone. Along with that the interest rates have been cut and the tax exemptions are gone. Rumours have it that large megastar corporate depositors were allowed and advised to withdraw their deposits at the highest rates of redemption and the shares of unknown companies were overbought to flush them with money. But the much advertised industrial regeneration has not come. As is usual the people who get this largesse have to pay back a substantial amount to those who give the advice. In such cases most of the money must have gone out of the country. The only loser is the middle class whose deposit forms the major bulk but from small powerless depositors. Some of the money will return before the next general election along with a further devaluation of the rupee to augment the rupee value of the deposits. Most devaluations of the rupee in the past twenty years or more have occurred prior to a general election to bring back more money, black or white at less cost.

In world history the ambitious intelligentsia of the middle class have often been its greatest enemies. It is specially so in our country. They grow up with a grudge and hate the law-abiding and god-fearing stagnant environment of their young days, often imposed by their god-fearing ethical elders never having enough of the goodies that other people with much less intelligence have. Lenin and Hitler are extreme examples but there are many examples in our democratic government. Psychoanalysis of corrupt politicians would often show a deprived childhood and growth period and instead of being sympathetic to the less privileged they become the worst exploiters.

Everything was going shipshape on this four-year plan of siphoning money from the middle class and giving it to the dogs. But then elections in three important states loomed on the horizon. The attention of the middle class had to be diverted. So the *mandir* issue was hyped up. It was brought out of cold storage and blown up to dangerous proportions. The unwise and unnecessary brinkmanship was taken to such dangerous levels that something had to give way somewhere. And it did give way in Gujarat. And the plan did not succeed in attaining its election objectives either. The 'Hindutvawallahs' forgot the advice of Vivekananda that an empty belly does not listen to religion. Can those leaders put one suicide squad on the soil of Pakistan? Can they show even a fraction of the conviction and grit of their supposed adversary? The whole project has failed and has pushed the country into grave national and international danger. The crisis in Afghanistan that nobody foresaw has exposed the weakness of government. No amount of rhetoric from exalted platforms and no amount of bribes paid in money is going to pull the country out of the mess. The government needs the backing of the patriotic middle class and the army comes mostly out of this class. But they have already been robbed. It has been the characteristic of the Indian Bania throughout history that they always try to bribe their way out of trouble. They have never raised an army as the East India Company did. When bribes do not work they have worked even to the political detriment of the country. There are many shameful examples in our history.

The advice to the government is to pay up the money that has been looted, because the middle class is generally patriotic and they know that the greatest danger to national security is a weak government at the centre. It is time to form a national government cutting across party lines and rejecting the corrupt, the casteist and the communalist.

2004

Crisis of Indian Democracy

The process of governance in India has been almost the same throughout the second millennium CE. A strong oligarchic central government in Delhi has ruled through its provincial outposts, benevolent or not. Rise of other power centres were either crushed militarily or absorbed in the hierarchy. People were programmed to think only of their immediate surroundings and no further. General education of the people was restricted to religious and scriptural education. The Brahmins and Maulavis ruled the blinded society. The British started general education to get the necessary manpower to govern but soon tried to wrap it up as it gave rise to nationalism. This was obstructed both by some members of the British society, some of whom lost support of their own ruling class, and Indians. Economic life was left to local nobilities as long as they paid the taxes. As a result there was total lack of enterprise in the population, which started only under the later part of the British rule due to western education, and this in its turn formed the root of Indian nationalism.

Before the freedom struggle could reach its zenith and win on its own, the British left India handing over power by arrangement along with partition of India. They had realized that in the post-Second World War situation they could not hold India any longer, and leaving her intact would leave a strong power centre in Asia in the form of a united India. Still wedded to the idea of global strategy as a legacy from colonial days, they sought to divide the country as quickly as possible before Mohammed Ali Jinnah died; surprisingly only the British government knew of his imminent death and not the leaders of the Congress, something hard to believe. The communal divide they had sown blew up and they beat a hasty retreat. They did the same thing in Palestine stabbing the Arabs in the back after winning and enjoying their loyalty from the time of the First World War and paid a lip service to the Jewish cause of a homeland, since the days of the premiership of Lloyd George through the Balfour declaration, and beat a hasty retreat before it blew up in their face. Sowing discord in occupied countries was the practised policy of British colonial rule.

A bewildered Indian polity took over, unsure of direction and depending solely on the structure left behind by the British with its entrenched bases of interests. Development started as if it were still a British colony or Britain herself and often on the plans already drawn up by the British. As a result emphasis was laid on heavy industries, massive irrigation projects and higher centres of learning at the cost of rural development and general education at the grassroots level. The Gandhian ideals were discarded along with the Father of the Nation. As the leadership struggled with the balancing act of the cold war years, often without success, the rural population burgeoned with a nearly one hundred per cent population growth since independence. This has eaten away all economic growth and left an impoverished uneducated populace. Education has never been a priority with any political party. What was once the basis of Indian nationalism has been neglected. Attempts have always been made to control the population by gimmicks by all political parties, be it Garibi Hatao or Hindutva or dictatorship of the proletariat.

In the meantime the world has moved on and its products have come in. Technology and progressively cheaper technology have brought media to every home and every hamlet. Expansion of the capitalist base of the world has brought investments and opportunities that can be grasped only by the top ten per cent of the population. The remaining ninety per cent can only stare at the television sets at the luxuries and fairytale lifestyles they cannot even imagine to access.

The disruption in the population is even more than in Mughal times. An Afghan in his hilly village cannot understand why he cannot live with his accustomed lifestyle and cannot have the goodies of the world. In India there are many Afghanistans. How can they hold on to the big picture of the Indian nationhood? The media, instead of educating, adds to the confusion because they also play up to the top ten per cent – that is where the money is. The media, the political parties, instead of providing education, try to brainwash the population. All political parties say that given the power they will do the right thing, but with power all of them do the same thing. Meanwhile the population increases, the expectation rises and the world moves on. And to add to all of this India has somehow become a superpower. We have become a superpower militarily but not in economic terms as all statistics would indicate. We have become a happy hunting ground in economic terms, the next El Dorado, and we are politically weak because of our big backlog of the impoverished and uneducated who cannot take advantage of the El Dorado.

That is the background against which the 2004 election has been fought. The NDA has fought on the plank of Hindutva and India Shining, leaving out considerations of the obvious impoverishment of the large middle class, the senior citizens and the poor. There is no projection of what they can offer. The Congress alliance and their collaborators fought only with the slogan of BJP-hatao and no positive economic programme. There were differences on disinvestments and fortunately it was left at that. The Left as always was playing with a number game in troubled waters to get a foothold at the centre with no positive policy of economic growth. Faced with such confused alternatives the electorate gave a confused verdict to the joy of the political mavericks like SP, RJD etc. Even after the elections the people are being confused with issues like *bideshini* or mother-and-child emotional scenes. Nobody is answering what will happen to Indian exports that will affect the poor as much as the rich if India shuts up and asks the foreign investors to get out. Nobody is answering whether the world will like an even remotely foreign finger on the nuclear trigger. There are many such issues that remain unasked and unanswered. Meanwhile the media pours out a hash prepared by the dishonest politicians for our consumption. The only casualty at the end is India and her unsuspecting and uneducated but politically sensitive people. Let there not be another bloodbath let loose by dishonest politicians.

2004

Loksabha Elections 2009

GREAT INDIAN CIRCUS: GOOD GOVERNANCE IS A DIFFERENT PROPOSITION ALTOGETHER

Another general election is round the corner and the familiar mayhem has started all over India where, as usual, the issues have gone into the background, mutual vilification and calling of names have come to the foreground, and Mother India is being torn to shreds by discredited politicians for a little toehold of a bargaining position and money through unprincipled alliances. The whole atmosphere is that of a national circus with the media busy converting it to showbiz with camera angles shooting exciting pictures. The campaign for the US presidential election is fresh in the memory of Indian media watchers. The hot debates revolved around national issues affecting the USA like terrorism and national security, economic downturn and unemployment, wars in Iraq and Afghanistan, energy solutions, climate change, governance and side issues like gay marriage, abortion, single parents etc. The debates were hot but to the point, both in large campaign meetings and on television. Experts debated on the solutions projected and people heard those debates to form their own opinion. Personal issues about candidates did come up but quickly snuffed out from a natural sense of decency and the realization that they were irrelevant in getting votes. It is not possible that every person who attends the campaign meetings or watches television debates will understand all of what is being debated. But the potential voter trusts people who understand, like those who advise the presidential candidates and those who are participating in televised discussions as honest opinion givers. He has the opportunity to pull them up and of course draw his own conclusions after he has listened to them.

India is beset with many more problems than the USA, calling for deep and serious reflection by all political parties rather than televised debates instigated by anchor persons who are more eager to vent their own opinions or are committed to the channels they serve and are quite often lacking in knowledge of history, real politics and statesmanship. Even the televised Lok Sabha debates dilute the issues, clouded by insincere one-upmanship and the desire to put up a good show. This is not to say that the debates should not be broadcast. It is the educational standards of the masses that naturally determine the behaviour of the politicians who represent them. But they are belittling themselves even to this electorate because an uneducated person is not necessarily a fool. The media has become the only guardian of governance but they are intent to get sensational scoops instead of analyzing the issues for the viewer. As a result there is very little incentive for governance that ought to be done through consultations between government and opposition on serious issues and if it ever happens it has no sanctity of secrecy. There is no other country where this happens.

Speaking of issues confronting India, there are so many that pages can be filled just listing them. The economic issues are of great importance at present. There are two sides to this, the internal and the global. The author had written before the general election of 2004 that two things inevitably happen before a general election, firstly money siphoned off from the market through one channel or another comes back increased as the rupee gets devalued. They provide funds for political parties and whoever can lay hands on them and the amount guzzled depends on the size and clout of a party but every party manages to get some. Before the 2004 election it was through collapse of the Unit Trust, a government sponsored mutual fund that went bust and the redemption value fell below the capital invested. But the big fish with the blessings of the then government redeemed their vast sums at the highest value before the bust set in; as a matter of fact this was the cause of the enormity of bankruptcy. For a few years before that a phenomenal rate of dividend was paid and the investment rocketed. As always it is the middle class who lost massive money. The history of pre-election rupee devaluation is older and has happened before every election. This raises the rupee value of the legal or illegal funds stashed abroad. All political parties and some individuals and corporate houses benefit. This author has written earlier that economists predicted in the mid-nineties that globalization will help money laundering that will stimulate global terrorism. Indian brains operating behind all political parties realized that it will augment money supply for the election. In the process their money has mingled with terrorist money in foreign waters.

This time the bourses had a prolonged bull run pushing the Sensex to 21K for which there was no apparent reason. The Finance Minister assuaged public concern by repeatedly quoting the PE ratio. People invested like mad and helped to push it up. Then it dropped sharply to 13K and held there driving inflated money out of the bourses back to where it belonged, both local big money and Indian foreign money invested through FII without actual transfer but invested through participatory notes. This far it was probably planned and the system could take it but then the government was caught unawares as the US meltdown hit the world and Sensex reached 8K. But every dark cloud has a silver lining and this time the value of rupee dropped automatically and dramatically. The Mumbai terrorist attack killed a lot of people but saved prominent politicians. It seems that our finance ministry does not have a cell of economic intelligence to honestly calibrate the money flow through different segments of the society and to monitor global financial movements, as is done in better governments,. A lot of political bickering would have been superfluous if we had that information. The finance minister of India has been changed prior to both the 2004 and 2009 elections, maybe a coincidence or concurrence!

The global financial movements are in a troubled phase. At the

G20 summit Gordon Brown, the British Prime Minister, wanted to institute checks and balances in the global financial systems through the IMF or similar organizations and stimulate government spending and prevent protectionism. What did he have in mind? Is it possible that some nations would be asked to deposit a significant portion of their wealth in the IMF or the World Bank or some such organization in exchange for credit cards? But what about the non-state laundered money, that will still remain, and will it help terrorism? France and Germany are unhappy and France has threatened to walk out if offshore tax havens are not abolished. China wants a new currency to replace the dollar, moving for more power on the world stage. Mr. Obama is more cautious saying that he would listen more than talk. The affluent G8 countries started globalization for higher profits but that money has been cornered and stashed elsewhere taking advantage of the unwholesome greed of the USA and other affluent countries. As they squashed China to their bosom in ecstatic love they forgot that she can bite. The US credit crunch was not caused entirely by the subprime housing loans but an unmonitored drain of dollars through poor regulatory mechanisms that also brought down the closely interconnected European banks. Now the call has gone out for America and Europe to close ranks. Close ranks against whom? Do we have the means, intellectual and practical, to handle this? We have a Prime Minister who is capable, but what if he is not there after the election? Even if he is there a consensus across party lines is essential without disclosing everything to the media for this is an area of global politics. The Left politicians are of no use for they will not even talk to the USA and allies whom they consider untouchable but are blind to the fact that Russia and China are capitalist countries too, with a ruling oligarchy, a risky combination, with virtually no media and both mentally eager to redeem their past glories, old or recent. India as a sovereign country cannot be a puppet of any other country and must find her place in the committee of nations and propagate her agenda for world development. That is the task, made difficult only by internal squabbling; there is no other deficiency.

There is another angle to the squabbling factor. After the Second World War when the British realized that they could no longer hold India, they sowed the seeds of discord and hurriedly arranged to leave by partitioning India before Jinnah died. This British agenda of keeping a finger in the pie has changed hands since then, first used by the USA in the cold war, then Islamic fundamentalists in different garbs and the Chinese. The British who planned it all have derived no benefit and are going to suffer more. Most conflict spots around the world are the product of Anglo-American global politics and they should do better now. Let us hope that things are not made worse by our squabbling politicians. It has already happened in relation to China.

The other big problem for India is communal harmony. Secularism is a much misused word that should be respected as a key word of our Constitution and not voiced casually and glibly. We have a department of minority affairs but no department of communal harmony representing all communities to discuss their problems mutually. Conflict resolution may not be easy to start with but it is necessary to keep talking so that some consensus on issues evolves gradually. A man of vision and learning should be given the charge as it is important for our development.

There are many other problems that need not be mentioned but the problems of economic development and communal harmony are at the core of all other problems and can be tackled only by good governance. Good governance does not involve only the ruling party at the centre but all parties both in government and opposition at the centre and the states. Splintering of parties has happened because of the money factor in politics as everybody who is anybody wants a seat in the Loksabha or the Vidhansabha. Even those who lose the election gain.

Politicians cannot be entirely blamed for putting up a show for the electorate instead of educating them. Majority of the electorate come to election meetings for the show and understand very little. Even an astute politician and administrator like Laloo Prasad Yadav puts up a show for his poor electorate in their language. Those who know Bihar know the attraction of the people for *nautanki* which is performed on roadside open stages during festive times. Similarly in West Bengal a candidate has to utter *janagan* (*aam aadmi*) in every alternate sentence. There is no scope for reasoning and the *nautanki* of the politicians extends to their offices. This time there is a larger proportion of educated youngsters and the Congress seems to be banking on those votes in urban and semi-urban areas. The result will be interesting to watch.

2009

MARXISM IN INDIA AND WEST BENGAL

Too Little and Too Late

CM Loses the PM Seat

Too little and too late seems to be a virus that has afflicted the Marxist movement in India since its birth. The Marxists did not join the revolutionary armed struggle for independence in Bengal and elsewhere in India though some of the revolutionaries joined the Communist Party later. They did not join the Quit India movement of 1942 from ideological objections that were not guided by the national interests of India. Then when the cold war started after the Second World War and the allies became enemies, they called for independence. But it was too late and the call was not even noticed. The country was in the grip of famine and communal riots. The Marxists started a peasant movement and armed struggle soon after independence when the nation was rejoicing in the freedom and trying to work out a democracy. The adult franchise and the ballot box, however imperfect, provided the first opportunity to the masses to participate in government after a thousand or more years. They were told that it was a false independence. When the armed revolution failed, the party came out of the underground and decided to participate in Parliamentary democracy. But it held on to its ideal of dictatorship of the proletariat through armed struggle. Long theories were propounded on a national bourgeois and bourgeois democratic revolution to be followed by a people's democratic revolution and so on. The whole prototype was worked out on the Russian model with no consideration of the ground reality in India. Only an external aggression or an internal destabilization by a workers' and peasants' movement could fulfill the dream of a revolutionary armed struggle. On the parliamentary front there began an alliance war. The war was more intense inside the party than on the outside. Meanwhile the Chinese Revolution had succeeded. Ignorant of international politics and history, some people started dreaming of China coming to liberate India. Even action plans were formulated in case of such an opportunity disregarding the patriotic sentiments of the people.

Then came the Chinese aggression, with the war on the Himalayas and the debacle suffered by the Indian Armed Forces. When the whole nation was astir with an intense emotional response, the leaders of the Communist Party started giving dubious statements. They did not condemn China but instead condemned the armed forces of India, whom they had categorized as a bourgeois army. That condemnation still continues. The party split soon afterwards producing a pro-Russian half, the CPI, and another, the CPI(M), which did not explicitly call itself nationalist but located itself somewhere in between Russia and China but leaning more towards China. The pro-Chinese faction later on split off producing the Naxalite movement. But China was least interested. They had more important tasks at hand. They had to rebuild their country. Mao said that they had to move faster than the rest of the world and the developed countries to overcome the handicap of fifty or more years of backwardness. The agenda of Chinese Communists has remained unchanged through twists and turns of politics and therefore they have received full cooperation of the people. The agenda of the Communist parties of India had never been development oriented and the leaders never had any idea of development. Everything that the people desired had to wait for the revolution but the leaders started to enjoy the fruits of democracy. This dichotomy has been covered over the years by polemical language.

As the Indian National Congress started to weaken, the alliance war started in full swing. People and parties were called progressive or reactionary, communal or secular, democratic or fascist depending on the convenience of the moment, more specifically on the convenience of the leadership. Party programmes or theories were not necessary for this. Gradually by highlighting local problems through destructive movements, personal vilification of opponents and producing alliances with splinter groups that had little or no commitment to Marxist or socialist ideals, the Communists came to power in three states.

Out of these three the longest serving government with most cohesive alliance partners has been in West Bengal. It was achieved because the people repeatedly voted it to power with a confidence that their lot will improve. But surprisingly that did not happen in spite of the personal integrity of most leaders backed by erudite intellectuals. Why did it not happen? Because the agenda was not development but to use West Bengal as a base for national revolution, the red fortress, and until that happened to keep it in captivity. For that the only necessity was to keep and enlarge the captive vote bank and keep the voting machinery in fine tune. All development and all the benefits given to specifically identified groups of people were aimed towards this end. It was also necessary to keep West Bengal psychologically and emotionally as far separated from India as possible. Education and industrial development had to be programmed to keep the captive population in toe. Outside investors were discouraged by an aggressive labour policy. Zamindari had been abolished in West Bengal under Dr B C Roy and land development was more advanced than other states. Further action could have been taken through administrative measures but a violent mass movement was launched to break the Congress vote bank and install its own. The agricultural output of West Bengal, contrary to claims made, has shown no improvement over other states. The conditions of the middle farmer and the landless labourers have not improved. The intellectuals in a communist movement are the saddest lot since the days of Lenin. They are supposed to put Marxism on the throne and then serve it without question or else. The few remaining intellectuals either became dumb or became accomplices. All this has happened because the programme of dictatorship of the proletariat and the pledge of development of a constitutional government could not be reconciled.

It is a common belief among people that capitalism is an enemy of communism and vice versa. Nothing could be further from truth. Capitalism uses communism whenever it suits it for it can buy it off most of the time. Lenin was sent to Russia by the German military high command in a special train. America wooed China with money and technology to hasten the fall of Soviet Russia. Who knows that something similar has not happened in India? Armed revolution in more revolutionary situations did not succeed in Algeria, Bolivia and Nicaragua but landed those countries in misery. This is not to derogate Marxism, but their continuous allergy to democratic socialism formed at the time of Lenin and the rise of Hitler has indirectly helped capitalism. Now that a credible socialist alternative does not exist in Indian polity, they still have to hold on to this old and obsolete habit.

The dream of participating in a national government has gone because of infighting. The latest party plenum has taken a decision to join a central government if the chance comes again. True to their tradition, the decision has been taken too late. But the agenda of dictatorship of the proletariat is still there like a skeleton from the past and as long as it is there, only shady alliances will be formed to the detriment of the country. The people of this country are not so ignorant any more. The change in policy is just too late.

2007

'De-Industrialization' of West Bengal

Once on a transatlantic flight I spent a few hours with an eminent American economist who told me that the world at large and economists as a community thought a lot of themselves but in reality they were nonentities for their reputation depended on politicians. I thought that was no wonder. Since the days of Adam, or should I say Adam Smith, great economic theories have made rich nations richer until very recent times when some humanitarian paints became necessary. It is no wonder that Alfred Nobel did not choose economics as one of his prize subjects.

I remembered that encounter as I read the brilliant interview given by Professor Amartya Sen and the debates thereafter. Professor Sen was two years my senior at Presidency College and his two illustrious batch mates, the Late Parthasarathi Gupta, who became Ishan Scholar, and the Late Sukhomoy Chakraborty, were my seniors at school. On that count I hope Professor Sen will forgive me if I refer to him as Amartya-da to remind him of our college days though he never knew me. In those early fifties we had no holy cows and would take on anybody on any agenda. From the heights of Baker Laboratory we looked down at the Arts building though we respected brilliance. But we were the new Mughals to build the new India. The days have changed much since. We are far away from *chitto jethā bhoyshunyo uchcha jethā shir* (where the mind is without fear and the head is held high), the dream of Rabindranath Thakur. The Bengalis today are like branded cattle. Anybody making any sound is inspected for political branding and the needful is done. Therefore only the media and the politicians make sound, while we the ordinary people suffer in silence.

The interview is brilliant because Amartya-da replied squarely to all sensitive questions except the contentious political issue of agricultural land and then hit us with this very technical word 'de-industrialization' without defining it. The word has had different meanings in different countries at different times. Modern Britain is de-industrializing as the industry's share of GDP and employment is going down without overall reduction, as the pattern of economic activity is changing. Germany and Japan were sought to be de-industrialized during and after the Second World War but the plan was reversed as threats of cold war grew. De-industrialization in small sectors has been studied as in the sawmill industry of Canada through the health status of workers. De-industrialization does not necessarily mean a slump in overall economic and social development. So where does West Bengal since the sixties of the last century stand and what are the parameters? Nor has it been spelt out how re-industrialization occurs and similar precedents, if any.

The importance of social psychology in industrialization has been recognized since the early days of the industrial revolution, and in early twentieth century Bengal stalwarts started national industries to make society industry-friendly when the colonial government ruled out state initiative. They started a movement called Bengal Initiative. Since then there has been rapid progress in Bengal and elsewhere, and after independence there has been a spurt in state investment. In the meantime the War, the famine of 1943 and the influx of refugees from East Bengal destabilized West Bengal. Everything went wrong thereafter. Resettlement of refugees outside the state was undermined and state administration was sought to be paralyzed by repeated political movements by the communists as many people, the refugees and others, not unjustifiably, thought that the Congress party had sold out Bengal. This was followed by militant trade unionism that increased as the Left parties gradually came to power and intensified and extended the movement into more violent ones. It was the main reason for de-industrialization but by no means the only one. Some day an impartial objective analysis will be done but that day has not come yet. Inefficient management, corruption, centre-state politics and flight of capital played their roles but the capitalists themselves remained securely ensconced in Kolkata as Amartya-da has said they always will. British colonialists could go to wild God-forsaken places to start business and industries but not the Indians even in these IT savvy days with much faster communication.

What has been the social fallout of all this? Many hundreds of small and medium scale industries have closed down, particularly those that were labour intensive and employed large numbers of workers, in addition to large industries including public sector industries. Kolkata has seen many beggars on the road driven to that state when they lost their jobs in industries. The incidence of suicides by ingestion of domestic acids, pesticides, kerosene and hanging probably reached levels comparable to late Stalinist Russia if correct statistics could be found. Some evidence can be found from medical literature. Decent middle class families living in rented houses became slum dwellers overnight, let down both by their employers and the unions.

Meanwhile land reform movements produced several effects. Many landless labourers and bargadars got their own land. Through some bloodshed, but not much, peace was established but not for long as jobless workers began to shift to land. The communist votes both in rural and urban areas were secure and the middle class petty bourgeoisie silenced, and all was well. Agricultural production increased but not entirely through land reform. Dr Norman Borlaug, who received the Nobel Peace Prize in 1970 for producing genetically altered seeds of high yield in the sixties and trained and worked with scientists of the Indian Council of Agricultural Research, can take more credit. He characterized his success as 'temporary success in man's war against hunger and deprivation,' a breathing space to deal with the 'Population Menace', words prophetic for West Bengal where uncontrolled multiple cropping and the cost of agriculture have brought down production.

Two generations of Bengalis have grown up with the experience that one could somehow survive on land through farming and small businesses but industry is a curse where one has to work harder with no security and remain servile to the union. The infrastructure of skilled and semiskilled workers has been depleted. Encouraging entrepreneurship locally with small and medium scale industries was suggested and the present government initially agreed. But it did not succeed. The social atmosphere is such that an entrepreneur has to include an extortion fund to his risk capital and has to have correct political branding and negotiate with market forces that have moved away from Bengal. The central administration has very little control on such peripheral demands, be it government agencies or local forces. So the government has taken the aerial route of mega projects that people have rejected. There is no politics in this. Politics is in the drama and the deals, not in the mind of people. They just do not believe political promises any more.

I would ask Amartya-da how industrialization should proceed on this social base. In this scenario I expected him to mention Japanese re-industrialization, linking big businesses with small entrepreneurship, instead of Manchester and Lancashire of ancient times. Mistakes are committed by every government in the world and are often recognized on hindsight and have to be corrected, usually by another. That is the advantage of democracy, not of a government in perpetuity. West Bengal politics has benefited India in some ways and has now produced a Central Plan for acquiring land for SEZ and mega industries but rejected by farmers, and investments are moving away from West Bengal. Can we re-install a convincing people-friendly industrial base and how?

2007

Communism or Socialist Democracy?

'Isms and preferences: The Time is Ripe for an Open Change to Social Democracy'

The media has raised a hue and cry over the statements of communist leaders giving socialism a minor rating in the context of West Bengal's capitalist development. Most of the critics did not seem aware of the historical, ideological and practical differences between Communism and Socialism and the long history of their struggle in Europe and equated the two, now being fought out in India. Communists rejected Social Democracy in Europe because it called for capitalist development of the economy and marked its protagonists as collaborators. Socialists rejected communism because Marxist economic theory had no formula for economic development. This struggle led to the Bolshevik revolution in Russia and Hitler's rise in Germany. Though fighting each other, both these powers took the road of capitalist development -- state capitalism in Russia and state-sponsored capitalism in Germany. The results were clear to the Europeans by the end of the sixties but only after suffering the horrors of the Second World War. Asians failed to read the lessons from their different socioeconomic milieus, lack of education and regional geopolitics. A rethinking amid rapid changes in the scenario is necessary both for our own economic development and in tune with growing international perception that unbridled capitalism does not augur well for the future of the world, with the inevitable threats from militarism and to the environment.

Going back to Euro-communism, the largest Communist party in Europe outside the Soviet Union was the Italian Communist Party (PCI). In the 1969 meeting at Moscow Enrico Berlinguer, Secretary General of the PCI, openly disagreed and dissociated from the political line of the Soviet Union on such fundamental issues as national sovereignty, socialist democracy and lack of freedom of culture that sidelined the Chinese Communist Party, though the PCI got massive financial help from Russia till 1984 and commanded around 35 per cent of popular national votes. The difference grew as PCI joined the Socialist International and in 1991 after the fall of Soviet Union the party changed itself to the Democratic Party of the Left (PDS) with a minority faction breaking away to form the Communist Refoundation Party. The communist movements in other West European countries followed similar lines. This consolidation of socialist forces forged a political stability and affluence that made them valuable partners in democratic governance.

Although Europe learnt early that Marxist economic theory had no development plan for poor economies, we in Asia did not know that. The Chinese communists being pragmatic enough to come to power leading a nationalist struggle, embraced capitalist development at the first opportunity after Mao's death. But ours preferred to stick to the utopian ideology of dictatorship of the proletariat, world revolution, abolition of the state etc. in name only, and after independence sought power and its fringe benefits through the democratic process retaining as much as militancy possible, which weakened both governance and national economic growth. To bring capitalism the Chinese created a capitalist class and they have a few hundred millionaires today diluted by the vast population. Our leaders did something similar, creating an isolated crony capitalist governing class using the ethnic diversity of India in a much smaller society. This is against national integration.

WHAT IS IN A NAME?

The Indian Communist parties are effectively participating in the democratic process and pursuing a socialist agenda and are practically social democratic parties. But the name remains important because it defines the party manifesto, organization and modes of functioning rooted in the ideology. Like the 'Hindutva' followers the religion of Communism is also very strict. These are important even if the ultimate aim is given up. This is a case of double standards in the worst Indian tradition. Democracy and socialism do not mean presence of armed cadres, a culture spreading to other parties across the country. This model cannot control the extreme left either. People have to be trusted and that does not mean the organized cadre alone, but a large number of free thinking citizens; to reject their opinion and ability to think rationally is a mindset unacceptable in democracy.

The dichotomy is harming in many ways. The Communist parties have a larger committed and qualified human resource at their command than most other parties. This wealth could be better utilised in the development of the country rather than devising ways and means to keep the party in power. Putting development above power may make the organization less closed but spread it wider among the people with a substantial lowering of the fear factor. It was the fear factor that Lenin and Stalin used but it has not stood the test of time. Violence begets violence and corruption accompanies violence, increasing in areas away from the power centre. It has happened in other countries, much worse in some. Identification of the enemy is the basis of Marxist political strategy and it becomes a habit, but in a democracy there is no permanent enemy or permanent friend and the same is true in the international arena. This modus operandi at the grassroots level is dangerous for all. The State apparatus in a Marxist state like the bureaucracy, police, party bureaucracy and *apparatchiki* are used more for keeping people in line and less for development.

Could the Indian Communist Party change to a Social Democratic party like the Italian Party even if they wanted to? The question is hypothetical but there was no opportunity. Soon after independence the Congress party outmanoeuvred the Socialist parties in existence at that time having such prominent leaders as Joshi and Lohia and took over the mantle of socialism themselves with the overwhelming personality of Nehru. Cold war politics brought India close to Soviet Russia and communists were at bay and the party was split. Social Democracy aims at prosperity through industry and business to ensure equal benefit to all sections by efficient administration and governance, not militancy.

The communist leaders in West Bengal have put socialism on the backburner to promote capitalism. But they have not discarded communism, at least in their avowals. The distinction has become fuzzy in West Bengal. Is communism friendlier to capitalism than socialism? Does this mean toeing the China line or sending a message to some people? The capitalists prefer to invest in an organized society, whatever be the mode of organization. They invested in Nazi Germany and in Communist China. Many prefer oligarchy, democracy asks too many questions, too many to pay. Marriage of capitalism and oligarchy has never been a happy one in world history.

Communism had different origins in China and India. In China it did not develop under colonial rule. In India communism was taught by the British. Most left of centre politicians, communists or socialists, were educated by the British Left. Somehow most of them never grew up to take their own decisions. It speaks highly of British education and policy that they could make highly developed independent progeny. The Indian communists in particular have always chased history instead of anticipating and making history. In a country that loves democracy, freedom and self respect the time is ripe for an open change to social democracy, instead of working through age old clichés, and submission to the national urge for pragmatic economic and cultural self reliance and probably God, in a largely God-loving nation nurtured in a true secular culture.

2008

GLOBAL ENVIRONMENT : WEST

The Boat on the Indus

The Anglo-American invasion of Afghanistan and Iraq has resulted in the rise of Islamic militancy in the region and globalization of the Kashmir problem. This has put us in a global hotspot as never before. The superpower policy of kicking and kissing the Islamic militancy may prove suicidal for them but is of graver danger to us. Bartering Kashmir for peace in oil rich areas may be a valid strategy for them but of grave danger to us. Therefore we must take a close look at our legacy.

In January 1831, a small flotilla was slowly sailing up the Indus from the Kutch. Lieutenant Burnes of the East India Company, an army officer inducted into the political wing, was in command.[1] The flotilla was carrying a gift of five huge dray horses from Britain for Maharaja Ranjit Singh of Punjab. The gift was in return for the Raja's gift of exquisite shawls to the King and Monarch in Britain. But why were the cold weather dray horses chosen for a hot country? Because they were impressively huge and would please the Raja as he had never seen one, and he loved horses. More importantly they could not be taken by the long and hot overland route but could be taken only by boat in winter. That was the excuse. But why go to such lengths for a boat ride? Because the unknown watercourse of the Indus had to be surveyed and its navigability checked from the sea to its upper reaches which the rulers of Sind and Punjab would not have allowed in the normal course. But why was it so important to know the Indus?

It was necessary because Persia had become a virtual Russian protectorate. Russian merchandise was moving freely through these regions and was being followed for their protection by detachments of the army and political officers and spies. The direction of their movement seemed to indicate an interest in Afghanistan and from there to India. Therefore to checkmate them British merchandise had to be pushed into the area inevitably followed by the armies, the political officers and the spies. The best way to send them was up the river to Peshawar and then through the mountain passes and the old silk routes into the bazaars of Central Asia. The key was Herat, the granary of Central Asia and a perfect staging post to move through Quetta and the Bolan Pass to India. Credit must be given to Ranjit Singh that he was not entirely ignorant of this global game and realized that Punjab could not remain independent, at least not after his death and that was not very far off. He had no other option but to remain friendly with the British for the security of Punjab and to protect Peshawar from the ambitious Dost Mohammed, the ruler of Kabul.

Five years later Herat was attacked by the Persian army helped by Russian advisers and detachments of Russian army, but the ten month long siege failed. This was followed by a great chess game of pursuits and sabotage, of bribery and lies, of espionage and diplomacy and was followed by two world wars, the rise of Communism in Russia and Eastern Europe and the independence of erstwhile colonies. During this whole period the British managed to cling to Afghanistan and neighbouring areas, the 'soft underbelly of Russia', and control it. One of their main weapons was promotion of Islamic nationalism that upgraded itself to religious militancy later on as they were betrayed. The stories of how this was done are well known and make for good bedtime reading.

Loss of colonies and decline of British power after the Second World War produced a power vacuum in the whole area. So the chess game started again. The games this time were the games of the Cold War. With the creation of Israel the powder keg was installed with a long fuse. Economic difficulties, betrayal of the Palestine mandate and public opinion progressively made Britain a minor player in the region. Americans moved in as the heir of the great Anglo-American heritage but with much less experience and expertise than the British. Wali Khan was the son of Khan Abdul Gaffar Khan, also known as the 'Frontier Gandhi', and was the leader of the Khudai Khidmadgar movement in Northwest India before the partition. He has written, after his release from long imprisonment in Pakistan, that Mr. Jinnah promised Pakistan's alliance with western powers against Soviet Russia before partition and obtained American tacit support for partition of India.[2] During the Cold War people were getting accustomed to its machinations with ups and downs in the Middle East and Central Asia.

Then the great thing happened, the Soviet Russia collapsed. In the process of collapse there was the ten year war between the Soviet army and the Islamic Mujahideen armed and trained by CIA and Pakistan with tacit support from China. Central Asia again fell into a power vacuum with the rise of terrorism. Nature abhors vacuum and especially so in Central Asia. To its strategic location is now added the enormous oil wealth. Meanwhile 'the soft underbelly of Russia' has been ripped open with the guts falling out. There is a lot of oil and gas in those guts and the Russian space endeavours that were internationalized with American money. So it is but natural that America would move in with Britain tagged along with token support from the erstwhile white colonies of Britain. It is also natural that the French, the Germans and the Russians would not like it. France has one erstwhile colony in Algeria with a predominantly Muslim population, Germany had lost all its colonies in the First World War and Russia never had colonies. What we are witnessing today would have been called imperialism in a bygone era. But political terminologies change with history. What should the terminology be today when there is no king but a President in USA and the power is so absolute that it can destabilize any government, annex anything, even without military power? How long will this last and where are we in all this?

Weakening of India seems a valid project to many from past history and we must prove them wrong. Though we are close to the conflict zone, we may be bypassed in most coming conflicts if we keep our balance and do not act foolishly. We may have to tolerate some minor ignominy but we can and we must build fast and silently. Foreign affairs are a matter of long foresight and discreet steps, like the boat up the Indus. Ideological stances and verbal rhetoric without backbone and teeth do not create diplomacy. The teeth need both economic and military strength and diplomacy starts from home. We are not a weak nation today. Our problem is that we have neighbours where sectarian interest dominates over national interest. Our policy must follow our long term national interests rather than permanent friends and enemies. We do not have the geographical advantage of the isolation of China. Therefore we must play the game. As inheritors of British India from where the Asian diplomacy was conducted and 'history was made in blood and iron' we have to be worthy successors.

References

1. Hopkirk, P, *The Great Game*. New York: Oxford University Press, 1990.
2. Khan, W, *Facts are Facts: The Untold Stories of India's Partition*. Delhi: Vikas, 1987.

The Desert Shrine of Hinglaj

A Bengali film named *Marutirtha Hinglaj* was made in the fifties. It was woven around a temple located in Baluchistan beyond the Sind desert, now inside Pakistan. The temple is very ancient and is one of the fifty-two *Satipithas*. In the puranic tale Sati, the wife of Lord Siva, died when her husband was insulted at her father's place. Siva went mad in sorrow and carrying her dead body on his shoulder started his dance to destroy creation. The gods became worried and approached Vishnu to save the world. Vishnu unleashed his *sudarshan chakra* to cut Sati's dead body in fifty-two pieces and scatter them all over the world and ordained that these will become the holiest places of pilgrimage. This then calmed down Siva. These fifty-two shrines are scattered over the Indian subcontinent and Nepal and are great centres of pilgrimage. The devout believe that whatever one wishes and prays for at one of these places comes true. These places extend from Kamakhya near Guwahati to Kanyakumari in the south to Vaishno Devi in the northwest to Nepal in the northeast and Kashmir in the north. All these goddesses are different forms of the Mother Goddess Durga or Kali. The westernmost shrine is in Hinglaj beyond the Sind desert. Pilgrims used to go to Hinglaj before Partition braving the hazardous journey, mostly on foot, through the desert. The film was about one such journey. Since independence and Partition Hinglaj has been slowly forgotten.

Whatever be the exact time of origin of the story of Sati, the geographical distribution of her fifty-two body fragments shows a brilliant means of psychological and emotional integration of India. It is doubtful whether at any time of India's political history, except under the British rule, all these four corners were under a single king. Yet the people were integrated culturally in spite of being divided into different kingdoms and even sometimes under different religions. To me the loss of the western outpost of the Devi at Hinglaj remained a real loss until I rediscovered her by chance.

I was invited to dinner with friends at the house of Adamjee at Karachi. He is a famous industrialist of Pakistan and formerly of Kolkata. A major chunk of the social elite of Karachi were there. I found myself next to a polished, kind looking gentleman whom I discovered to be the celebrated editor of the *Dawn*. We started talking about this and that and about Karachi having a cosmopolitan culture since the old days and still preserving it. We talked about some of the old places. He was keenly interested and volunteered to show me around after dinner. After dinner meant after midnight and this kind gentleman, who was quite a few years older to me, himself drove me around old Karachi till the early hours of the morning. The new Karachi is modern and beautiful. The old Karachi looks more like a city out of a history book with its dilapidated and deserted houses, narrow dark lanes, and men in dark tattered clothes sitting around even at that hour doing nothing. Most of the places look like a city after an earthquake where people have not all left. There were old deserted Hindu households with temples in the courtyard, some occupied by squatters, though legally owned by the government.

It was so fascinating that I went back next day in the late afternoon with another local friend. Even in daylight the area looked the same, only more ghastly and with more people loitering idly. My friend became very enthused about locating old temples. They were now government properties and godless without the idol. At last in falling darkness a tall man in Pathan suit sitting idly on what must be called the roadside, who did not seem quite on the right side of the law, took us through a narrow lane to what seemed like the back of a godown. He called out for somebody who refused to come out. After repeated coaxing and being told that there were foreigners to see him, he cautiously opened the door. From his features this was definitely a Hindu Brahmin. He confirmed it. There was an elegantly carved wooden temple door standing incongruous in his modest dwelling and he hesitated to open it. I told him I was from Kolkata and his eyes dilated. He opened the door and took me inside a small room full of pictures of gods and goddesses and a funny image painted on a piece of rock. I asked him what that god or goddess was and he answered that this was Devi Hinglaj. I was dumb with amazement. Then he told the whole story. He belongs to the traditional priests of Hinglaj and through trials and tribulations they have never left her alone. Here in the ruins of old Karachi he and others before him have survived, mingling with the poor Hindus, some of them belonging to scheduled castes, poor Muslims, many of them refugees from Bihar and known to us only as the trouble makers of MQM. Here in the underworld of old Karachi they survive in a commonality of interest and hardship and he worships Hinglaj in her city abode. I asked about the temple in the desert and he said it was still there, undamaged in its isolation, forgotten and left out. He goes there once every year on the special puja day and worships the goddess. It is a difficult journey taking seven days to go and come back.

I was exhilarated by my discovery. In her isolation and among the ruins the goddess is waiting for her devotees. Will Hindus be permitted to visit her as the Sikhs are allowed to visit the Nankana Sahib? Will Mr. Vajpayee ask this of Mr. Musharraf?

Postscript. This was my first trip to Pakistan as member of a citizens' delegation from Bengal Initiative, a Think Tank established in the early twentieth century by the great men of those days for economic and social resurgence of India. The NGO was revived in the early nineties. During this visit in 1998 to Lahore, Islamabad, Muree, Karachi, Peshawar and other places to socially meet top leaders of Pakistan and prominent people, so called Track 3 diplomacy, the state of the Hinglaj temple and the continued presence of the Goddess in her abode was not known or at least not known to me. I think it was so since Partition. I accidentally discovered the home of the Hinglaj Priests hiding in Karachi amid dark streets and ruins, worshiping a replica of the Goddess in a closed room and living in great fear. It was just before the Kargil War and the arrest of Nawaz Sharif, whom we had visited at his home as he came hemmed by army men in plain dress and there was fear in his eyes. The people of Pakistan knew something was coming. After publication of this article, in the interlude of peace after the Kargil war, two trips were made by journalists and political leaders with protection from the Pakistan army, but I do not know of anybody visiting prior to 1998. Roads have since been built in the area for the Chinese-Pakistani port of Gwadr and the industrial commercial area around and a few people are now going.

Another interesting event in this tour was a meeting with the Lahore Chamber of Commerce where, during break, one gentleman asked me about Vedanta that he wanted to read but no books were available. I knew that no religious books other than Islamic ones were allowed to enter Pakistan but promised to send him some on my return and asked him to acknowledge receipt by email as a safe channel for him if they ever reached. I kept my promise but the Kargil War broke out three days after we returned and I could only request the Pakistan High Commissioner personally after the war ended to send them. He put me in touch with a very beautiful lady I had met during our pre-tour meeting whose designation, I later learnt, was of an intelligence officer and she promised to send. That was the end of the story. There was no acknowledgement from the gentleman or the High Commission and no internet contact.

Searching Hindu temples in a Karachi night meant asking local big brothers as they knew where to find the Hindus and shouted their names but they were behind closed doors and refused to open. One man named Debu shouted back he was not a Hindu but a Harijan. I shouted back that I was a Hindu from Calcutta and a small shrivelled young man came out demurely but refused to open his mouth and quickly vanished inside. Standing amid that ruin at late night with my sari clad wife beside me was an eerie sensation. Our hosts, a nice couple, with a Pathan driver, took us to Karachi Club, a British legacy, to a cordial welcome as they were having their AGM and men lamented we should solve Kashmir and be friends. There were no women. We were taken to a lavish dinner in a posh restaurant and then to their home and family and sent back with gifts.

1999

Pakistan Today 2003

There is a wind of change in Pakistan today that will be evident to anyone visiting that country. At last they seem to be growing up to the realities of globalization and realizing that politics of confrontation and hate is no longer valid in the present day world. One may ask what the basis of this optimism is.

In the words of the Foreign Minister Khurshid M. Kasuri the politics of hate is no longer paying. In an elected Parliament of 372 members the seats are almost equally divided among women members (sixty nominated and thirteen elected), the Pakistan Muslim League, the Pakistan Peoples' Party and the MMA, the rest being divided among the various reserve constituencies and small factions.

The participation of women in the democratic process at the centre, provincial assemblies as well as more peripheral levels is really remarkable. One sees more women driving cars on the roads of Lahore and Islamabad than even five years back, more women in colleges and universities than before and often doing better than men. The procedure of Talaq has been substantially modified right up to the village level and can no longer be accomplished by just uttering the word three times.

There is a genuine interest in expanding business with India though there are problems of tariff and mechanisms to be solved. Joint ventures in mining, power and several other sectors are welcome. Trading in tea, jute and textiles are welcome. Engineering goods are not viewed with the same suspicion as before as these are being already imported from other sources like Korea and affecting local industries. Joint ventures in these areas may actually salvage some of them.

What has brought all these changes in attitude? Ask anybody and the reply will be the same; it is the personality and vision of President Pervez Musharraf. He is a directly elected President through national referendum and above the legislature that gives him a more or less free hand. The democratic structure may not be like ours but we have no right either to judge or to pontificate because democratic structures vary. The important thing is whether it works. Newspaper articles criticizing the functioning of the state appear regularly and the editors are unanimous in saying that censorship of press is minimal and they are actually consulted in determining policy.

In relationship with India the well-known irritants are there – like the Kishenganga dam and Baglihar Hydel Project in Kashmir, the LOC and Kashmir, Siachen and a few minor ones. A major concession on Kashmir is their expressed wish to move away from the UN Resolutions on plebiscite. India being a larger country, they want us to be more generous and not make Pakistan feel small and insulted. Both governments have decided to solve the problems through negotiations and both have declared that process to be irreversible.

All this may sound too good to be true. A cynic could ascribe everything to the antiterrorist war, pressure from the USA and the economic gains from a gas pipeline to India. But there is a genuine desire among the educated class for a friendly relationship and they demonstrate it through their hospitality, which was so evident during the recent cricket series. They also realize that economic backwardness of South Asia is due in part to a senseless conflict for 57 years and they now see India forging ahead. There is even the dream of an eventual South Asia without borders that has been articulated officially, a thing that could not be dreamt of a few years back.

But are there no dark clouds to be wary of and can the guard be lowered? On the Pakistani side there are cynical views that all this is a show put up by the establishment on their side for international consumption for the time being, and the critical articles mainly in the

English newspapers are published under orders from the very top to demonstrate freedom of the press. In Parliament and in newspapers more orthodox parties like MMA lambast their government over suspected concessions on Kashmir and they do not desist from hate India speeches.

Some experts in the Institute of Strategic Studies in Pakistan do not believe that the armed strength of India is not directed against Pakistan. They do not understand or accept our strategic needs. From our point of view the international situation is in a flux, heightened by big power rivalry and impending energy crisis in the world, as fossil fuels may not last through this century because of higher consumption throughout the world. China is constructing a new port at Gwadr on the Baluchistan coast and the Chinese navy will be using it. With this China will virtually encircle India from Chittagong through Bangladesh, North East India, Nepal, Tibet, Aksai Chin and Gwadr with the Chinese Navy frequenting the Indian Ocean. Strategists in Pakistan jokingly say that the American Navy and the Chinese Navy will be berthed side by side at Gwadr. We have a friendly relation with both countries but a close embrace even from a friend may be uncomfortable sometimes. Just one man, General Pervez Musharraf, controlling the Pakistan army and continuing in power in Pakistan and extending a friendly hand towards India, cannot offset this alarming strategic situation. But on the other hand a strong and friendly Pakistan on our western frontier will be great security. Throughout history all Indian Empires have sought friendly and powerful states on that frontier. It is too early to predict what can happen with Pakistan. In the meantime we must increase bilateral relations and people to people contacts with Pakistan to increase the confidence of people on both sides and reduce tension. At the same time we have to succeed in the second industrial revolution starting with IT and extending on to the frontiers of technology, alternative energy sources and space research.

We, therefore, have to be very careful and very alert and not lower our guard, both to the external and the internal threat perceptions. After all eternal vigil is the price of freedom.

Israel Revisited

SHOULDER TO SHOULDER

I visited Israel last in 1980 and then revisited in September 2006 during a lull in the war in Lebanon. I was in for a striking contrast. Much has happened in the world in these 26 years and much has happened in Israel and in the India-Israel relationship.

In 1980 I was invited to a medical conference in Israel but advised to get my visa in New York. Even that was a change because earlier the Indian passport did not allow a visit to Israel. I got my visa from a heavily guarded Israeli consulate in Manhattan. I had to take the flight to Israel from Rome and return to Rome for the flight back to India as no aircraft taking off from Israel was allowed to fly over the Arab countries.

In 2006 I was scheduled to go to Egypt from Israel and then return home. Ordinarily there would have been no problem but because of the war in Lebanon no Arab airline was prepared to issue a joint ticket with El Al. The only convenient flight to Israel and from there to Egypt was a twice-weekly El Al flight but return by the same route would be a difficult schedule. But somehow these problems were solved by Internet booking, not available in 1980. How fast the world is changing and hopefully wars between nations would be obsolete but not the dirty wars.

THE NEW GENERATION

The El Al flight was full of Israelis touring India in large numbers. The few dark passengers were Indian Jews returning to Israel. The aircrew was polite and most Israelis speak English with a decidedly un-American accent. Many of them are descended from Russian and European parentage as the major lot of Jewish immigration to Israel in the past few decades have been from there.

Since my last visit the new generation in Israel has blended into an assured nationhood. Their holiest site, the wall of the Temple of Solomon, which was called the Wailing Wall, is now known as the Western Wall because the Jews no longer wail, that I had seen even in 1980. Instead there is an air of festivity around the wall and in the large open courtyard in front that was not there 26 years back. The Hebrew language has been made suitable for modern use and new indigenous technology has developed in many fields. To their brain has been added brawn and self-assurance. Signs of prosperity and culture are obvious. Despite many roadblocks they want to develop into a multiethnic society. Terrorist bomb attacks that were commonplace in Jerusalem still happen but are fewer and they have developed disciplines to control those effectively. I had the opportunity to see one such incident though it turned out to be a false alarm.

THE RELIGIOUS DIVIDE

The Arab-Israeli conflict of today is deep rooted in antiquity. The three Semitic religions – Judaism, Christianity and Islam – have their origins in the same roots in the Old Testament and some of their holiest sites exist close together. In Jerusalem the Mount Moriah or Temple Mount, the rock on which God ordered Abraham to offer his son Isaac as a burnt offering, was the site of Solomon's temple, and on this very rock Prophet Mohammed sat on a horse riding all the way from Mecca in a dream and was lifted to heaven to meet God. Caliph Umar I built the Dome of the Rock in memory, which the Crusaders made their headquarters when they came to protect the Church of The Holy Sepulchre where Jesus Christ was crucified and entombed. All crusader or Templar churches in Europe since those days are octagonal in shape like the Golden Dome of the Rock. This one site is symbolic of all the conflicts in the region. Solomon's temple was destroyed by Nebuchadnezzar, King of Babylon in 587 BCE; rebuilding began in 536 BCE under Persian occupation; was decorated and ornamented by the Roman king Herod in 37 BCE; and this second temple was razed to the ground in 70 CE; and only the Western Wall remains. In the meantime Jesus Christ came and preached, hiding in the corridors of the temple from his pursuers. Himself a Jew, he was sentenced to death by the principal Jewish Council or Sanhedrin that had its seat on a hill that is called the Hill of Evil Counsel, where the United Nations are located today.

HISTORY OF CIRCLE OF HATRED

The beginning of the history of Israel or the Land of Canaan can be traced back to 1300 BCE when the Hittites and Pharaoh Rameses II of Egypt fought bloody wars in this land of Canaan and both exhausted armies returned home proclaiming victory. They left the land desolate and empty where the Jews fleeing from Egypt led by Moses and Aaron came and settled. As Moses said, it was their promised land. They formed their kingdoms under Saul, David and Solomon. A seafaring people called the Philistines, from whom the modern Palestine took its name without any historical connection, populated the narrow coastal areas. After a relative peace lasting a few centuries, a stream of conquering armies continued encroaching till the present times. They included the Assyrians, Babylonians, Persians, Greeks, Romans, Byzantines, Arabs, Crusaders, Mameluks, Ottoman Turks and finally the British after the First World War with the Palestine mandate and the Balfour declaration of 1917 to create a Jewish homeland. The Jews scattered around the world suffering the anti-Semitism of the Christians because their Sanhedrin had sentenced Christ to death. The Christians hated the Muslims for they rejected the divinity of Christ and the Muslims hated the Christians because they replaced the concept of single God by the trinity of the Father, the Son and the Holy Ghost not found in the Gospels. The Muslims called the Jews cursed people for Moses had cursed their forefathers after coming out of Mount Sinai with the Ten Commandments. The Jews called the Muslims usurpers as Mohammed claimed to be the true follower of Abraham and recognized and claimed Palestine through that dream. Islam recognizes Adam, Noah, Abraham, Moses and Jesus as prophets like Mohammed, but Jesus is neither son of God nor any part of divinity. This laid the foundation of the circle of hatred of the three Semitic religions. Through a history of five thousand years national boundaries have meant very little, only people have mattered, fighting for religions in intermingling cultures which was often a fight to finish, but nothing has finished. Everything has come back in different garbs proving the futility of human conflict on Earth.

MODERN TIMES

After the Second World War the exhausted British made a hasty exit leaving a mess in Palestine as they did in India. The USA took up the management of the Middle East, the soft underbelly of Russia, with much less expertise. Cold war politics played havoc with the Middle East with the inevitable rise of Arab and Islamic nationalism. The balancing acts of the two big powers kept a semblance of stability and Israel became a virtual American protectorate. Collapse of the Soviet Union left the USA the sole player, but the world is afraid of their aggressive acquisitive culture. Every folly of the USA has boomeranged on Israel and the latest and most dangerous one is Iraq. Israel is coming out of the American shadow and establishing her independent nationhood.

INDIA AND ISRAEL

India-Israel relations have gone through ups and downs as with no other country of the world. The foreign policy of non-alignment that India adopted immediately after independence took her closer to the Soviet bloc in the days of the Cold War and military pacts like CENTO and SEATO, to encircle the two communist countries, Soviet

Russia and China. Pakistan was the natural geopolitical ally of the allied powers. An Indian passport in those days debarred entry to Portugal, South Africa and Israel. After the fall of Goa the name of Portugal was erased; after fall of apartheid the name of South Africa was erased. The Non-Aligned movement lost its momentum and then there came the fall of Soviet Russia. India's relationship with Israel was gradually improving during this period due to commonality of interest. An Israeli consular office was opened in Mumbai and gradually full diplomatic relation was established. Israel is a great country, their scientific inventions and innovations have surpassed those of many developed countries as also their social engineering. Culturally we have an affinity born out of two most ancient religious heritages with written texts. An ancient historical connection has been revealed by the lost tribes of Israel and a genetically identified ancient Jewish population in India has been settled for two thousand years. Islamic militancy is plaguing both of us with cross border infiltration. Israel for her own survival has invented technology and methods to control it and we need them badly. Agricultural research in Israel is turning the desert green that we need very much and Israel needs a share of the huge Indian market. Geopolitical tensions are there but both are democratic nuclear armed nations in a hostile environment. Similarities and commonality of interest, more than differences, have brought us closer.

THE ROAD AHEAD

In our globalized world brought about by technology, economic compulsions and climate change, a permanent military solution to international problems is not possible. This is as much true for us as for Israel. How to bring about changes for a peaceful solution is a difficult road to tread. We have to learn to live in peace with neighbours and they should also learn. Until that happens a policy of containment has to be pursued. We have no right to pontificate to Israel nor can they to us. The problem of Israel is the acceptance by surrounding Islamic nations of the existence of sovereign Israel. Until that is in place unequivocally and from the heart, no progress is possible. It would only then be possible for five million Jews in a country no larger than several districts of India and an even smaller number of Palestinians to live together in peace. Unless they come out of the history books and forsake the fight to finish tradition in the Middle East they will be burned along with a sizable part of humanity whereas jointly they can be proud pathfinders of the future world. The situation is similar with us. Globalization of terror has made things more complicated and rich countries have not yet forgotten hegemonic desires.

Economic empowerment and pride of achievement within their traditions and way of life make a people responsible citizens of the world. It is the same everywhere, in Israel and Palestine, the hills of Afghanistan, the jungles of India and the desert of the Middle East. This is a fact often forgotten in the corridors of power.

A Hundred Years of Troubled Iran

SUMMARY OF A HUNDRED YEARS OF POLITICAL PROBLEMS

1901 D'Arcy, a British national, individually obtained Iran's concession to drill for oil and struck oil in 1908 but had gone bankrupt by that time. In April 1909 the Anglo-Persian Oil Company (APOC) was founded and took over from him and D'Arcy was made a director, giving the British effective control of Iranian oil reserves for 60 years. APOC changed to the Anglo Iranian Oil Company in 1913 and then to BP. The financial support given by Burmah Oil and the British Admiralty to D'Arcy in his bankruptcy was made an excuse to refuse him directorship in the new company and he died a broken man.

1905 The Iranian Constitutional Revolution, pioneer of modern era in the Middle East

1921 Iran's Constitutional Monarchy falls when Reza Khan Mirpanj forces a coup.

1951 Democratically elected Prime Minister Mohammad Mossaddeq nationalized the British-owned oil industry after talks failed for a fair sharing as between Aramco and Saudi Arabia and all hell broke loose. Unable to resolve the issue single handed, post-World War II Britain looked towards the United States to settle the issue. Initially America opposed British policies. After American mediation failed several times to bring about settlement, American Secretary of State Dean Acheson concluded that the British were 'destructive and determined on a rule or ruin policy in Iran.' By early 1953 Eisenhower was elected President of the USA and US policy towards Iran changed. Despite Mossaddeq's open disgust with socialism, Churchill told the United States that Mossaddeq was 'increasingly turning towards communism' and was moving Iran towards the Soviet sphere at a time of high Cold War fears. In October 1952, Mossaddeq declared Britain an enemy, and cut off all diplomatic relations. In November and December 1952, British intelligence officials suggested to American intelligence that the prime minister should be ousted. Eisenhower and Churchill agreed to work together towards Mossaddeq's removal. In March 1953, John Foster Dulles directed the CIA, which was headed by his younger brother Allen Dulles, to draft plans to overthrow Mossaddeq. The Operation Ajax was launched and by internal subversion through propaganda and money by agents like Donald Wilbur and external blockade the situation became serious and Mossaddeq, though enjoying popular support, had to take tougher measures and played into the hands of CIA. On **19 August, 1953** Mossaddeq was rounded up as the CIA-backed coup came to a successful end and the Shah returned to power. He was then tried, imprisoned for three years and kept under house arrest until he died in March 1967. It has to be said as a postscript that Mossaddeq is regarded as a great democrat who did everything he could to defend the people of Iran. He was a secular person who refused to make Mehdi Bazargan Minister of Culture because he could have 'put the veil on the head of all the girls in schools.' Mossaddeq was the most pro-American prime minister Iran ever had. He never blamed the USA for the coup and mostly blamed the British.

1954 The Shah gave an international consortium of British

(40%), American (40%), French (6%), and Dutch (14%) companies half the profit from its oil to run the Iranian oil facilities for 25 years. Iran was not allowed to audit consortium accounting records.

1960s Stability returned with economic growth that benefited only a few, and the liberal pro-Western policies and culture alienated certain Islamic religious and political groups.

1970s Widespread religious and political opposition to the Shah's rule and programmes like depredations of his secret police Savak caused him to flee Iran on 16 January 1979.

1979 US Embassy in Tehran seized by militant Iranian students holding 52 embassy employees hostage for 444 days from 4 November 1979 to 21 January 1981, the first day of Reagan Presidency. Jimmy Carter had earlier tried Operation Eagle Claw to snatch the hostages, but that failed with death of US soldiers, and Carter lost his reelection.

1980 Iraq, with secret encouragement from the Carter administration invaded Iran in September 1980. Iraq was supplied with conventional arms, biological and chemical weapons technology even to the extent of cyanides in spite of protests from the world community and the precursors to nuclear capabilities in the garb of dual use technology and also direct supplies by the Reagan administration and its allies, China, France, Italy and others. Soviet Russia, who originally armed Iraq, cut off supplies when chemical weapons supplied by the West were used. The offensive capabilities of supplies increased as Iraq went on the defensive with massive Iranian counterattacks. The arms bazaar of the whole world joined in to supply both sides. Iran's weaponry was mainly of US origin supplied during the Shah's time. When spares and ammunition from the US were stopped, Iran had to shop from just anybody, and all nations joined openly or clandestinely. Banca Nazionale del Italia through its major branch in Atlanta provided a Five Billion dollar undeclared loan to Iraq on secret approval of US administration for supply of high tech equipment for guided missile technology and nuclear weaponry and production of chemical weapons and the same administration later convicted the bank official. Most suppliers actually supplied both sides either directly or through channels.

1986 Reagan Administration covertly sold anti-tank missiles and spare parts to Iran in what is known as *Iran-Contra affair.* The weapons were sold via Israel officially to use the money to release American hostages from Hezbollah but actually to fund the Contra rebel fighters installed by CIA in Nicaragua. Protests rose worldwide and Reagan apologized to the nation that he as the President of the USA knew nothing!

2005 Mahmoud Ahmedinezad, an ultra conservative, was elected President of Iran. With a powerful base inside the Alliance of Builders of Islamic Iran, he has been criticized by Western governments for his statements that Israel should be wiped off the map, his support of Hezbollah, controversial comments he has made on the Holocaust and the legitimacy of Israel's existence, and his alleged drive to develop nuclear weapons. In the last five years the confrontation has escalated to the point that armed action against Iran has been threatened by Israel and supported by lobbies inside other governments. In the meantime election to the parliament has been held re-electing Ahmedinezad, and the world has seen violent protests on the streets of Tehran. On past records such scenes can be created in Iran by both the MI6 of Britain and CIA and also by Islamists, but this time the Islamists are on the side of Ahmedinezad. The world is watching with concern what happens in the next decade.

COMMENTS

This condensed view of Iranian history looks like madness or as the Greek divine tragedy of Prometheus chained and bound and his eternally regenerating liver eaten by an Eagle. Iran for a hundred years is fighting external and internal wars. The external war was with Britain to start with, and then Britain, and USA as the latter shouldered the 'white man's burden' from Britain although Iran trusted them and joined CENTO initially. The internal war is between the secular educated population in the cities and the vast population in the countryside educated and controlled by the Islamist clergy.

In the external conflict one side is driven by what they consider the key to their medieval greatness and believe the same is valid for present and future and, shackled by the clergy, their diplomacy is crude and erratic and lacks finesse.

The other side, in spite of their gift of knowledge, culture and material progress of humanity, believe in their God-given right to a major, if not exclusive, share of the wealth of the world and any means to keep it. They have poisoned the earth's air and water but want to do the least and keep their lifestyle unchanged while advocating others not to emulate. The ancient wisdom of India held that knowledge is not a property since it is based on the pre-existent knowledge base of human society. The west believes in intellectual property rights but they did not invent the zero, numerals, paper, wheel, time, mathematics, astronomy, medicine, architecture and art and not even gunpowder. The world is grateful to them for building the huge superstructure but that does not give them rights to the world. Saner elements must prevail for their own good.

Iran needs nuclear energy. The economy of Iran is dominated by oil and gas exports which constituted 50 per cent to 70 per cent of government revenue and 80 per cent of export earnings between 2006 and 2008 but it is not going to last. It has a large public sector, large religious foundations, or Bonyads, and rigidities that undermine the development of a private sector and employment. President Ahmedinezad proposed replacing energy subsidies with targeted social assistance to the Iranians. However reforms do not go well in Islamic countries and previous efforts have met with resistance, violent protests and collapse of government. High oil price in recent years led to huge profits, yet this increased revenue has not eased economic hardships, double-digit unemployment and inflation, and has prompted Iranians to seek employment overseas, resulting in a significant brain drain that they can ill afford.

Are they making a bomb? Opinions are consolidating against them but there are responsible contrary views. Another Iraq with a Rumsfeld and WMD fiasco will not be good for anybody. Iran cannot use nukes except clandestinely and that is not easy. The rebound will destroy them. Rationality is not an important feature in many Islamic countries. Is Iran in that category? Unlikely but hard to tell. The rhetoric is definitely to keep people on the edge. It is likely that they will negotiate once they feel secure. This author had written in March 2003 at the start of the Second Gulf War that there was a hidden agenda of getting close to Iran. Let us hope that assessment was wrong.

2009

GLOBAL ENVIRONMENT : NORTH TIBET

Journey Through Tibet: Nature's Call on the Roof of the World

I heard Professor Samdhong Rinpoche, Kalon Tripa (Chairman of the Cabinet), Central Tibetan Administration of the Dalai Lama, in private discourse at the Ramakrishna Mission Institute of Culture, Kolkata. Respected the world over for his wisdom and clarity of expression, he said there is no such thing as Tibetan Buddhism, a term coined and used by the West, just as there is no American or European Christianity.

Buddhism went from India and the Tibetans faced difficulty in interpreting and translating the real meaning of the Sanskrit texts, inventing expressions jointly with Indian scholars that enriched the Tibetan language. It took centuries. He spoke on the stream of consciousness and spirituality of man in Hindu and Buddhist traditions. To me, they seemed so close! Will this heritage be annihilated by the Chinese version of global capitalism? A Communist state with capitalist economy is uncharted waters with lurking dangers. I had to see Tibet.

In June last year, I went by road from Lhasa to Mansarovar and Kailash, the holiest pilgrimage of Hindus, Buddhists and Jains and the ancient Tibetan religion Bon, and also to see Tibet, the holy land where the treasure of Buddhist learning and history of the ancient world were transferred from India in the seventh century and the main bulk in the eleventh and twelfth centuries by Atish Dipankar

Srjnan and others after the Muslim invasion of India. These were kept for posterity, a wealth similar to the destroyed library of Alexandria. The modern world laments that destruction but does nothing to preserve the wealth in Tibet. They hold the history of many nations and religions of antiquity, including Christianity.

Tibet is an independent nation. In the thirteenth century, Gengis Khan conquered most of China and his successor Kublai Khan conquered Tibet, unifying them under one Yuang empire. The Mongol rule of China ended but the Chinese claim on Tibet stands on that colonial historical basis. If that is justified then so is our claim to hold the boundaries of British India as the legal boundaries today. That claim of China existed on paper only in later centuries. The relationship was more of mutual respect. The fifth Dalai Lama was the spiritual guide of the then Qing emperor. The Tibetan language is different from Chinese and there were no Han Chinese in Tibet before the Chinese invasion. In the Peoples' Republic of China the belief seems to be that all the people with shades of Mongolian features are part of the old Chinese empires. Will it include Bengal some day! Tibetans repulsed two British attacks in 1888 and 1903 without any help from China. Will the wealth of Tibet survive?

We reached Lhasa by air from Kathmandu and spent three nights to acclimatize to the altitude, visiting Potala Palace, Jokhang Temple, Drepung Monastery, and Sera Monastery among others. We then started our drive towards Kailash and on Day 1, we travelled to Gyantse; Day 2 took us to Lhatse via Shigatse. On Day 3, we reached Saga and camped in the open. On Day 4, we reached the camp in open grounds beside a stream outside Paryang. On Day 5, we reached Manas and camped in the open by the western shore of the Sarovar. On Day 6, we performed Puja and Hawan beside the Mansarovar, visited Tirthapuri and reached Darchen, the base camp of Kailash. We spent three nights at Darchen, the team breaking up into those who went on an outer *parikrama* or inner *parikrama* or stay in the travellers' lodge performing Puja.

On Day 10, we returned to the eastern shore of the Manas, took holy dip on a full moon day, spent the night in camp amid a mild snowfall and on Day 11, drove back to Saga. On Day 12, we went back to Nyalam near the Nepal border, spent the night and the next day, crossed the border and drove to Kathmandu.

China has invested and earned in the development of the Tibet Autonomous Region (TAR) that is less than half of the original country. The rest, including the rich provinces of Amdo and the eastern half of Kham have been absorbed in China proper. The effect is visible in the populated cities of Lhasa and to some extent in Gyantse and Shigatse. Beyond that there is only the arid mountain region and deserts of shingle and stones with small depopulated villages and hamlets with no development.

My interest is in the people and what the occupation has done to them. The modern airport of Lhasa was a surprise as was the drive to the city through lush green fields that extended along the Brahmaputra river valley to Shigatse.

Agriculture has been mostly collectivized by China. In this whole trip I saw only one poor farmer pushing a plough with a yak on the silted river bed. Lhasa is a modern city with rather curious decorative street lighting like an Indian marriage ceremony, not seen anywhere else in China, a legacy of the Lhasa festival. The people were an almost equal mixture of Tibetans and Chinese. Many Tibetans were carrying prayer wheels as they were streaming out to morning work as if in silent assertion of their separateness. There were devotees prostrating on the road on their way to the temples. This scenario disappeared as one left Lhasa and only dirty clothes and poverty devoid of any religious emblem marked the Tibetans. Unlike the burly Tibetans in my school days in the Himalayas, the thin malnourished Tibetans of today seem to have lost on all counts.

The huge paved area around the Jokhang temple is a bazaar with open stalls of Tibetans, whereas shops with mostly Chinese and English signboards line the clean wide roads. There are Chinese medicine shops with polite attendants where we bought herbal medicines for high altitude which allowed us to climb unfamiliar heights in harsh weather despite age. The main ingredient of the medicine is the rhodiolla root. They are very effective and should be available in our country.

The monasteries hold thousands of monks. Drepung alone houses 7,700 of them and the largest, the Sera, more than ten thousand. Ancient manuscripts lining the walls and candles in front of the altars of the Buddha or earlier Dalai Lamas are a familiar sight. There is little communication between the monks and the people and one hardly ever sees a monk outside, unusual in a Buddhist country as one would see in Thailand or Burma.

Beyond the Brahmaputra valley, the landscape changes and sanitation, water supply, hospitals and schools disappear. The bare windswept hills and plateau of Tibet have a rugged beauty with a burning sun, ultramarine blue sky of strong ultraviolet rays and freezing high winds that never stop blowing sand and dust.

The streams beside the camp have freezing water in high summer. The major highway to the west is a pressed down track of stone and rubble, throwing up blinding clouds of dust. The whole of Tibet is a lavatory with people defecating everywhere, even on their own doorstep, and water is scarce. Dry and extreme cold weather kill the bacteria and protect them from disease, but for how long? Approach to a village or hamlet is often heralded by the stench. The travellers' lodge at Darchen for international tourists has nice rooms with good beds, whose sheets are changed but not washed because water is scarce, and one can step on human excreta as one comes out of the building if not careful.

The journey exposes one to dangers of accident, sickness and death. The clinic at Darchen that comes within a day or two of driving, has poor health facilities even for minor afflictions. This is the picture all along the major tourist route. A single official, who is never seen, governs the entire Manas–Kailash area and collects all the revenues, even from the poor horse or yak owners whose animal is hired by the tourists. The collector on behalf of the governor is a Chinese lady in very improbable Ascot attire. The poor horse-yak owners are terrified of her. The Chinese one meets are crude and not the educated people of China. The Tibetans are just poor.

The experience of three days at Kailash and the sight of the mountain from close range that has through the ages raised awe and respect in every traveller and explorer, as expressed in books from all countries and religions, was indescribable. Personally I followed the inner *parikrama* route as far as I could go and that was not small – up to a height of 18000 to 19000 feet, and stood face to face with the south face of Kailash, an unforgettable experience. The stay at Darchen was followed by the full moon night beside the Manas, where *apsaras* or divine dancers come down and dance at midnight. Some of us were awake and went out in the severe cold with high freezing wind almost blowing off our clothes and wrappers and were mesmerized by the stark beauty of full moon on blue waters and the sheer white body of the Guru Mandhata range, as if it is where all our *Puranic* stories took origin. We did not see any *apsara* except white clouds floating in very bright full moonlight in a blue sky.

On our return journey from Manas we entered a small village Ghorasu to look for some provisions. The village is about a kilometer long collection of poor hovels and waste water running through the middle of the central dirt road and camera-shy children playing in the dirt. There is only one red brick building at one end with solar panels, dish antennae and tall aerial masts with a high boundary wall, manned by one Chinese woman whom we saw from a distance. She is the ruler and representative of government wielding the long arm of law and governance.

People are terrified of the green uniform even if they are not police or army. One such uniformed road worker invented a deliberate ruse to beat up our burly Tibetan driver and the man whimpered until we intervened. In large towns there are two classes of citizens – a small number of well dressed Chinese and the mass of Tibetan menial workers and idlers. In the glass front of one Lhatse shop are pasted posters of three Indian film stars, Preity Zinta, Mithun Chakraburty and Rani Mukherjee, amid all the squalor. Is this the only relief for the marginalized Tibetans?

Visited by a large number of Indians and visitors from all over the world, this area should become a UNESCO heritage site with easier road access from India. The income can be used by the Chinese to develop the place with better amenities and supervision. This would be a friendly gesture from China.

2007

Who Owns the Sixth Dalai Lama?

There is a recent (1 November 2007) statement by Mr. Zhou Gang, former Ambassador of China to India, presently advisor to the Chinese Foreign Ministry and an expert on South Asian affairs, demanding that India must make substantial adjustment in the eastern sector, including returning the Buddhist enclave of Tawang to China, to reach an early settlement of the border issue. His statement as published continues, 'I cited the following example that during my tenure as Chinese ambassador to India, I made it clear on many occasions to the Indian public—Tawang belongs to China, it is the birthplace of the sixth Dalai Lama and the Dalai Lama is China's Dalai Lama, who cannot be India's Dalai Lama. I think if the Indian side can make substantial adjustment in the East sector according to the principle of mutual understanding, mutual accommodation and mutual adjustment, the Chinese side will make its adjustment in the Western sector accordingly.'

China has never accepted the McMahon Line as the eastern boundary between the two nations and has made many demands on different sectors of Arunachal Pradesh, though in the recent past our foreign minister Sri Pranab Mukherjee has reiterated that Arunachal belongs to India. But the claim on Tawang is a new one, since by the ceasefire following the hostilities in 1962 the Chinese were supposed to withdraw beyond the Sela Pass. Actually they have continued to occupy the heights of the Sela Pass and Chinese infiltration of Tawang has continued. The people of India have been kept in the dark about this. Conceding the Tawang enclave brings the Chinese army to the outskirts of Bomdila and close to Tezpur in Assam. This is a dagger capable of severing the Northeast from the rest of India. The new road being built from Gyantse in Tibet to Nathu La pass in Sikkim will probably have a diversion to the top of Sela. This road is being built very fast with heavy earth moving machinery. It is funny that the justification for the fresh demand is the Sixth Dalai Lama.

THE FIFTH DALAI LAMA

The Sixth Dalai Lama is a peculiar character in the lineage of the Dalai Lama. The Fifth Dalai Lama was a powerful and astute statesman and spiritual leader. In 1640, when civil unrest arose in Tibet, the Fifth Dalai Lama, Ngawang Lobsang Gyatso (1617-1682) applied for assistance from his associates, the Mongols. Gushi Khan, a Mongol warlord, conquered Kham in 1640 bringing the Sakyas and the lords of Kham and Amdo under their control. His victory over the prince of T'sang in Shigatse in 1642, completed the unification of the country, displacing the rival dominant school of the Karmapas. The Dalai Lama also established warm relations with the Shunzhi Emperor of China, the second Manchu emperor of the Qing dynasty, during a state visit to Beijing in 1652 after several earlier invitations. He set out accompanied by 3,000 men and stayed at the Yellow Palace which had been specially constructed by the Manchu emperor to house him. The emperor met the Dalai Lama in January 1653 when he was only 14 (15 by Western reckoning). The Dalai Lama stayed in Beijing for two months and was honoured with two grand imperial receptions. Some historians claim that the emperor treated the Dalai Lama as an equal while others dispute this claim. The Emperor subsequently granted him the honorific title *Dalai Lama, Overseer of the Buddhist Faith on Earth Under the Great Benevolent Self-subsisting Buddha of the Western Paradise.* From this meeting onwards, the Dalai Lamas were considered priests to the throne by successive Qing emperors. He then recognized the authority of the Fifth Dalai Lama, making him the ruler of the whole of Tibet. It was after their subsequent pacification of the nation, that the Mongols invested him with complete political control. The Fifth Dalai Lama thereby became the spiritual and temporal leader of Tibet. So capable was he in both temporal and spiritual realms that this Dalai Lama is often referred to as the 'Great Fifth'. The Chinese, who are very particular about history, have forgotten this action of their Mongol Emperors as also the fact that this 'Great Fifth' became Guru of the Emperor and thereby China.

THE SIXTH DALAI LAMA

The sixth Dalai Lama was Tsangyang Gyatso (1 March 1683 – 15 November 1706). He was a Monpa by ethnicity and was born in the present-day region of Arunachal Pradesh in India. The claim by Mr. Gang that he was born in Tawang is not adequately specified. He led a playboy lifestyle and disappeared near Kokonor, probably murdered on his way to China in 1706. Tsangyang Gyatso composed poems and songs that are still immensely popular in Tibet to this day. Although Lozang Gyatso, the fifth Dalai Lama, had died in 1682, the Regent Desi Sangye Gyatso kept his death a secret, partly to continue the stable administration, and partly to gain time for the completion of the Potala. The five-year-old reincarnation was discovered in 1688, but immeditely sent to Nankartse, not far from Lhasa, where he was kept concealed by the Regent, Sangye Gyatso, until 1697 when he sent a delegation to the Chinese Emperor in 1697 to announce that the Fifth Dalai Lama had died and the Sixth had been discovered. Tsangyang Gyatso enjoyed a lifestyle that included drinking, the company of women, and writing love songs. He visited Lobsang Yeshe, the Fifth Panchen Lama, in Shigatse and requesting his forgiveness, renounced the vows of a novice monk. Tsangyang Gyatso had always rejected life as a monk, although this did not mean the abdication of his position as the Dalai Lama. Wearing the clothes of a normal layman and preferring to walk than to ride a horse or use the state palanquin, Tsangyang only kept the temporal prerogatives of the Dalai Lama. He also visited the parks and spent nights in the streets of Lhasa, drinking wine, singing songs and having amorous relations with girls. Tsangyang retreated to live in a tent in the park near the northern escarpment of Potala. Tsangyang finally gave up his discourses in public parks and places in 1702, which he was required to do as part of his training. In the spiritual and monastic traditions of world religions this Dalai Lama is a most interesting character and has been analysed from a spiritual viewpoint. Already chosen he could not be unseated. So the elders took the decision that during the day he will fulfill his functions as the Dalai Lama wrapped in a shawl and at night he could leave Potala and go wherever he wanted. To the devoted Tibetans the deception held even after he was murdered probably on his way to China. That is why in all Tibetan monasteries the small statue or picture, whatever it is, of the Sixth Dalai Lama is kept completely wrapped in a small Thankha, his face cannot be seen even now. Do we now have to give up Tawang to an atheist China because of him? What a humiliating demand! And the present fourteenth Dalai Lama is the property of China to keep or kill! Any day now they will demand Gautama Buddha!

IN THE PRESENT SCENARIO

The Chinese politicians are not garrulous like ours, who keep talking to build their image, keep the media happy, journalists employed and people misinformed. Chinese political statements are deliberate weapons with a purpose and need to be addressed not only for their contents but also the timing and the place of release. Sometimes their statement is in action and not in words as in the recent shooting down of one of their old satellites during a visit by the Israeli Prime Minister, the journey probably undertaken with American blessing. Similar was the attack on India in 1962 when our leaders were fooled, and it is doubtful whether they have learned yet. It is the old Mongol technique. On the contrary the Indian political firmament is a cacophony of noises.

It is not difficult to imagine the reason for this statement emanating from Beijing at this time and from a known person in high position.

China has officially kept a low profile on the Indo-US nuclear deal professing their neutrality, treating our political emissaries with cold politeness and encouraging their own supporters in India. Why this sudden demand of Tawang at this sensitive time? Most likely this is a reaction to the visit by Kissinger and party to India. The message is both to India and Mr. Kissinger. What is the likely message to Mr. Kissinger? Can it be 'don't give them what you gave us for they can't deal with you as we did against the Soviet Union' or may be 'the world has changed since you last saw it; do not make it more difficult than you can handle?' What can they be saying to us? May be 'buzz off, kids, this is an adult game; go play your little money games elsewhere.' This is the typical Chinese way of sending messages to multiple targets that hit. The message to us may be humiliating but may be right! Almost unwittingly we have entered the big game, the danger game. Can we play it with danger lurking on both sides? All these years we have played as linesmen and now suddenly we are pushed to the playing field. We need a statesman of stature as manager, which we do not have.

Our political system does not allow drastic proactive policies. Even the party agenda comes after self, making the Parliament irrelevant. Some have found sudden faith in our able scientists, who toiled with obsolete Russian designs for decades till the collapse of the Soviets, to recreate the world from scratch with whatever we give them. Some are kids who love to play 'pull the rug' and wait silently till it is time to pull. Some are so blindly attached to an ideology that they refuse to see its failures even if shown time and again. Our country has suffered for long from ideologist leaders who cared more for their ideologies than for the people. Majority of Indians, if not all, are programmed only on money and make it their God, definitively and literally, and are unconcerned about the integrity and security of the society. That is why we have betrayed our nation again and again. Is this a proper team for a big game?

With reference to the present crisis, on the credit side we have the opportunity to join the big league of technology and financial powers of the western countries headed by the USA and on the debit side we cannot afford to upset our traditional friends, not just China, nor get embroiled in disputes that are no immediate concern of ours. Other talks of being stooges of United States are only rabble rousing. A weak nation will always be a stooge whether of the USA or China or someone else. We must be strong as fast as we can and that needs massive inputs both in quality and quantity. There must be a middle way through this crisis and it can be found if all political forces join hands leaving aside partisan and individual interests. That is what the nation expects of its politicians and will reject anyone who betrays this.

2007

GLOBAL ENVIRONMENT : EAST

Bengal and Burma

The relationship goes back to antiquity. It is traceable at least to the fourth and fifth centuries CE and was closest between the eleventh and thirteenth centuries. The kingdom of Pattikera in the Tripura region, whose origin can be traced to the seventh century and whose capital has recently been located near the Mynamati hills to the west of Comilla in Bangladesh, extended at one time from the flow of the Ganga to the northern Burmese kingdom of Pagan or Bagan. The royal family had familial and filial relationships with the royal families of Arakan and Bagan and folklores of royal love stories survive even to this day in *Hmannan Yazawin*, an ancient Burmese book. Prome, the capital of Arakan, was at one time a major centre of Sanskrit and Bengali language and culture.

Muslim conquest of the riverine terrain of southeast Bengal did not happen until the end of the thirteenth century and did not extend far into the Burmese territory, which has remained largely Buddhist to this day. Aurangzeb pursued his brother Suja to the borders of Arakan where the latter sought refuge but his subsequent fate is unknown. The British fought three Anglo-Burmese wars. In the first in 1824-26 they conquered Assam, Tenasserim and Arakan; in the second in 1852 they conquered Lower Burma and then in 1886 conquered Mandalay and exiled King Thebaw to India where he died. Earlier they had exiled the last Mughal Emperor Bahadur Shah Zafar to Rangoon where his last remains lie. Burma remained a part of the

British Indian Empire until 1937. In 1942 Japan invaded Burma from Thailand and the country became ravaged by war. After the war Burma gained independence in 1948.

During British occupation Indians went to Burma in large numbers as labourers, civil servants, professionals, clerks and businessmen, and the Bengalis formed a large part of it in the last four categories. One of the illustrious émigrés was Sarat Chandra Chattopadhyay, the novelist who has immortalized Burma of those times in his writings. Revolutionaries from Bengal used Burma for refuge and transit. Netaji Subhas Chandra Bose was imprisoned in Mandalay jail for more than two years where his health broke down. Later he brought the INA through Burma to the borders of India. Chandra Bose is still a familiar name in Burma.

The Indians had to evacuate Burma twice. The first time was during the Japanese invasion when there was no organized evacuation of the civilian population who had to move on foot through hostile, lawless jungles and swamps leaving all their belongings. Large numbers died, the survivors were robbed of everything including clothing, and the women were raped. The British Governor of Assam, unable to arrange relief during wartime, requested the Ramakrishna Mission to help and the then Head of the Shillong Math and Mission, Swami Bhuteshananda, moved to the borders of Burma and singlehandedly established camps and brought about a rapport between the local population on both sides of the border bringing the fleeing Indians to safety.

After the war was over the Indians started trickling back to retrieve whatever they could of their property and slowly got established again. In the newly independent country they got a safe haven and flourished, as there was insufficient talent in the indigenous population. Almost seventy per cent of Rangoon's population were Indians in 1962 when the civilian government abdicated power to the military and General Ne Win established the Socialist Republic. The government nationalized all business and industry. Literally overnight the Indians, most of whom owned business, became paupers. A second evacuation started but was more organized than the first one. Nevertheless many had to travel over land as they had lost everything and had no means of support to wait for a place on a ship. The second exodus was almost as complete as the first, leaving only the labourers, who had nowhere to go and could survive only by adjusting to the local conditions. These were people from Bihar and the South and they still live in Myanmar, consolidated in their own localities, stateless, numbering about four lakhs and the succeeding generations never having seen India.

There are Bengalis too, between fifty to sixty families, surviving and clinging to their culture. They speak Bengali with a Burmese accent. Some of their children cannot even speak the language and some have intermarried with local population. Yet they remain stateless needing special passes to go out of the country even for short visits. They say the passes cost a lot of money in bribes, though the Indian Embassy refutes that, and they dare not leave for fear of not being able to get back. Their life revolves around what used to be the Ramakrishna Mission, which was closed down by General Ne Win. The large hospital run by the Mission was handed over to the government but the Mission building and the small temple on the rooftop, which had escaped Japanese bombing, remained in the hands of a local society of devotees. Their lives revolved round it, without any contact or support, for more than three decades until in the mid-nineties a senior monk visited them twice as soon as travel restrictions were lifted. People who have never seen their homeland took initiation from him in large numbers in Yangon and Mandalay.

The socialist government of General Ne Win was isolated from the world and went bankrupt. Amid public unrest democratic elections were held and the party led by Aung San Suu Kyi won. The new military government refused to hand over power and arrested her followed by a student revolt and severe repression. Thousands of young people, mostly students, were killed. The government changed its name to Society for Peace and Solidarity with military officers looking after different departments as secretaries of the society, socialism was rejected and replaced by an open market policy and the name of the country was changed to Union of Myanmar. Burma had always been a difficult country to rule with warring tribes and their private armies ruling in respective border regions though the majority was the Burmese living in the plains. The name of the country was changed to Myanmar to give a greater sense of national identity to all tribes. There is a flourishing trade in opium and narcotics in the golden triangle at the joint border of Burma, China and Thailand. The government faced internal revolt, international pressure and economic sanctions, the drug trade and hostility of warring tribes in a crumbling economy. They have suppressed student revolts, have pacified warring tribes by giving them virtual autonomy and have taken army action against opium growers and distillers with international help. They have undertaken large scale building of infrastructure with roads and bridges so that the opium growers can revert to cash crops and get to ready markets and an industrial infrastructure can be established. But they are reeling under international economic pressure with devaluation of currency, low foreign exchange reserves, adverse balance of payments and poor industrial growth. Even foreign companies find it difficult to send money out legally as the reserves are low. In spite of the so called open market policy the country is still partly closed with very little banking connections and banning of Internet facilities and cellular phones. E-mail facilities are open with surveillance. The government promises to lift these restrictions soon. They accuse widespread maligning by international media as the cause for restrictions. They are very sensitive to allegations of forced labour and child labour in international media. They have been admitted to the ASEAN but complain that the purse strings of the ADB (Asian Development Bank) are not open for them.

How is it to live in Myanmar today? Not too bad if one is not dabbling in politics. The law and order situation is very good and one can drive far out of Yangon on the newly built highways without fear. The cost of living is very low. Myanmar is a country of fifty-one million in a landmass one-sixth the size of India with very fertile plains, rich and wide navigable rivers and tremendous natural wealth of gold and precious stones. Hunger and abject poverty are absent. The people are polite, the work force in industrial zones is disciplined, and the cities are very clean with big plush hotels. There are posh restaurants where a good dinner or lunch will cost only two or three US dollars. A five star hotel room is surprisingly cheap. The country has been opened for tourists who are welcome but so far there is only a slow trickle. The old archaeological sites in Bagan and Mandalay have been beautifully restored and are unforgettable. The new airport at Mandalay can rival any in India. On the debit side the local population can get a midnight knock on the door from the police, as they are not allowed to keep a guest or even a relative overnight without informing the local police. There is also allegation of widespread corruption. Art and culture are controlled by the military and are stilted. Universities remain open for a minimum period of time and college courses are short. People allege that the drug trade is still on. But life for the outsiders is peaceful if they keep the right contacts, which a business community usually does.

The Indian community is slowly trickling back with businessmen and professionals and are doing well. But they have a competitor now. The Chinese are entering in large numbers both in business in large cities and infiltration through the borders. North Burma has a direct road link to China. A road link with India is under construction. Border trade with India was large until barter trade was stopped. There is no definite banking route as yet but is in the offing. The balance of trade with India is in favour of Myanmar, exporting pulses and cereals to India in exchange for pharmaceuticals and some engineering goods. The possibility of expansion is substantial. There is a proposal for a gas pipeline to India as Myanmar has large gas reserves. Such a pipeline may benefit the eastern states. Similarly, help and cooperation in medical facilities, which they seek, will be helpful to both. Communication is easy as English is spoken freely. Political difficulties with India are negligible. It is time that a greater initiative is taken. The dialogue for democracy is on in Myanmar and the government promises to return to it in a gradual manner. A helping hand of support and friendship for the people will be insurance for the future and people to people contact may help the process of democratization. We are advocating this process in Pakistan to reduce hostility and Myanmar is strategically and economically no less important. They have a judiciary and a civil service that provide a better democratic infrastructure than many nations. Who knows what the international attitude might have been if Myanmar was a large market and militarily powerful?

2001

Human Faces in Two Chinas of the Nineties – Beijing and Taipei

Beijing

In 1991 a foreigner landing at Beijing airport would pass over vast cultivated lands with small widely isolated hamlets and wide asphalt roads but devoid of people or cars, in fact totally empty. On the ground, black market dollar exchange and booking of private taxis in place of metered taxis would be encouraged. The black market rate gave slightly more than the official rate but the foreigner was expected to carry NEP slips and not cash Yuan. The wide four-lane highway out of the airport had very few cars and those that were there were large in size and guzzling a lot of petrol. There were very few, if at all, privately owned cars. On both sides of the road high rise apartment blocks were coming up, some of them finished already. But there was no one to be seen at the windows or around them, no sign of life. Privatization of the taxi was the first step towards capitalism after the fall of Soviet Russia but there were so many taxis! It was impossible that so many had gone into business. Every driver only smiled and shook his head when asked whether he owned the taxi.

On both sides of the road were lanes for slow moving vehicles. There were a large number of bicycles, a picture that was so familiar to the outside world. But what was not so familiar was the equally large number of people in very ragged clothes walking down with loads on their heads or on pushcarts or rarely on a donkey cart. The common ware was brooms of some sort. These were very poor people not looking to right or left, not at the roadside open canteens selling cheap food but just trundling down the road monotonously. These were 'lucky' villagers who had received the permit to enter the city.

On the road one was accosted by beggars, more after dark, and they were very persistent pulling at one's jacket sleeves for alms. They were everywhere, even in the newly coming up posh business districts. The beggars were mostly females, some with babies in arms and men were more visible after dark. They mingled with smartly dressed men and women who took no notice. I took a picture of a group of beggars in front of a western style hairdressing saloon for ladies with no customers, beneath a large billboard of Hitachi. At another place in a tourist area there was a high white wall all along one side of the road for a distance of more than a kilometer. There were a few small doors in the wall and all of them were tightly shut except one that was slightly ajar, the lock having broken. I walked down, pushed it open a little more and peeped through, all the time afraid of a police whistle or something like that. It was the worst possible ghetto with millions of wall to wall dilapidated thatched roof houses but no human being or any other animal in sight. The poor people must have been moved wholesale for developing the place. This would have been impossible in a democratic society with a free press whether one likes it or not.

One day I bumped into a man I had noticed in the periphery of my working place. He was a handsome young man with proficiency in English, obviously a government functionary. It was his day off. We started talking and I put him at ease. It was extremely interesting. During the Cultural Revolution this man had been taken from high school and employed to clean toilets in a remote rural area. His father, an architect, his mother, a university professor, his elder sister, a postgraduate student, a brother, a school student, were similarly treated, all in different corners of the vast country, and he has never seen them since. When he came back after it was all over, he had nowhere to stay and he was too old to get into college, which still gave free education. So he worked as an ordinary labourer in one of the many building sites of Beijing and continued his study privately at night, mostly by the street lighting. Eventually he graduated from the Open University. With his proficiency in English acquired in the early school days he landed a government job, married and had a daughter, the only one allowed by the State. He now lived in a small house whose small subsidized rent was deducted from his salary and he was not allowed to invite me home, as he shyly said, the traditionally hospitable oriental. The expenses for his daughter were borne by the State and that included higher education, which he could not afford with his salary of about a hundred dollars a month. The exchange rate was about six Yuans to a dollar at the time. He shopped in subsidized government shops, although newly built department stores in Beijing were overflowing with fashionable goods. The prices in them were exorbitant. Those were for businessmen who did not pay taxes, he told with a sneer. He has vacation for two weeks in a year when he takes his family to the seaside in a designated area in one of the designated hotels. I pointed at his jacket and remarked, 'that is an expensive jacket.' The man blushed and said he acquired that on a foreign tour when he went on a delegation with the minister. Everybody wanted to go on a foreign tour when you are given a lot of things. Every student in China dreams of migrating to America or at least to get a job in a multinational company that are called joint ventures in China as there are no fully held ventures. He said, 'The Cultural Revolution pushed us backward by fifty years. It eliminated all our top intellect.' 'Do you feel bitter?' 'No, not bitter but feel sad. What is past is past, life must go on.' I said, 'But today your education is no longer free. As a matter of fact it costs quite a bit compared to what you say is the salary of a well-established person like you. The education of your daughter is free. But what about the countless talented children there must be all over the country to whom that cover is not available? There must be a large number of scholarships and grants.' I was thinking of the poor village folk on the roads. 'Some pay for their own studies. Others must write to Chairman Deng. There are no scholarships as such,' was his reply. 'What, thousands, or probably millions must write to Chairman Deng!' 'Yes, he then finds sponsors for them, often from the joint ventures.' 'For those who pay, the wages that they can expect to get at the end of their studies does not match the cost of education.' 'Yes, that is true now but we expect newer avenues of income will open up very soon.' And they have opened up for this pragmatic and industrious people.

It was wonderful to wander around in Beijing, something that the westerners never did. There was no lawlessness. Language was no problem, hand signals and gestures were enough if you knew how. People were friendly but at a loss for words. A smile and shaking of head were enough. Youth were as usual crazy about the newly opened McDonald shop. I entered the old winter palace of the emperor, converted to a museum now. There were souvenir sellers but not as persistent or as professional as in the West and had not yet learned to cheat. Even the taxi drivers, the hotel boys did not accept tips, in fact sometimes looked uncomprehendingly when offered. Entering the winter palace I moved from pavilion to pavilion up the hill looking at the exhibits from ancient China. In a medium size hall were the legacies of Buddhism, in fact about Buddhism as it came from India. It contained golden statues of ancient gods and goddesses from Mahayana Buddhism, some of them serene, some of them violent and ugly with many hands and heads. Each of them was named and the names were all Indian. There were statues of nine Buddhist monks or Acharyas who were the first to come to initiate China to Buddhism. Their facial appearances were Chinese but the names were Sanskrit, some of them familiar. We have no record but the Chinese remembered them. This is one of their many great qualities. It was almost like seeing a page of Indian history in flesh and blood. There were big signs of 'Photography Prohibited' all around.

I looked around and found a female Red Guard guarding the hall in her usual dress of navy blue trousers and red jacket. She was a young and unusually pretty girl, putting on a grave face as befits a guard. I took out the camera and asked for permission in sign language. The girl looked at me severely, pointed at the signboard and wagged her finger, all with as much severity in her face as she could command. I continued to move around the room, looking at the same objects over and over again. In the third round I came close to her and begged again with as much pathos as possible. The girl was still very severe and she had a chain in her pocket, which was probably connected to a whistle but she was not asking me to leave the pavilion though I must have taken at least three tours around the room for nearly half an hour. I thought that I might be looking young in jeans and sneakers with a designer top and the girl, even though she was a red guard, must be curious. I now chose a moment when the pavilion was empty apart from the two of us and came to the girl again, this time miming and clowning and apparently trying to explain that I was a student whose life depended on taking those pictures and asking for her permission to take them. The girl kept looking at me severely but there was a smile in her eyes. Gradually the smile spread hovering around the corners of her mouth and then she laughed. It was a very sweet and shy laughter shaking her bobbed black hair and, by a mock order asked me to photograph quickly. She went out of the entrance and stood guard. I took as many pictures as I wanted and came out and thanked her and the thought of a kiss on her cheek crossed my mind but immediately cancelled, it was still a forbidden country. She was probably a student who could not understand what harm could come to communism by taking pictures of some antique statues and had probably never seen an Indian before. They are really a pragmatic race.

Taipei

I have a great deal of admiration for the Chinese for their ability for hard work, a down to earth attitude to life and the new determination they have acquired. This is a civilization that found most of their own solutions, invented technologies by themselves, removed as they were to one corner of Asia, separated from the rest of the land mass by fearsome deserts and high mountains. They have given more to the world before the modern days than they have taken, from paper to ice cream to gunpowder. Is it possible for a race to hold onto its characteristics over several millennia, in spite of the changing demands of the time and ever changing political and economic geography? The basic traits of a race can lie dormant for long periods of difficult times and flourish when the historical conditions become appropriate. It may look like a new culture but the basic traits remain the same. It was essential for the ancient civilizations to know their roots and heritage so that the progress in the modern world is orientated in keeping with the traditions for natural and easy acceptance by the masses. The greatest example is Gandhi. His mass movement was in keeping with the traditions and emotions of India and therefore caught the popular imagination. In any other country the same method would have failed and has failed. Similarly, in the case of China the mental attitudes of Maoism and Confucianism are very similar. It was Confucius who had said that the people have a right to forcibly overthrow a king who has lost the characters that prove his divine mandate to rule. Chinese people have overthrown many kings. Every nation, like individuals, has its strong points in character and the weak ones. An intelligent leadership must evolve policies in keeping with the strength of the nation and guard the weak ones. China and India are two great ancient civilizations, which are still linked to the past. There is continuity in spite of the changing world, continuity in mental attitude and language. With a favourable world situation they will flourish and the subjugation of the individual would eventually go. A great experiment is on. In India development is being attempted by freeing the individual and in China by subjugating the individual to the State whereas the historical tradition of both countries is somewhere in between. Each country had to find its own solution, its own road to prosperity and creativity. The economic and political theories are only approximations, not sacrosanct in themselves. Therein lay the wisdom of the leadership to find the balance. How was it in the other China?

My Taipei visit was a short one. I was sitting at the vast air conditioned lobby cum bar of a very big hotel idly sipping a drink watching bullet lifts going up to the sun roof of the high rise and pretty Chinese waitresses with long skirts side-slit almost to the waist fleeting noiselessly from table to table. This was something not to be found in Communist China. Large contingents of business travellers from Japan were coming in and at the reception pretty young Chinese girls were coming and getting introduced and attached to each man. It seemed to be all prearranged as part of the visit as if it came with the air ticket from the travel agent. There was no hustle and bustle, no hugs or kisses, no endearing addresses, just by quiet arrangement they picked up their briefcases and their girls and went off to their rooms. I made a mental note for a future comparative study of the sexual habits of the oriental and the occidental, having seen the American business traveller, noisy and expressive, not cool and matter of fact like the Far East. There were foreign businessmen in Communist China too, but if they had such facilities it was not so overtly visible. In Taipei even if there is no prior arrangement the bellboy settling the guest in his room asks whether he wants to spend the night alone.

At the workplace everything was efficient and cool. The Chinese were serious and efficient at work but liked to enjoy their evenings. In Communist China there was very little opportunity for night life at that time, in Taipei there was plenty. The many snake restaurants were special. On both sides of a small street known as snake alley there were small restaurants on both sides and all of them served snake dish. The snakes were kept in large wooden crates at the entrance. You chose your snake as you went in. The snake was taken out, hung by its neck from a rope and its chest was cut open. The main artery from the heart was cut and the blood poured into a glass half filled with a strong local rice wine. As you drank, the snake was cooked in the way you wanted. There were special shops dealing only in poisonous snakes, some types of vipers, and it cost a fortune. There is the common belief that eating snakes and drinking the blood increased virility, and a lot of the customers were old men.

The culture of Taipei was entirely American and everybody had an American nickname. Even today American NRIs are not as much adjusted to it. I had a young assistant named Ruby. I asked whether that was a Chinese name. She said it was not but the Chinese name was too difficult to pronounce. I said, 'Cut out the American crap. We have pronounced each other's name for thousands of years.' I do not think she understood that but said her name was Yin Yang. I always called her by that name. When the project was coming to an end she said one day while serving coffee, 'Do you know that you are very handsome?' The reply was 'hmmm'. She continued, 'Our island nation is very beautiful. There are beautiful places to see. Why don't you take a few days' leave after the work is finished and rent a car? I shall take you around and show you beautiful places. It will only take a few days.' I took her hands and said, 'Thank you, it would have been lovely. But I have to save some money since I promised my wife that I shall take her to Europe for a holiday next month.' I had a short stay at Taipei.

Chinese Expansionism : Why and How

HISTORICAL BACKGROUND

The first dynastic kingship in China dates from the Xia dynasty in the late Neolithic period from the twenty-first century BCE that lasted till the sixteenth century BCE. They were followed by the Shang dynasty, which developed language and social organization, but were overthrown by a nomadic king named Zhou. The Chinese were welded into a nationality under the Zhou dynasty through conquest and spread of the language and the culture developed by the preceding Shang dynasty. The Zhou dynasty lasted long from 1021 BCE to 223 BCE and much of Chinese historical traditions have continued from this period. It was the philosophers of this period who first enunciated the doctrine of the 'mandate of heaven', the notion that the ruler the 'son of heaven' governed by divine right but that his dethronement would prove that he had lost the mandate. This is one of the doctrines formed and propagated by Confucius along with others such as the need for a secular bureaucracy selected through a central examination where all citizens irrespective of social standing were eligible to participate. This examination used to be held in the Royal Palace until the last king was evicted by the communists. Legitimacy of changing an ineffective government by any means has extended through history from Confucius to Mao as has that of an efficient secular bureaucracy irrespective of regime change selected on merit alone. The political tradition of 'if you win you have it' is similar to the American one of 'winner takes all', almost a tribal culture but effective. This is why the heritage of the Mongol dynasty and emperors like Kublai Khan are accepted by the Chinese Hans; the Mongols were overthrown but their conquest of Tibet justifies today's occupation. These are such strong legacies that the western concept of revolution has a different meaning in China. People expect a non-performing regime to be toppled by another and success proves divinity. The communist government is actually a dynastic successor of Mao and in spite of all his faults only Mao's mausoleum is in Tiananmen Square and will be.

This practical philosophy is balanced by the spiritual philosophy of Lao-tzu, the slightly senior contemporary of Confucius and the father of Taoism, whose book *Tao-te Ching* has been valued by Professor Suniti Kumar Chattopadhyay as an Upanishad formed outside India proving the perennial value of that philosophy. A reading of *Tao-te Ching* should make that obvious at least to an Indian and explain the later popularity of Buddhism.

EARLY EXPANSION : TO THE WEST

The first expansions of China occurred after the Zhou period. During the reign of the Han emperor Wu-ti, China was plagued by attacks from a tribal people, Hsiung-nu, from the north. Wu-ti, trying to find a way to defeat the Hsiung-nu, heard of another tribe to the west known as Yueh-chi who were also fighting the Hsiung-nu. Considering the possibility of attacking the latter from both sides he asked for a volunteer to cross the territory of the Hsiung-nu and contact this other tribe. A young adventurer Chang-Ch'ien set out in 138 BCE with a hundred cavalrymen but the Yueh-chi in the meantime had already suffered several defeats and in the last battle their king was beheaded and his large skull was used as a drinking vessel by the Hsiung-nu. Chang rode straight to the arms of the Hsiung-nu who killed most of the soldiers sparing the life of Chang and ten soldiers. They treated Chang well, gave him a house and a wife probably because of Wu-ti's royal token of a yak's tail. After living with them for two years Chang fled with his followers westwards to continue his mission. In the meantime the Tokharian speaking Indo-European tribe Yueh-chi had retreated, one group going to populate Tibet and the larger section far to the west along the foothills of the Tienshan range north of Taklamakan desert and found fertile land around Amu Darya River and then spread southwards to the region of Bactria. Later a section of them, the Kushans, came to India and conquered the country. Curiously they were Shiva worshippers before they entered India. Failing to encourage them to war with the Hsiung-nu, Chang toured Central Asia making maps of the region and heard about the distant land of Rome. He saw the large Ferghana horses and returned home with a few samples. He was again intercepted by the Hsiung-nu and again managed to escape, this time alone with the horses after 13 years of travel.

This was China's discovery of the Silk Road and first expansion to the west. The Indian discovery of the silk road was at least a couple of centuries earlier by Buddhist monks crossing the Himalayan Passes and spreading along the roads 'discovered' by Chang. From Khotan, founded by Indian settlers at the time of Asoka, they later spread both to the west and to the east by the northern and southern silk roads and along the southern edge of the Taklamakan desert almost to the peripheries of China proper. Settlements with stupas and temples were built deep into the desert, south of the Tarim basin, bringing water through underground tunnels, some of which persist till today. Emperor Ming-ti in the first century CE saw in dream a golden figure floating across his room in a halo of light and wise men interpreted that he had seen the Buddha and an envoy was dispatched to India. In 2005 the Chinese ambassador to the USA in a lecture made reference to the special relationship between India and China by saying, 'For twenty centuries, India conquered and dominated China without ever having to send a single soldier;' and went on to describe the voluntary search for spiritual enlightenment, pilgrimage and learning of a high order. It is curious that the two people in two large countries with geographical proximity and close cultural ties spanning two millennia could be so different and still are. While the Chinese are practical, pragmatic to the point of being inscrutable and have kept accurate historical, scientific, travel, navigation and geographical records, we with equal achievements in all those fields have never kept any records except the religious ones and sometimes glorified records of kings by the court historian. The trend is still the same.

EARLY EXPANSION : TO SOUTHEAST ASIA

The same thing happened in Southeast Asia at the same period of history. The history of this area started in the first century CE when Indian ships appeared, followed some two hundred years later by the Chinese. The artifacts from Oc-Eo in the Mekong Delta from the second century CE indicate the eastern seaboard of India as the source. Indian trade with China through Northeast India to the Bay of Bengal was suffering at this time from the attack of nomadic tribes on the frontier. Improved shipbuilding and navigational knowledge pushed Indian ships eastwards towards South China. The earliest Chinese records from the third century CE are of the state of Funan in South Cambodia and South Vietnam that was Indian in culture, Brahminical in religion with a language from the Mon-Khmer family of languages. The Chinese considered Southeast Asia a land of barbarians. Indians cared little for history and little about exploration except in the line of trade, but brought their socio-religious culture that bonded the small coastal maritime settlements into ports and then into cities followed by states which had Indian names. That history has been recovered only recently from copper plaques or other mementos left in honour of some God or stone inscriptions. The kings with Indian names were mostly not Indians. Kings of Cambodia have carried the title of Varman till the present day but none of them were Indians. Indian influence in Southeast Asia was more Indianization than Indian colonization in keeping with our culture. Indians expanded when conditions in India were good and the Chinese expanded when they were not good. Apart from indigenous people the Chinese form a major part of the population in Southeast Asia today.

MODERN DAYS : THE SECOND WORLD WAR

Evolution of human history is a continuous process, the causes and effects operating through time and space becoming manifest in apparently disjointed periods and locations. The pace has accelerated in recent times; changes that would have taken centuries are now happening over decades with the acceleration in the development of human knowledge and psyche. The history of humanity can no longer be divided into isolated epochs or nations. History traditionally has no near vision. But now there is greater need for man to understand his environment fast. Therefore, at the risk of misjudging some of the things, current analysis is essential. This is done mainly by politicians, strategists and think tanks against the background of history. When traditional historians come to judge our times, we may be long dead and gone. So the choice of the Second World War as the starting point of modern times in China is acceptable. China was visited at the beginning of the last century by two travellers from Bengal, Indumadhav Mullick (inventor of the Icmic cooker) and Benoy Kumar Sarkar, whose travelogue gives an Indian perspective.

The World War II started for China in 1937 with invasion from Japan. Soviet Russia supported China ending China's prior cooperation with Germany. Starting at Shanghai, Japan pushed Chinese forces back, capturing Nanjing in December. The Second World War started in Europe on 1 September 1939 with Germany invading Poland and the declaration of war by Britain, France and the Commonwealth, Hitler having already taken Austria, Hungary and Czechoslovakia and signed a pact of non aggression with Stalin. The Sino-Japanese war had stalemated by mid-1940. In August 1940 Mao Zedong led communist forces in offensive against Japan in Central China and Japan started harsh measures in occupied areas to reduce resources for the communists. Tensions between Chinese Communist and Nationalist forces ended their cooperation in January 1941. In April 1941 Soviet Russia, worried about Germany in spite of the non-aggression pact, signed a neutrality agreement with Japan to move armies from Manchuria to the west and stopped arms supply to China.

China never forgave Russia. In the dying moments of the War, Russia, in between dropping of the two Atom Bombs, snatched Manchuria from Japan.

In Europe Mussolini was killed by partisans on 28 April 1945, German forces in West Europe surrendered on 29 April, Hitler committed suicide on 30 April and his successor Grand Admiral Doenitz surrendered to the Russians on 8 May. War still continued in Asia with the allied forces occupying Japanese islands and reaching the doorstep of Japan. The Japanese were however advancing in China occupying the cities of Changsha and Heingyang and China-occupied Myitkyina in North Burma. Japan refused to surrender and accept the Potsdam Treaty till the atom bombs were dropped and finally surrendered on 15 August 1945. After the surrender of Japan, the civil war in China continued in right earnest and after four years of war Chiang Kai-shek fled with his followers to Taiwan to establish the nationalist government, and Mao declared the People's Republic of China (PRC) on the mainland. For China the war lasted 12 years, and for fifty years it was a hungry nation. PRC was a bankrupt nation to start with, but recovered quickly, reaching pre-war level of production in 1953 but slid down with the Great Leap Forward economic plan that failed, soon followed by the Cultural Revolution. Change followed Kissinger–Nixon visits in 1971 when agreement was reached between the Americans and Mao and Chou en-Lai for the Chinese, to contain Soviet Russia in exchange for American capital and technology. Under Deng Xiao Ping, who came to power in 1978, China made drastic changes in economic policies and is now the fastest developing nation. Deng was purged three times before he came to power and had to walk the streets of Beijing wearing a dunce cap, ridiculed by red guards. His famous cryptic quotes are: 'Whether a cat is black or white makes no difference. As long as it catches mice, it is a good cat'; and 'Poverty is not socialism'; or ridiculing the Cultural Revolution as 'better to be poor under socialism than rich under capitalism'. Hunger is a relative thing and in a single party China the hunger for food has been converted to hunger for land.

MODERN DAYS : EARLY DAYS OF PRC

In 1949 the PRC had a massive People's Liberation Army (PLA) and a reduced civilian population. This large army in fighting readiness had to be given tasks. Mao had foreseen the problem and chalked out a plan. Before guns stopped smoking, the struggle for 'lebensraum' started for the Chinese. This Hitler agenda was used by Pravda to describe China. Soon after the founding of PRC on 1 October 1949 Radio Beijing broadcast that PLA will liberate all Chinese territory including Tibet, Xinjiang, Hainan and Taiwan.

Tibet. PLA units moved to the Tibetan border in 1949 with propaganda of imminent capture. An attempt at negctiation to stall the military advance was attempted on India's suggestion but failed. China demanded complete merger of Tibet with China. In October 1950 PLA defeated the weak Tibetan army of 8000 men and captured Chamdo, capital of the eastern province. In November Tibet handed over all powers of State to the Dalai Lama, who left Lhasa for Dromo, close to the Indian border. Tibet sent an appeal to the UN. A resolution was tabled in the General Assembly by El Salvador on 17 November but on India's suggestion that a mutual solution could be found it was withdrawn! Nehru loved to see Chou en-Lai smile and this was the first of many! In April 1951 a five member Tibetan delegation with no executive authority went to China for discussion but they were given a 17 point agreement to sign that the Government of Tibet had never seen. Almost at gunpoint the delegation was forced to sign the document and before they could return and report to the Dalai Lama, the agreement was broadcast on Radio Beijing. The Dalai Lama, shocked by the so-called treaty, returned to Lhasa to renegotiate, but PLA units advanced to occupy Lhasa, Gyantse and Shigatse. Chou en-Lai smiled again! Dalai Lama fled Tibet and only on 20 June 1959 he could reject the treaty and tell the world how it was signed. By that time it was an accomplished fact and Tibet was divided into three fragments. Amdo, the largest province in the north, was fragmented and integrated with surrounding Chinese States and so was the eastern half of Kham, the eastern state. The arid province of U-Sang and western half of Kham were joined to make the Tibet Autonomous Region (TAR) that contains the Lhasa prefecture. Appeals of Tibet's friends for autonomy are for TAR only, the rest two-thirds have been given up along with their Tibetan population.

Xingjian. This westernmost province of China, called the Xingjian Uighur Autonomous Region (XUAR), was under Chinese control off and on through history, and was home to about 20 million people of 13 ethnic groups, the Uighurs comprising more than half the population in the forties, and virtually no Hans. Uighurs are Muslim by religion and have a separate existence since antiquity when they had been employed by Mongol armies as civilian officials because they were educated. Ethnically they are close to the people of Turkistan and groups like East Turkistan Islamic Movement (ETIM) in XUAR oppose Chinese occupation, and struggle for independence or greater autonomy. After the fall of the Qing dynasty in 1912 they enjoyed independence until the Nationalist Chinese took nominal control in 1933. They declared independence in 1944 under Soviet support but were taken over by PLA in 1949. The PLA started large scale migration of Han Chinese under the name of Xinjiang Production and Construction Corps (XPCC) who are armed volunteers for agricultural production and frontier defence. They established settlements that gradually enlarged, followed by large scale Han immigration so that the Han population has increased from 5 per cent at the beginning of the Chinese settlement to more than 40 per cent now holding the best jobs and businesses. Being Muslims the Uighurs are sometimes suspected to be part of the global terror network linked to the Al-Qaeda but with no proof. Because of this suspicion their support on the world stage is not as strong as for Tibet.

Russia and Outer Mongolia. In the early days of PRC Mao extended help to Outer Mongolia, a Soviet satellite state with one million population, and a 4000 strong blue dressed Chinese work force landed in Ulan Bator. After a short time they were returned en masse back to China and the reason for that is not so speculative. But the 4000 mile frontier with Russia was never quiet. In 1964, the Times Magazine referred to a Pravda article that said that China had published a map in a school textbook that claimed large parts of eastern Russia as China territory that puts the frontier about 300 miles inside Russia over a long stretch enclosing 1.5 million square kilometers, including Mongolia. It included Sakhalin and Kuril Islands – one to be given to Japan and one to China. The interesting thing is that this area was actually wrested from China by the Czarist Russia in the nineteenth century. Pravda called Mao a red Hitler.

North Burma. China and Burma have a border that is virtually open to the Chinese as the control of the government of Burma is distant and nominal. The road connection from China is excellent. This is also the region of the Golden Triangle, junction of the three countries of China, Burma and Thailand, one of the world's largest sources of narcotics. The production and marketing is controlled by China, both PRC and Taiwan, the warlords, and to a small extent by the Burmese government. The warlords are Chinese or of mixed origin and very rich. Drugs pass through Yunnan and Sichuan provinces to Kunming and Hong Kong to Taiwan and the west. Part of the money funded the Communist Party of Burma until a division in the CPB and the rise to power of Deng Xiao Ping; the drug traffic has reduced as large numbers of Chinese are getting addicted. The Chinese influence is strong in Burma as they are almost the sole supplier of arms to the military government. What they get in exchange is a land bridge to the Indian Ocean, port facilities for the Chinese Navy and possible installation of sensing and tracking facilities in the Malacca Straits, the Indian Ocean and the Bay of Bengal on the sea route to Chattagram and close to the Andaman and Nicobar Islands.

MODERN DAYS : PRC AFTER MAO

Mao embraced communism when, working as an assistant in the Peking University library, he was convinced that democratic liberal socialism was unsuited for China as time was short and history would not accord her the privilege of a gradual change of a relatively painless and orderly evolution. For PRC his target was that China must overtake western nations in 50 years. That haste is the key to modern China.

The author was in China when the curtain was lifted to attend an international medical conference, probably the first of its kind and opted out of the post-conference conducted tour and was allowed to spend five days in Beijing freely roaming and talking to people. What was seen may not be seen in Beijing today, but what was inferred has been confirmed by many others visiting China since. It was safe to condemn the Cultural Revolution at that time and a senior government official said that China had been pushed back by more than 20 years by the Cultural Revolution as the brain of China was destroyed. I asked about integration of the society and he said there was only disintegration.

During that visit I saw huge empty slums concealed behind walls right beside the Forbidden City, gangs of very determined beggars, a continuous stream of people in rags on wide avenues tiredly pushing handcarts with household items, a picturesque countryside devoid of people. A large scale population movement was on, but where were they going?

I visit two medical colleges and doctors take me through clean and painted but empty wards and when I ask where the patients are, they tell me those wards are for foreign patients. The faces are inscrutable and I shudder. Are the rumours of trafficking in human organs correct? Not one crowded ward was shown to me. They said the Chinese are healthy.

Education was no longer free after Deng came to power and the tuition fee in, medical college was about Rs. 25000 per semester, it was Rs. 100 in our government colleges at that time, but the Professor's salary was in the range of Rs. 1000-1200 per month. Why should anybody study medicine? Because they can migrate to America and private practice may be allowed in future. There are large decorated stores of Chinese indigenous medicine and those doctors are allowed practice, and the Professor shook his head.

Cost of school education is high. City dwellers can cope because most of them are government servants and education of one child is free. What happens to meritorious students from poor parents in villages who are not government functionaries? They write to Chairman Deng and the deserving are sponsored through foreign multinationals and permanently separated from their parents.

In short the entire population is divided between who can be developed and who cannot. The second category either disappear by attrition or go to outlying corners like Tibet or Xingjian. Most smart athletes seen on TV never see their parents and have no family attachment. What psychological profile does that produce and what sort of nation?

New department shops are overflowing with foreign goods but no buyers. I ask my friend the officer and he says they are for businessmen who do not pay taxes and he sniggers; he buys from designated shops. He was wearing an expensive foreign jacket and I point to that. He blushes and says this one he got during a delegation abroad, they get a lot of things on such occassions; everybody wants to go on a delegation or migrate to the US. He says his salary is about Rs. 800 per month, has a house on nominal rent, wife, one daughter with free education, two weeks' holiday in a year, to go to a particular seaside hotel and spend the paid holiday. Is he happy? He shrugs the resignation of the east at the end!

I watch on CNN the meeting of the Chinese Trade Union Congress held every 5 years and speakers just repeat that in a workers' state there is no room for agitation and their only duty was to concentrate on workers' recreation so as to increase productivity.

All the people I met were polite and helpful. Why are they so hard and threatening in politics and outside China proper, as I saw in Tibet in 2006? Travelling across Tibet I found that the green uniform evoked terror even if worn by a civilian worker attached to PLA. In TAR the large investment in infrastructure is only to tighten the grip of a colonial regime, not to improve the life of the Tibetans. The monks live in large monasteries and are educated and refined but they are never seen outside mixing with common people, which is common in other Buddhist countries. In Lhasa Tibetans carry prayer wheels, probably a show for the foreigner, because outside Lhasa religious emblems are banned.

We entered by chance a small village named Ghorasu, made of packed lines of hovels with poor people on both sides of a dirt road, filthy water flowing down it and dirty children playing in the muck. We saw one well dressed Chinese lady at a distance and my guide said she was the terror of the village and she lives there; he pointed to the only decent brick house with high boundary walls and solar battery and disc antennae on top. She has to press a button to bring law enforcers as fast as she wants.

At the root of this expansive trend of China is Mao's idea to catch up with the world in 50 years. This haste, the reason behind the rapid growth of a military industrial society whose ultimate goal makes even rich nations uneasy, not to speak of the nearer ones like us, is wreaking havoc in China's own society tearing her out of her own roots. China's deputy minister of environment gave an interview to the German newspaper *Spiegel* on 7 March 2005 and I quote excerpts. 'This miracle (of China's growth) will end soon because the environment can no longer keep pace. Acid rain is falling on one-third of the Chinese territory; half of the water in our seven largest rivers is completely useless, while one-fourth of our citizens do not have access to clean drinking water.' 'We are using too many raw materials to sustain this growth. To produce goods worth $10000, for example, we need seven times more resources than Japan, nearly six times more than United States and, perhaps most embarrassing, nearly three times more than India.' 'Even now, the western regions of China and the country's ecologically stressed regions can no longer support the people already living there. In the future, we will need to resettle 186 million residents from 22 provinces and cities. However, the other provinces and cities can only absorb some 33 million people. That means China will have more than 150 million ecological migrants, i.e. environmental refugees.'

'The economic growth fanatics in Beijing are still playing the lead role – for now. For them, the gross domestic product is the only yardstick by which to gauge the government's performance . . . We are convinced that a prospering economy automatically goes hand in hand with political stability. And I think that's a major blunder . . . If the gap between the poor and the rich widens, then regions within China and the society as a whole will become unstable.' It is known that the gap between rich and poor has widened considerably. It is known that all refugees are not ecological refugees but a large number are evicted from land, a million times of our Singur. Brutal evictions are continuing and have been witnessed by Indian engineers. Some of them have seen how people run out of their houses in terror when clearing starts. Protests are also increasing. Westerners know it all but make no comments because they are earning from China and clapping. The effects, they think, are not going to touch them. No commentator asked during Olympic 2008 what happened to all the people who lived at the sites. Incidentally there is a parallel with Germany. Hitler used the Olympic Games of 1936 to demonstrate the organization and technical might of his superior Aryan race where the television was beamed for the first time in the world.

It is not known whether the minister is still in office but the concerns mentioned are supported three years later by the *National Geographic Magazine*, May 2008 issue. The Yellow River or Huang Ho described as China's Nile that supported the massive agricultural production of North China, is so polluted that not only fish but even goats fall dead by drinking from its tributaries, and agricultural production has gone down drastically. The leaders of the PRC have produced political, military and economic revolution, but even more than that a demographic revolution of unimaginable proportion. The only precedents are Germany and Russia before and during the Second World War, and not only has it destroyed them but the whole world has paid the price. Population policy to evict farmers and deport them to Siberia and rapid industrialization under Stalin depressed Soviet agriculture so much that it could never recover and led to the collapse of the Soviet Union. Stalin had a valid reason in warmongering Germany, but what is China's reason apart from the chauvinistic dream of Greater China, like Hitler and Mussolini? Who in this world will be foolish enough to dream of conquering China militarily? Demographic projections show that by 2015 China will have a shrinking work force because of the one child policy since 1979, and there would be a diminution of youth with no parental connection and controlled solely by the State. By 2050 one-third of the population will be over 60, diverting resources to pension and securities or to chaos. Time for correction is short.

The direction of China's politics and intent needs to be examined, along with the agenda of the present political leadership and their economic, social and strategic compulsions, judging events objectively and ignoring the rhetoric and not through her history or culture. The word 'embarrassing' mentioned by the Chinese deputy minister with relation to India is the key. India evolving to prosperity within its democratic structure and with its human rights intact is very 'embarrassing' to China and completely negates the ideology of her revolution propounded by Mao and is a great danger to them, both internally and externally, apart from a loss of face that the Chinese hate. Internal danger is greater. External danger can be in competition in finance, trade and commerce, which the Chinese are experts at controlling, or in war. China knows that India will never declare war on China, unless pushed into a global war which is very unlikely and whose ramifications are unpredictable for every nation, including China. But China is capable of limited military action when conditions are favourable as they did in Tibet, in India in 1962 and in Vietnam in 1979. They were defeated by Vietnam in the northern border and in Cambodia and suffered heavy casualties; hostilities ended with a border agreement in 1989 and in 1990 Vietnam ceded some territory, to China and evicted all ethnic Chinese from their territory but normalization of relations had to wait till 2007. China used only ground forces in all three wars but is better prepared now for total war.

Why is China surrounding India militarily? From the Malacca straits through Myanmar, Chittagong and Bangladesh, Tibet and Sub-Himalayan region, to Ladakh and Pakistan and the new naval base being built by China in Gwadr in Pakistan, the encirclement is complete; and the Indian Ocean is visited regularly by the Chinese navy using the open port of Colombo. They are continually intruding or using diatribes against the border regions of India. In addition they have a missile force that can strike anywhere in India. What is an alternate site of attack for this missile force? Madmen both inside China and the USA talk about biological weapons to depopulate the USA and repopulate with the Chinese. What does USA gain by attacking China or the latter USA, except to indulge in paranoia, not quite acceptable in two very pragmatic nations? The present economic difficulty of USA does not need that as a solution. Then why encircle India with a threatening posture?

The answer lies in the 1962 war whose logical goal was to stall the economic development of India. That is the best case scenario. The worst case scenario is that they covet territory in the northeast by severing the land connection to the eastern states by pushing a dagger through Tawang or Bhutan or Sikkim to Bangladesh and creating a diversion in Kashmir. They also want to take command of the South China Sea and Indian Ocean. India can be weakened by terrorists from the west and the east, by propaganda and pinpricks from the north, by ideological subversion and communal and other tensions inside India, to force her to keep a large force in the Himalayas, to maintain a large police force, to maintain a minimum credible nuclear deterrent. China takes advantage of our free press that does not always behave responsibly, especially in confusing talk shows with ignorant media managers who behave like political gurus whereas she has put down the ETIM revolt in Xingjian brutally with a reverse propaganda against Muslims in Central Asia. China also knows that historically Indians cannot keep continuous vigil over long periods of time, yielding to the enemy at a weak moment and that moment can come in a democratic setup. Indian democracy has to remain united and vigilant against the threat from outside, mainly China at the moment, for a long time to come, and it must be realized by all concerned that covert diplomacy is essential in international politics and everything must not be brought to the open. We have no experience in the big game of global politics as we have never ventured out of our country in our long history. We only have the short experience of British India when armies went out to Afghanistan, Tibet and Burma. It is from their diplomacy that our administrators have learnt and learnt well. That should not be negated by selfish political wrangling by inexperienced politicians. The Chinese people have greater experience and tenacity. They have beaten us diplomatically and militarily several times in the past sixty years and it must not happen again.

It will be better for both countries if China puts her own house in order as she has seldom been an aggressor against neighbours before modern times and never against India; or else China will prove the truth of Lenin's theory that Imperialism is the last stage of Capitalism, whatever the political, historical and religious tradition of a country might be. China must be made to realize that even short wars in search of clean arable land is more risky than slowing down the pace of economic growth gradually. Greed born of unbridled capitalism and autarchy make a dangerous combination.

2008-2009

THE ROAD AHEAD

Economic Wars: New Challenges in Multilayered Societies

At an international seminar dealing with problems in medicine, participants from a number of countries were debating the different theories and directions of research. The discussions were animated with everyone passionately defending their positions. A bit of nationalism also comes into play on such occasions. During a coffee break someone remarked to a delegate from another country, 'You know I can argue and fight with you for hours but I understand your language. But I cannot say the same thing about a lot of people from my own country. For example I do not know what to talk about with a stockbroker from my own country.'

MULTIDIMENSIONAL

This is fast becoming a global reality. We grow up in a culture that we share with fellow countrymen. Our emotions are related to that culture. But today a large number of men and women are involved more intensely than ever before in their professions or vocations. In a competitive world, professional demands become high and the culture of the profession often prevails over that one is born into. Some like it and some of us condemn it. The older generation usually condemns it using terms like workaholics. But is it such a bad thing?

In a great departure from the work cultures of the yesteryears, these professions often provide built-in methods of relaxation. It may be a spontaneous defence mechanism against boredom and inefficiency. In any case the recreational life of the individual also often revolves around the profession because of emotional bonds with colleagues. Work, as far as we know in this country till the present era, was really an extension of school life, a duty extending from ten to five. All the fun is afterwards when the workplace is completely forgotten.

Today it is not possible to forget the workplace. In more developed countries this is a more general picture. In our country it is fast moving to that situation. Whether we like it or not there is no other option because this is the only means of making a society efficient.

The older generation will point out that this culture, taken to the extreme, produce people with closed minds, those who know nothing beyond their work—somewhat like the *Brave New World*. This of course is an exaggeration. Many of these men and women are highly intelligent and, therefore, multidimensional.

SOCIAL COMPLEXITY

However, it is true that pressure of work limits general intellectual development to some extent, even among the intelligent. A more general picture of this type is seen in the USA where general knowledge and sensitivity beyond the workplace is not a matter of great importance, and the prototype is perfected in a few years of intense fighting in the corporate or the professional world. General knowledge of the world and the human race, even among the educated, is amazingly poor in the USA.

Such competitive professional life produces very aggressive people. This aggressiveness is, of course, much better than in any other form of aggression. Nevertheless, it has been seen that living continuously at the edge of economic aggressiveness is not a healthy living, either for a society or an individual. In the history of many nations and civilizations, after a period of aggression and expansive development comes a slow decline, a sort of a quieter autumn, after it reaches its zenith. The society becomes most livable and more humane during this autumnal period. It has happened to Rome, to us and to Europe.

The modern technological age is, however, substantially different. Apart from the shrinking of the globe, due to rapid communication, there has been a multiplicity of professions never known before. Society has become very complex and multilayered. People living in the same society do not understand each other. Emotionally the nation sways together much less. For example, the intense emotion of some on the Ayodhya issue leaves many others of both communities totally cold. If the 11 September attacks had been less drastic and earth-shaking than they have been, many, even in the USA, would have given it only passing attention. On the other hand, even a small event inside one's own layer or profession generates intense reaction.

NEW PARAMETERS

Societies today are so multilayered, and there is so much responsiveness inside one's own layer across national boundaries that one wonders whether the human and national boundaries that are vertical today will one day become horizontal and nations in the present sense will cease to exist. Such a change will be better for humanity and that is why the modern technological age is a boon. This surprisingly corresponds to our ancient ideals of social organization.

The problem is that all countries are not shareholders of this change. Less developed countries have very few layers and are the breeding grounds of mass emotions. If humanity wants to survive, the world economy should take a new turn and from a highly competitive nature become more egalitarian to bring nations at par. The nature of today's world economy is such that its parameters like productivity, profits, value of shares and stocks, GDP etc. must either go up or go down. The economic competition among nations that this mechanism produces is not in keeping with the concept of a global village or global economy. Unnecessary augmentation of desire to obtain a larger market share breeds despair and violence. Attempts to corner larger shares of earth's resources have produced two world wars and are still continuing at the risk of a third. New parameters and new steady state economic theories instead of competitive theories must come into being to make the world a more peaceful place.

2002

Pains of Industrialization: 'People's Industry'

Industrialization of a country from a pre-existent agrarian economy has always been a painful process. Industry needs land, energy, capital and trained manpower. The land has to come from the agrarian base. That agrarian base has a surplus manpower that can be trained but not all of them. Industry, especially in modern days, needs technical manpower and as small an untrained labour force as possible. So where does the surplus manpower from land go and what happens to the agrarian base?

In the United Kingdom the industrial revolution started in the eighteenth century with coal as the main energy source. Large deposits of coal were available in Wales and the northwest. Displacement of farmers and the woes of the coalminers saw the beginning of organized trade union movements, the eventual rise of leftist ideologies and some excellent literary works. The surplus manpower was shipped out to the colonies or engaged in shipping to win more colonies. These colonies, of which India was the principal, provided both the capital and the market for the industrial revolution of Britain. It took more than a century and many wars to balance population with internal productivity and till the end of the nineteenth century many areas of London remained a nightmarish den of unemployed labour, vagabonds, rogues and prostitutes. Till the early twentieth century the coal miners' movement remained the breeding ground of many left wing politicians who became famous in later days.

In the United States of America the hunger for more land for expansion of industry led to the formulation of the principle of 'Manifest Destiny' by the Jackson Democrats in 1845. A painting by Gast in the thirties shows Columbia in the form of a lady, pushing west behind progressing railroads driving the American Indians from their land. This was followed by the slogan of 'All Mexico' and culminated in the annexation of California, Oregon, Texas and some parts of Mexico. These acts of banditry have been filmed later in Hollywood as romantic heroism.

In Germany the process started a little later and not having colonies to ship the surplus population they looked elsewhere and Friedrich Ratzel in 1897 raised the political agenda of 'Lebensraum'. Von Bernhardi used it for practical politics in 1912 and said that in the next war Germany would seize the lands eastwards up to the Urals to settle the German population in a greater Germany. It continued as practical politics of the Second World War. The theoretical justification was based on the Darwinian hypothesis of 'filling of ecological niches' by a superior adaptive race. These lands in Tsarist Russia were sparsely populated and were being filled up by encouraging large-scale migrations from other countries though citizenship rights were not given to many. This ultimately proved to be a problem. After the First World War the Nazis took up the cry for Lebensraum and Alfred Rosenberg drew the map of a future Germany with 'Reichscommisariats' ruling European Russia including Byelorussia and Ukraine and all of Western Europe excluding Spain, Portugal and Finland. Hitler was not the originator of Lebensraum but added an internal version by eliminating Jews.

Industrialization of Russia under Stalin has been studied as data became available after the fall of the Soviet Union. In summary Stalin reversed Lenin's New Economic Policy of distributing land to the farmers that had ushered in a marked rise in agricultural output. Capital was needed for industrialization and it was scarce. The middle class who could invest was decimated by 1926. Stalin saw that there would be only one way for the State to raise money and accumulate capital, and simultaneously transform the economic base of Russia from farming to industry. The solution for Stalin was to collectivize agriculture, forcing the peasants into communes, destroying the kulaks, controlling agricultural output, and fixing the prices of wages and food. The surplus labour on land was deported to industrial centres in the east. Half of the food grain production was appropriated by the State at a low price and sold in towns at a higher price thereby forming the capital while it produced famines in the rural areas. In eight years from 1929-30, 25 million peasants were forcibly evicted from land to distant industrial centres, 25 million small peasant farms gave birth to one lakh collective farms, private consumption of gross GNP went down below 50 per cent (in an economy at take-off stage it should not go down below 80 per cent), rebellions broke out as famine spread in many states and Stalin initiated his policy of 'final solution' of the nationalities in Ukraine, Kazakhstan and some other areas amounting to virtual genocide. The industrial production however went up spectacularly, making Soviet Russia the second largest economy and a military power in eight years, but agricultural production continued to decline through the war and afterwards and could never recover. One has to say in Stalin's favour that he could see the growth of the Nazi war machine and was never in doubt about Hitler's intentions in spite of the friendship and non-aggression treaty they signed at the end of this period and he had to industrialize rapidly away from the theatre of war.

China started industrialization in earnest after the waves of the Cultural Revolution had ebbed. The growth rate has been spectacular so far with an annual growth rate in GDP close to 10 per cent that many in India look at with envious eyes. But industrialization has a price to pay no matter where and how it is done and the faster the rate the greater is the price. China is paying that price as evident from an interview given by China's Deputy Minister of Environment to the German magazine *Der Spiegel* about a couple of years back and quoted elsewhere in this volume. China has since decided to cut down the pace of industrialization and aiming for a more moderate growth in

GDP as unrest is growing and there is a growing difference in income. China has space to resettle refugees in Qinghai, Sichuan and Tibetan provinces and the TAR, but that produces unrest in those areas. The intention here is not to denigrate the great Chinese development but to emphasize that the problems of industrialization are similar everywhere and there are no magic solutions. Each country has to find its own roadway.

So what is the road for India and particularly West Bengal, a State with high population density? The recent growth in the Indian economy has been mainly through the IT sector, service industries and entrepreneurship in foreign countries that do not need massive land space, and West Bengal with its frittered human resources has regrettably been a late starter. This Indian growth cannot be sustained without infrastructure, heavy industries and manufacturing industries in different sectors for which suitable land is of prime importance. West Bengal is credited with a land reform programme that has empowered the rural population and increased agricultural production that is now showing a downward trend. The rural people are more educated now and cannot be brushed aside in a democratic country. Land acquisition programmes are seen as a betrayal of what was promised. There is also a large educated underemployed urban middle class.

The State is not new to resettlement problems following the partition of India. At one time plans were made to resettle East Pakistan refugees in the Andaman that was thwarted by political opposition with the result that Tamil migrants to the Andaman cornered most of the economic activities and the small Bengali population has remained poor. The refugees were then resettled in the more inhospitable region of Dandakaranya. An exodus from there occurred at some time towards the Sunderbans, more specifically Marichjhapi, and police resorted to firing to discourage those farmers. Now the story is being repeated in places where the government is trying to establish mega industries and the political sides have changed. While we do not have the 'advantage' of a totalitarian state to move populations at will and nor should politicians think that we have, we have the advantage of being one of the most open democracies in the world and are proud of it. The people are responsive to change for a better tomorrow if they are made partners. Democracy automatically prevents excesses in any direction however frustrating it may seem, and acts as its own check and balance. Development is a national priority like defence of the nation, and political parties should act in unison in the best democratic traditions and decide on the strategy of development as partners and not as enemies. Politics today does not encourage freethinking and honest people without personal and group interests to help the process and give democracy a chance.

2007

Globalization and The State in Indian Perspective: Think Global, Act Local

This article has been written after considerable soul searching on whether a common man without expertise can write about the massive changes happening in the world around us. And the answer is yes because the common man decides the fate of theories as he reasons with his guts and suffering. The present economic process affects the common man globally and drives him to analyze. Judging from the Indian perspective is important not only to an Indian but also globally as India occupies a critical place in the world today. In today's North-South world India sits at the centre, has been recently given a fringe seat in the North, but actually lives in the South. We are a large democracy with an elected government through adult universal franchise, a large poor population with a few very rich and very wide income differences. There is a large educated upwardly mobile middle class who can think, a rule of law that is flawed, an entrenched bureaucracy, inadequate regulatory standards for financial institutions and corporate affairs and the usual monetary and other pressures of democratic governance. But the government is unlikely to crumble like Somalia under the pressure of globalization though it is not quite efficient under pressure.

Globalization today means globalization of capital. The pursuit of surplus accumulation has provided a principal and powerful spur to globalization. Contemporary globalization has left no country untouched, and even relatively small concentrations of transborder capital have had far-reaching effects in various countries of the South. capitalist and arch-speculator George Soros deposed before a US congressional enquiry on 19 September 1998: 'The global capitalist system . . . is coming apart at the seams'. He has since expanded on this in a book entitled *The Crisis of Global Capitalism.* He divides the 'global capitalist system' into a centre (US, Western Europe, Japan) and a periphery (Asia, Latin America, Russia, East Europe, Africa). Under this system capital flows from the centre to the periphery and back, supposedly to the mutual benefit of both. He sees the danger of disintegration coming from countries on the periphery taking steps to stop the free flow of capital in a bid to avoid the negative effects of the system's instability on their economies and populations. Soros continues, 'The functions that cannot and should not be governed purely by market forces include many of the most important things in human life, ranging from moral values to family relationships to aesthetic and intellectual achievements. Yet market fundamentalism is constantly attempting to extend its sway into these regions, in a form of ideological imperialism.'

Joseph E. Stiglitz wrote in 2006, 'Trade liberalization puts downward pressure on unskilled wages (and increasingly even skilled wages), increasing inequality in more developed countries. Countries trying to compete are repeatedly told to increase labour-market flexibility, code words for lowering the minimum wage and weakening worker protections. Competition for business puts pressure to reduce taxes on corporate income and on capital more generally, decreasing funds available for supporting basic investments in people and the safety net. And international agreements, such as Chapter 11 of NAFTA and the intellectual property provisions of the Uruguay Round of trade talks, have been used to short-circuit national democratic processes.

'Yet Sweden and the other Scandinavian countries have shown that there is an alternative way to cope with globalization. These countries are highly integrated into the global economy; but they are highly successful economies that still provide strong social protections and make high levels of investments in people. They have been successful in part because of these policies, not in spite of them. Full employment and strong safety nets enable individuals to undertake more risk (with the commensurate high rewards) without unduly worrying about the downside of failure. These countries have not abandoned the welfare state but have fine-tuned it to meet globalization's new demands.'

India is not Sweden that has a long tradition of highly skilled capitalist economy and one of the highest per capita GDP in the world for decades, combined with a level of social security for its people not present in any other country of the world. The unemployment benefit of an ordinary citizen of Sweden is more than the budget of a middle class family of India.

In an article published in *International Affairs*, Vol. 73 no. 3, July 1997 pp. 427-52, 'Global capitalism and the state', Jan Aart Scholte extensively researched in the era of enthusiastic optimism for globalization in the west. Much has happened since. The article focuses on the character and activities of the state in relation to transborder accumulation. Here it is argued that global capitalism has contributed to: (*a*) the end of sovereign statehood; (*b*) a rise of supra-territorial constituencies; (*c*) possibly, a decline in interstate warfare; (*d*) increased constraints on state provision of social security; (*e*) a growth of multilateralism; and (*f*) the impracticability of achieving democratic governance through the state alone. In sum, then, although the state survives under globalizing capitalism, it is in at least six important respects a different kind of state.

Reading through these articles one has a feeling that nobody had any definite idea about how globalization would develop and how to handle it. It has been and it still is like six blind men trying to figure out an elephant and coming to different conclusions. In the present state of a complex disease running through the world economic and monetary systems, it would seem that all the diagnoses are partially right and it is a complex mixture of all of them in varying proportion from one country to another. As a result the treatments prescribed are also all different. The general reaction of nations is like frightened animals desperately trying to get back into its hole, but the road of straight return is no longer there.

Going back to Soros, he says that uncontrolled capitalism has come into prominence as a result of the collapse of communism, and Soros is not a Marxist and has full confidence in the capitalist system. He says elsewhere, 'according to market fundamentalism, all social activities and human interactions should be looked at as transactional, contract-based relationships and valued in terms of a single common denominator, money. Activities should be regulated, as far as possible, by nothing more intrusive than the invisible hand of profit-maximizing competition. The incursions of market ideology into fields far outside business and economics are having destructive and demoralizing social effects. A transactional society undermines social values and loosens moral constraints. Social values express a concern for others. They imply that the individual belongs to a community, be it a family, a tribe, a nation, or humankind, whose interests must take precedence over the individual's self-interests. But a transactional market economy is anything but a community. Everybody must look out for his or her own interests and moral scruples can become an encumbrance in a dog-eat-dog world. In a purely transactional society, people who are not weighed down by any considerations for others can move around more easily and are likely to come out ahead.' Capitalist economy by its very nature goes through cycles of booms and busts and never attains an equilibrium state. When it is enlarged to global proportions the variations are bound to become mind boggling and a danger to human civilization in its present state. The control then again comes back to every nation for themselves.

Submission of the state power structure to the transborder flow of money started actually at the end of the last century only a decade after the G8, or the group of eight richest nations, thought of globalization of capital or allowing their huge capital to cross their border and enter other markets and expand. This supra-territorial capitalism cost contemporary states one of the principal marks of sovereignty: namely, complete and exclusive control of the national currency and associated financial markets. For example, globally circulating monies have greatly complicated a state's management of its money supply, exchange rates and interest levels. With volumes on the world's wholesale foreign exchange markets running at $1,230 billion per day in 1995, even the most powerful states could not singly maintain their target exchange rates. Meanwhile, global banking offered ample scope for money laundering, tax evasion and reckless lending. Indeed, laundered money, which in 1995 moved as much as $500 billion per annum through banks in the United States alone, has financed mafia-type organizations that have grown to rival the state in certain districts of Brazil, China, Colombia, Italy, Pakistan, Russia, and Thailand. We know what it has done to our country. Rumour has it that the unaccounted Indian money in foreign banks may be as much as a trillion dollars. It is also rumoured that China has an even larger amount of money in its banks and poses a threat to the US economy. The difference between China and India is that it is non-state money in the case of India, but state money in the case of China. The offshore banking of rich nations and countries like Luxembourg and Lichtenstein have huge volumes of transferred capital from other nations that is overloading them

The US economic meltdown was produced by the greed of the very rich that asked the poor to spend more and provided the money. The poor in the USA are poorer than many other countries and live by forward spending without any savings. But the poor in other countries are worse sufferers as the money was siphoned off from those countries by mechanisms installed that they scarcely understood and they will pose problems through disintegration and revolt and rise in terrorism unless the course is corrected. But India has only a weak role in that correction. It cannot correct the foreign multinationals whose accountability and business ethics in India are much lower than in their countries of origin. India cannot control the greed of its own people not to speak of the foreigner. The government has given no cogent explanation why the sensex rose to 21K and why it fell to 13K before the US meltdown started and then it fell to 8K. What prompted the rise and the initial fall? Then the government was surprised by the economic debacle in USA and Western Europe and the Finance Minister kept on chanting the P/E ratio. It is just pure luck and the intelligence of a few that the debacle pulled the money out of the bourses but could not touch the banks to that extent. But there is no time to relax, the worst is not yet over. The rulers have to have the confidence of the people that they are honest and able to tackle the problems in the nation's interest.

In a short span of ten years at the most, globalized capitalism has completely altered the social structure and social mores of India. The only thing that has saved India so far is the 'instinct of savings' of the Indian poor and middle classes, not the gold of the very rich. Therefore India's pullback can only come from feeding money into that level, the infrastructural level of the *aam aadmi.* If that is helpful for the interim budget of an election year then so be it. After all a nation has to have some luck too. In this country who knows how many Ramalinga Rajus there are in the corporate world? May be the *aam admi* knows instinctively but he is powerless.

2009

Politics of Probabilities

Global politics is a game of probability and flexibility and for India it is total in today's world politics. Until the 9/11 destruction of the World Trade Centre, we were local players. With the rise of global terrorism world conflict is at our doorstep.

Our nation was born in the middle of the Cold War. The British had actively encouraged the creation of Pakistan since the beginning of the Second World War. American support was obtained at a meeting on 1 May 1947, the participants being Jinnah, Mountbatten and the Americans Ronald A. Hare, Head of the South Asia Division of the US Foreign Office and Thomas E. Well, Second Secretary in the US Embassy. There Jinnah emphasized Pakistan's support to US against Russia. Mr. Jinnah, the 'Father of the Pakistan Nation', a minority leader of Muslims before the War, sold the child before it was born! We have bemoaned the partition because of the terrible human suffering it caused in the subcontinent, but sixty years down the line if we think objectively, the creation of Pakistan has buffered us from direct involvement in the Cold War and, apart from the Chinese aggression of 1962, allowed us two decades of relatively peaceful development to enable us to lay the foundation of our human and other resources. The failure of Pakistan to develop as a democratic nation lies in their involvement in the Cold War and has now produced the Taliban. Almost all frontline states in the Cold War have had unstable or autocratic governments. As for China, we should have involved other nations in the problem of Tibet by raising it in the United Nations but we actually prevented it; the debate on the motion raised by El Salvador in the General Assembly was withdrawn at India's request. Standing in Gyantse in front of the Palchoi monastery, the seat of the Panchen Lama, I thought that the Panchen Lama helped China take over Tibet and we gave asylum to the Dalai Lama and the Tibetan government in exile when the world did not care. That may be greatness but not politics. In foreign policy strategy ideology has to be matched with the nation's interest.

Indian communists are rigid in world affairs because of a stagnant ideology that has never risen above national interests in Communist countries. Russia, China and Vietnam have fought bitter wars among themselves. In 1979 China attacked North Vietnam with 600,000 soldiers and 400 tanks from Kunming, Chengdu, Wuhan and Guangzhou Military Regions attacking on three fronts. Some troops in this war, engineering units, railway corps, logistical units and antiaircraft units, had assisted Vietnam in its struggle against the United States just a few years earlier. Vietnamese crack units and border militia fought back leaving huge casualties, much more for the Chinese who retreated with a scorched earth policy burning villages and farmland. Peace came in 1990 as North Vietnam ceded territory to China and threw away its Chinese population to the sea to become the famed 'boat people'. Normal relations were established in 2001. Deng Xiaoping, on a state visit to the USA in 1979, was shown the Chinese troop deployment recorded by spy planes and satellites and acknowledged. Vietnam was attacked because they attacked Khmer Rouge communists in Cambodia, responsible for the most severe genocide in modern history. Three other important events happened in 1979 – the Shah of Iran abdicated, the Egypt-Israeli pact was signed, and Soviet troops entered Afghanistan.

It is the same thing with religion. Those who are blinded by old history are incapable of taking correct decisions. History should provide knowledge, not bias. Let us think, would it have been nice if we had a friendly Pakistan on our western border? The answer is obviously yes. That should make us think if there is anything we can do about it, not now but if such a situation arises. Things change in this world, one should anticipate change.

Who are the Pakistani Taliban? They are mostly Pashtu speaking people residing in the border areas of Pakistan and Afghanistan. They were our friends. Khan Abdul Gaffar Khan, the Badshah Khan or Frontier Gandhi, was a staunch opponent of partition and supported the Congress. Wali Khan, his son, wrote a wonderful history of those years after being in Pakistani jails for years. Pakistan decimated that generation of Khidai Khidmadgars. Later they were also worried about Daoud Khan's intentions for a Pashtunistan or Pakhtoonistan. After the end of the monarchy of King Zahir Shah in Afghanistan in 1973 the Marxist PDPA party gained strength. Zahir Shah's prime minister Daoud Khan captured power. He was assassinated in 1978 and Nur Muhammed Taraki of PDPA became President. The party had many factions, and factional struggle split the party and the attempted social reforms produced rebellion. Taraki was killed and Hafizullah Amin captured power. Rebellion spread due to Amin's zeal to push social reforms. The CIA stepped in with training, arms supply and propaganda against the 'godless' Marxist regime with the aim of dragging the Russian army to their Vietnam. CIA's proxy war through Pakistan, helped by China, succeeded in bringing the Russians into the fray. The Soviet army entered in 1979, a slow trickle at first, progressivly increasing in numbers and force. The mujahideens trained and armed by the USA and helped by ISI and the SSG (Special Services Group) of Pakistan and the enormous dollar aid to Pakistan that inflated the economy and intensified the war forced the Soviet army to retreat back to Russia in 1989. Najibullah's Marxist government survived for a short time and then the mujahideens captured power.

The Afghan and Pathan population are fiercely independent people devoted to Islam but generous and large hearted. The British lost two wars against them and then found it was better to befriend them and through treaties made Afghanistan secure against Russian advance. The Americans used these people against Russia and then forgot them in a land decimated by war. Flourishing orchards became fields for poppy cultivation to produce narcotics to fund terrorism.

During the years of war many Islamic mercenaries, Arabs and Central Asians joined the Afghans – the so called Arab Afghans. One of them was a young Saudi named Osama bin Laden. The Islamists who fought believed that they were responsible for the fall of the Soviet Union. Osama claimed that the credit for 'the collapse of the Soviet Union . . . goes to God and the mujahideen in Afghanistan . . . the US had no mentionable role,' but 'collapse made the US more haughty and arrogant.' This led to the development of a large mercenary force. Osama and al-Zawahiri are creations of the Arab-Israeli conflict. They hated the Egypt-Israel pact. Pakistan has used terrorists over the years to receive aid without developing their own economy. The society has been corrupted by bribe from birth.

We have no role in this conflict but we are getting involved in what is America's creation. We are being advised to be kind to Pakistan so that they can redeploy their army in the east to tackle the Taliban in the west. But that is a hoax, for terrorism is profitable to them. We have never been aggressors. Our programme so far has been only containment of infiltration in Jammu and Kashmir. But the Pakistani Taliban have free access in Pakistan territory and have virtual control over Baluchistan, Peshawar and NWFP. They are progressing in the north and have come to Buner. In the north, near Taxilla, Pakistan has important nuclear installations. That is the urgency in America that prompted the address of Hilary Clinton to Congress; and in immediate reaction Pakistan's rulers 'drove' them away for a couple of billion dollars!

The American push in Afghanistan has pushed the mixed Taliban to the east, and Pakistan is using them to earn money and arms. But that game will not last long or else the structure of terrorism may change with access to the nuclear arsenal. The NATO army has so far succeeded in keeping areas around big cities like Kabul, Kandahar and Herat under control, but for how long? As long as it takes? But it is stimulating fundamentalism. They should be able to lead their life as they like and reform their society. The Karzai government has taken lessons from the past and is slow in pushing reforms. America could have helped development when the Soviets left. They have to somehow do it now. There is already a de facto Pashtunistan in Baluchistan and NWFP. The refugees from Swat valley are the same people as the fighters. Would paying Pakistan help the development of the Pashtu speaking people? If that had happened the whole area today would not have been one united terrorist territory. The social situation on both sides of the Pak-Afghan border is similar and hence the unity. To the American people the people of Asia for a long time have been a faceless multitude. They are not conscious of cultural barriers within and instead of taking advantage of that as the British did as colonial rulers, they break down the barriers by force and unite terrorism. America vaguely considered the possibility of a Pashtu state at one time but was afraid of the Russians getting to the Indian ocean. That fear has gone and now there is the fear of China and greater cohesion with China policy. But they have other options and access from Central Asia. They can find another Ahmad Shah Massoud to prevent that. Very few people know that this Tajik warlord, supporter of western style democracy and used for blocking the Russians, was nominated for the Nobel Peace Prize in 2002 but was assassinated before that could be awarded. In this jigsaw our option is only to sit quiet but watch closely. The British sent 'advisers' to what is now Taliban land and up into Central Asia. Let us hope we also have watchers around and a sensible and able government in Delhi without ideological or religious hang-ups.

2009

Thanks for Saving us from Fatka

As an ordinary citizen of India I have read through the principal parts of the budget of the Hon'ble Sri Pranab Mukherji and some of the media discussions. We the descendants of the Bengali *bhadralok* of the last century saw the last remnants of an arrogant culture of hardly half a century of intellectual and cultural eminence. During this period new words appeared in the Bengali language of which *fatka* is one, meaning speculative financial activity. The Bengali *bhadralok* looked down on that word. Much water has flown down the Hooghly and we have paid dearly for that arrogance. We are not parochial and have always been Indian at heart, but our frivolous sense of superiority to strike out on paths different from others has not been abandoned. Strangely enough in the three decades of Left rule that isolation was even inside the Communist parties bedevilling many issues and preventing Sri Jyoti Basu from becoming the Prime Minister.

The loss of individuality and enterprise and crippling of three generations of students by eliminating English from the major school curriculum impoverished Bengali society both in education and wealth during Left rule. That has forced many to enter *fatka* of different kinds, becoming prey to those who have traditionally controlled those activities. I do not know how common the scenario is in the rest of India of people investing their entire savings, their meagre provident fund and other assets in instruments like Sanchaita, UTI, company deposits, mutual funds pushed up by false bull markets and a few others. No such statewise statistics will ever be available. The need for 'extra money' to survive with rising prices in an inflationary and speculative economy has bedevilled the lives of poor innocent people. It has driven them to corruption that has spread to the grassroots of society.

CAPTIVE POPULATION

The rest of urban India is not aware of the harrowing tales of the middle and lower middle classes, the underemployed, not to speak of marginal villagers in Bengal. This is a captive population who voted the Marxists to power repeatedly, having no alternative and hoping to be looked after, but they increased only in numbers not wealth.

The budget has diverted funds from 'growth economics' to the infrastructure. In a nutshell growth economics meant corporate growth in manufacturing and service industries increasing exports, higher dividends, more FDI, upswing of share prices and the bourses. It is essential for economic growth creating more jobs, stimulating downstream medium and small industries, increasing productivity and employment. By its growth momentum it should spill over to less developed areas like agriculture and agricultural industries, better marketing of produce with higher return to farmers, backward areas and population that were unproductive coming into the growth circle, in short, installing a growth chain. With globalization and market economy, the State's participation in economic activity reduces and people themselves run the economy, the State installing checks and balances through the legal structure. In the short period of relatively open economy we had spectacular growth before the global economic downturn for which the developed countries were responsible. Poor economies were exploited and money stashed in tax havens, and they called it poor governance of global economy when it hit them.

In our case the growth has stalled, exports both of manufactured goods and services have reduced and FDI and FII have dried up. They will not improve unless the global economy improves with revival of consumerism in the west. Will it revive, when and how much?

There is no final prediction, but reading through the small print it is clear that it is very unlikely that they would revive to the original levels. That means exports need to be more competitive in price, quality, diversification and innovation, and that means growth economics will have to look more inwards for market than before – a whole new deal with more competition inside, as the world will not allow a closed market.

What has been the performance of short lived growth in our economy? In short it has been dismal, mischievous and unpatriotic. The amount of Indian money stashed in foreign tax havens is now 1.4 trillion US dollars, roughly Rs.70 lakh crores (*DRC Journal*, July, 2009) by conservative estimates, almost doubling in our short growth period. Much of that money never comes back to India except through dark channels to produce bull run in bourses and drain out more poor man's money with each bear run back to where it came from. This is not considered terrorism against the nation! Some of it is used to buy assets in foreign countries, sometimes even sick industries, to what purpose is not known but definitely of no use to the ordinary Indian.

So the rich do not need low lending rates or tax concession and other incentives. Why cannot they work as FDI and help others downstream, which was the culture of Japan's industrial revival after the Second World War? The government is powerless and unwilling to bring that money back, which is double our GDP in 2007-08, the peak year. The very rich have sold Mother India through the history of the last millennium and ordinary people have fought and died for the country.

INSTRUMENTS FOR INCLUSIVE GROWTH

But we are grateful to that half of the population below any statistics and another thirty per cent above them for not losing our bank deposits, provident fund and life insurance in global downturn. Inclusive growth is a redundant word for growth means inclusive growth. In our country it has to be specified because of the large poor-rich divide. Empowerment at the bottom of the society cannot be achieved by stimulating *fatka* as has been done by two previous governments. Impoverishment of even a small segment of Indian society is a risk to the society, and therefore growth has to be inclusive.

A lot of investment has been done in infrastructure and alleviation of poverty accepting fiscal deficit. The government seems to be considering partial disinvestment. It seems a logical step to help those who helped the country. But would it ever reach the people it is meant for? Experience has shown that the act of governance not only has holes but is actually a shower bath. It has been amply seen in places like Lalgarh and Maoist infested areas, the poor farmers who commit suicide, who have no margin of safety. Just one Ayla cyclone has killed farmers in rice growing areas of West Bengal who lost their Boro crop after taking heavy loans. Crores of rupees given through political jugglery when it was all over is like giving oxygen after the patient is dead. Politicians who are expert at killing or undermining those with political dissent have never known or loved their people. An Italian gentleman loving India was in my car as we drove on a potholed road in Howrah and remarked that such roads would create a revolution in Italy. Most minor roads in urban and semi-urban areas are like that. The people of India tolerate much more, not just roads. Inclusive growth has to be inclusive of politics, for all people and not segments.

FDI AND FII

Foreign money is welcome to any developing country. It was welcomed by Hitler's Germany, Communist Russia and China. All those countries had controlled economy and the money came in a development chain for a longer term commitment and not as a visit to whorehouse through pimps to inflate the bourses and depart, duping a large segment of the middle class and poor population as in our country with poorly controlled economic laws. Foreign institutions get away with violation of laws and principles that is punishable in their country of origin. This budget, at least, has not installed any mechanism to help in that matter, drawing a hue and cry from the capitalists and their mouthpiece organizations, money manipulators and their crony media. It is uncertain how long the government can hold back *fatka* but till then from an ordinary citizen they deserve many thanks.

2009

Epilogue

The Indians through their long history of evolution have been individualistic people. The culture of individualism was established on a philosophical base long before the formation of cities, city states and kingdoms dating probably from the nomadic days of tribal migrations. Thus the philosophic boundaries of Indian-ness and India were formed long before history started and beyond any political or ethnic boundaries even unto the present times. Archaeological and anthropological tracing of ancient history thus leads to a prehistory that dissolves in the enormity of time itself. The earliest treatise on politics, economics and statecraft indicating formation of organized states available to date is the *Arthashastra* by Chanakya Kautilya Vishnugupta – his name indicating that he was the son of Chanaka belonging to kutila gotra having the given name Vishnugupta. Legend has it that he was a Brahmin from the region of today's Kerala, ugly in appearance, who studied in the university at Taxilla, and enraged by an insult from the Nanda King Dhanananda of Pataliputra, was determined to destroy him and trained and helped Chandragupta Maurya to conquer the throne of Pataliputra. He lived in 321 BCE during Chandragupta's ascent to the throne. Those who dispute this on various grounds put the latest date as 150 CE, no later. There is no cogent reason though to disbelieve the legend. That Megasthenes did not mention the name of Chanakya in his book *Indika* might well be because his name was not mentioned in the royal court because he had left after putting Chandragupta on the throne, as the legend states. It is common among scholars, especially the westerners, to question our legends and infinitum, but those legends are what we are made of and the basis of our culture. After Chanakya we have two thousand years of history but before him we have four thousand years of history till the time when sailors from Lothal and adjoining ports sailed to the ancient Sumeria and left their archaeological marks there. Even those ancient times merge in prehistory.

What sort of society was it, for whom Chanakya wrote the *Arthashastra*? He did not write like Bismarck or Machiavelli or Marx. Here I have to quote from L.N. Rangarajan's introduction to his book *Kautilya: The Arthashastra* (1992; Penguin Classics):

'From time immemorial, the great aims of human endeavour (the *purusharthas*) have been classified in India as being four – *dharma, artha, kama* and *moksha,* roughly translated as moral behaviour, wealth, worldly pleasures and salvation. Of these *moksha* has always been held, unanimously and unambiguously, to be the highest ideal to which a human being can aspire. It is not easy to define *moksha;* it is, basically, self-realization through liberation – the liberation from earthly bondage by realizing the divine in the human, the spiritual in the physical and the *Atman* or soul in the mind-body complex. It is the final beatific and timeless state of the enfranchised soul, and it is not possible to achieve it by mere mental processes and literary thought. However the pursuit of the three objectives – *dharma, artha* and *kama* – can contribute to the attainment of *moksha.* Of the three objectives capable of being studied and practised, *dharma* has always occupied the premier place. *Dharma* not only signifies an absolute and immutable concept of righteousness but also includes the idea of duty which every human being owes to oneself, to one's ancestors, to society as a whole and to universal order. *Dharma* is law in its widest sense – spiritual, moral, ethical and temporal. Every individual, whether the ruler or the ruled, is governed by his or her *dharma.* To the extent that society respected *dharma,* society protected itself; to the extent the society offended it, society undermined itself.'

He continues elsewhere, '*Artha* is an all-embracing word with a variety of meanings. In (1.7.6-7) it is used in the sense of material well being; in (15.1.1), livelihood; in (1.4.3), economically productive activity, particularly in agriculture, cattle raising and trade; and in general, wealth as in *Wealth of Nations*. *Arthashastra* is thus 'the science of politics' as it is used in (1.1.1) or (1.4.3). It is the art of government in its widest sense. The subjects covered include: administration, law, order and justice; taxation, revenue and expenditure; foreign policy; defence and war.'

In the *Arthashastra* war or acquiring new territories for colonization is a natural corollary of economic growth and expansion. A ruler should not only look after his treasury or the wealth of the nation of which he is only the guardian but also the wealth and well being of the common man to whom the benefits must flow or else the state will be weakened. In politics and foreign policy Chanakya has been accused of immoral or unethical methods, but in recognition of that necessity he has laid down stringent conditions for pursuing them and always on the practice of *dharma* in its wider sense, and these can be seen in the *Mahabharata*. These methods, when adopted, should be followed by restitution of values or *dharma*. Thus he says, 'The conqueror shall not covet the slain king's land, wealth, sons or wives but give the members of the family their appropriate positions. (7.16.26,27)'

These principles have laid down rules of governance in India for the next two thousand years, and rulers have followed them successfully or unsuccessfully leading to successful or unsuccessful states. This is rooted so deep in the Indian psyche in spite of the admixture of races and religions that it cannot be otherwise The final goal of *moksha* is so individual that the pathways to it, the other three *purusharthas*, got to be partly individualistic, both for the ruler and the ruled. Only a very few will reach or aspire to reach *moksha*, but that individual choice, within limits in the interest of the king and the society, goes down the line to *karma* of creativity in all spheres of activity following the principles of *dharma*. Chanakya has quoted extensively from earlier works of Manu, Brihaspati and the Shukracharya schools of thought and the three Vedas Rg, Sama and Jajuh, collectively called *Trayee* and from *Atharvaveda* and *Mahabharata* to establish his conclusions. 'There are in all one hundred and twelve places in the text where a number of earlier authorities and opinions mentioned by them are mentioned . . . From a number of quotations and references in later works, we know that there were at least four distinct schools and thirteen individual teachers of *Arthashastra* before Kautilya. Unfortunately all the earlier works are lost and Kautilya's is the earliest text that has come down to us.' This was due to the extensive handling of all subjects of statecraft with logical solution for each eventuality that has made this a monumental creation and much of it is universal and relevant even to the present day.

Thus the guiding principles of *Arthashastra* existed well before the times of Chanakya Kautilya. But how far beyond? The origin of the philosophy of four *Purusharthas* is the key and is hidden in timeless antiquity. They are rooted in the Vedas whose exact timing is debated and have developed through later *Puranas* and *Smritis*. Since all these texts were orally transmitted for unknown lengths of time, their exact dating through texts written much later are difficult. But there are archaeological and anthropological evidences of their existence in the earliest Indus Valley civilization. The meditating head of Mohenjodaro is a much later refined example. There are many evidences from Early Harappan times. Archaeological evidence of early Harappan settlements has been found all over the plains of India. The inscribed tablet recovered from the ziggurat at Ur from 4000 BCE shows the commodities brought by Indian sailors as offering to the god in the temple. The list of items shows that they have been procured from all over India as far as Assam. The UNESCO museum on human heritage at Ankara displays extensively artifacts and figurines from the Sumerian and Hittite civilizations that show similar style and expressions as the early Harappans. It has to be mentioned that the four *Purusharthas* – *dharma, artha, kama and moksha* – are not religion-specific but fundamental to man's earthly existence. In India *moksha* has been placed as the ultimate attainable, but achieved by very few, just as very few get Nobel prizes but many dream of and work and innovate, and have created our culture. The difference is that *moksha* is attainable by the ordinary common man without preconditions of education and erudition as much as by the erudite and a common social value base is established. At the end both may reach a stage of apparently lonely life of inner satisfaction and peace like Spinoza. *Arthashastra* prescribes complete honesty that can come only with complete detachment, the combination of a king (*raja*) and sage (*rishi*) but with energy and wisdom in action to those who rule, for a successful kingdom or nation and lays down possible modes and principles of functioning to achieve that. In spite of variable fulfillment of that ideal in kingdoms through the millennia, without the political unity of a nation state the achievements of Indian culture are not mean compared to the few hundred years of western culture after the individual was freed from the restrictions of the Christian Church in the European Renaissance. This actually proves the importance of freeing the individual and indicates the potential of greatness of a united India.

Proper integration of individual freedom and social organization has always been a problem in human society, probably more so in India because of its greater diversity and, especially during the last millennium, from foreign occupation, colonialism, famines, overpopulation, poverty and wrong politics. It has to be reestablished. In one article it has been pointed out that human society can never be organized like a society of bees or ants and that is true for all societies. The force of individual choice through the development of the human brain has been the driving force for thought and innovation in human society. Instead of an organized society as in the gorilla and higher apes the biped hunter gatherer man walked out in search of a different life in the dawn of humanity and they are still walking. The human social organization must allow for individuals to walk out of the beaten path in search of different pathways of body and mind. That is what is embodied in Indian philosophies since antiquity, the choice of the individual to seek his own *karma*. Integration of that desire with social organization has not always succeeded and those periods show social disintegration. Such imbalance occurs in the history of all nations. The two German theories of Fascism and Communism evolved out of a period of German history and in their application severely curbed individual freedom. But democracy can also be tyrannical and has to be guarded against. If we can develop the science and parameters to examine nations and societies from bottom upwards instead of from the top, and use those parameters as indicators to judge societies, both during their periods of growth and decay, the 'bits' may explain the 'it' better as the unit predictors of growth.

Index

Abul Abbas, 47-48
Advertised industrial regeneration, 138
Afghans, 118, 120, 142, 256
Akbar, 101, 103-104
Anglo-Persian Oil Company (APOC), 185
Anti-Semitism, 36, 181
Antiterrorist war, 177
Appeals of Tibet, 228
Arab and Islamic nationalism, 182
Arab tribes, 45
Arab-Israeli conflict, 180, 256
Armed revolution, 153, 156
Arthashastra war, 265
Artificial hills, 19
Aryan theory, 113
Aryan tribes, 113
Asian Development Bank, 210
Asiatic Society, 93, 115
Astronomy, 88, 114, 189
Aswathhama, 61-62
Aurangzeb, 95, 101, 104, 207
Autonomic nervous system, 62
Azmer Sharif Dargah, 95

Babylon, 33, 112, 181
Baglihar Hydel Project, 177
Balfour declaration, 38, 141, 181
Baluchistan, 14, 102, 171, 256-257
Bay of Bengal, 13, 16, 224, 229
Bialystok University, 97
Bioindustry, 56
Biological system, 76
Biosciences, Perspective of, 69
Biotechnology, 82
Black Madonna, 43
Bolshevik Party, 62
Bolshevik revolution, 71, 78
Book of Genesis, 29
Border infiltration, 183
Borobudur hills, 7
British colonial rule, 141
British colonialism, 95
British power, 168
British-owned oil industry, 185
Buddha temples, 21
Buddhism, 21, 90-92, 94, 99-100, 102, 104-105, 113-114, 193, 216, 222
Buddhist king of Ceylon, 27
Builders of Islamic Iran, Alliance of, 188
Business community, 211

Cairo University, 48
Cambodia, 14-16, 18, 224, 234, 254
Cambodian war, 19
Campaign meetings, 144
Capitalism, 82-83, 156, 162, 164, 213, 226, 236
  feudal, 83
  globalized, 252

globalizing, 249
state-sponsored, 161
unbridled, 161, 236
uncontrolled, 250
Capitalist development, 161
Capitalist system, 250
Caspian Sea, 111-113
Caste status, 14
Caste system, 90
Casteist forces, 99
CENTO, 182, 189
Centre-state politics, 159
Chemical weapons technology, 187
Child policy, 234
Chinese and English signboards, 195
Chinese Communist Party, 162
Chinese development, great, 245
Chinese expansionism, 221
Chinese pragmatism, 94
Chinese Revolution, 154
Chinese Trade Union Congress, 231
Christian era, 16, 64
Christian Missionaries, 43
Civil war, 15, 226
Civilized society politics, 84
Cold war politics, 164, 182
Colonial days, 140
Colonial era, 128
Colonial policy, 95
Colonialism, 76, 267
foreign, 105
Communal antagonism, 6
Communism, 156, 161, 163-164, 168, 186, 217, 250, 267
discarded, 164
embraced, 229
rejected, 161
Communist movements, 155, 162
Communist Party of Burma, 229
Communist Party of India, 154
Conflict resolution, 148
Conflict zone, 170
Confucianism, 218
Congress Party, 158, 163
Consumerism, 259
Contemporary society, 116
Conventional arms, 187
Cultural Revolution, 214-215, 226, 230, 244

Dalai Lama, 193-194, 196, 199-202, 227, 254
Danger zones, 137
Day of Atonement, 39
De-Industrialization, 157-159
Democratic Party, 162
Desert Shrine of Hinglaj, 171
Determinism, 78-79
scientific, 78
social, 78
Development of oligarchy, 134
Dialectic conflict, 64
Dinosaur era, 74
Displacement of farmers, 242
Divinity of Christ, 44, 181
Divorce, 43
Dolorosa, 38, 40
Dome, 37, 39-40, 180
Dualism, 54-55, 65

Early Harappan settlements, Archaeological evidence of, 266
East India Company, 115, 139, 167
East Turkistan Islamic Movement (ETIM), 228
Economic analysis, 82
Economic development, 70, 148, 161, 235
Economic empowerment, 184
Economic Prosperity, 118
Economic revolution, 233
Economic theory, 81, 161-162, 241

Education
cost of, 216
free, 214, 231
general, 47, 140-141
liberal, 127
scriptural, 140
Educational standards, 145
El Dorado, 142
Euro-communism, 162
European liberalism, 115
Expansive development, 240
External conflict, 189
Extortion fund, 160

Facultative development, 74
Favouritism, 105
FDI, 259-261
Female divinity, 43-44
Festivity, air of, 39, 180
First World War, 141, 181, 243
Flying carpet days, 96
Foreign power, 105, 123
Fratricidal war, 104
French Revolution, 105, 133
Frontier Gandhi, 169, 255
Fundamentalism, 44, 101, 256

G-20 summit, 147
Gandhar art, 92
General Theory of Relativity, 78
Global Capitalism, Crisis of, 248
Global villages, 241
Globalization of terror, 184
God of dualism, 55
Government-sponsored mutual fund, 138
Greek rule, 33
Guided missile technology, 188
Gulf of Aqaba, 112
Gwadr, Chinese-Pakistani port, 174

Hammurabi Code of Babylon, 25
Han immigration, 228
Hebrew University, 32, 36
Hezbollah, 188
Hill of Evil Counsel, 35, 181
Hindu backlash, 104
Hindu incarnation of God, 102
Hindu liberalism, 116
Hinduism, 4, 21, 95, 99, 102, 116, 129
revived, 94
saved, 114
Hindutva, 141-142, 163
Hinglaj temple, 174
Hinglaj, 102, 171-173
Hippocratic Oath, 24-25
History of humanity, 124, 225
Hitler, 113, 137-138, 156, 225-226, 233-234, 243
Holocaust Museum, 36
Holy hills, 43
House of Honour, 65
Human history, Evolution of, 225
Humanism, 44, 49
Humanistic rationalism, 28
Hundred Years of Troubled Iran, 185

Ibrahim Lodi, 119
Ideological imperialism, 248
Imperialism, 169, 236
India Shining, 142
Indian Bania, 139
Indian Council of Agricultural Research, 159
Indian Democracy, Crisis of, 140
Indian Institute of Management, 126
Indian marriage ceremony, 195
Indian Muslims, 115
Indian outfit of white pyjamas, 47
Indian Philosophy, Conquests of, 86
Indian soil, 105
Individualism, 263

Industrial centres, 244
Industrial commercial area, 174
Industrial development, 155
Industrial revival, 260
Industrial revolution, 72, 158, 242
Industrial society, 232
Industrial zones, 211
Industrialization of Russia, 243
Industrialization, 158, 160, 242-245
Industrialized countries, 62
Industries
  agricultural, 259
  cottage, 3
  heavy, 141, 245
  large, 159
  local, 177
  manufacturing, 245
  mega, 160, 245
  sawmill, 158
  sick, 260
Institute of Computer, 97
Institutions
  democratic, 133
  financial, 247
  foreign, 261
  running, 80
Intellectual development, 86
Intellectual liberalism, 115
Internecine war, 101
Iranian Constitutional Revolution, 185
Islamic fundamentalism, 95
Islamic nationalism, 168
Israeli society, 47
Italian Communist Party, 162

Japanese re-industrialization, 160
Jehangir, 104-105
Jesus Christ, 34, 180-181
Jewish council, 35, 181
Jewish festival of Yom Kippur, 39
Jews, 33-34, 38, 42, 44, 47, 180-182, 243
Jinnah, 148, 169, 253
Jokhang Temple, 194-195
Judaism, 39, 45, 180

Kali temple of Dakshineswar, 116
Kalinga war, 104
Kargil War, 174
Kashmir Shaivism, 6
Kashmir, 102, 118, 171, 175, 177-178, 235, 256
Kautilya, 100, 266
Khan
  Badshah, 255
  Chengiz, 119
  Daoud, 255
  Genghiz, 94, 121, 194
  Gushi, 200
  Khan Abdul Gaffar, 169, 255
  Kublai, 94, 194, 222
  Preah, 19, 21
  Reza, 185
  Wali, 169, 255
Kulen Hills, 18

Land of Canaan, 33, 181
Land reform movements, 159
Land reform, 159
Lenin's theory, 236
Lhasa festival, 195
Lord Shiva, 3, 8-9, 171
Lord Vishnu, 19

Mafia organizations, 251
Magic of Angkor, 13
Mahabharata war, 61
Mahayana Buddhism, 19, 94-95, 216
Maoism, 218
Marginal villagers, 259
Market fundamentalism, 248, 250
Marriage of capitalism, 164

Marxism, 71-72, 76, 78, 80, 82, 129, 151, 155
classical, 129
derogate, 156
embraced, 129
Marxism-Leninism, 72
Marxist communism, 76
Marxist contempt of India, 89
Mass movement, 218
Materialism, 82, 86
dialectical, 76, 81
Mecca, 40, 45, 180
Medium scale industries, 159-160
Mesopotamia, 25, 87-89
Middle Ages, 43-44, 46
Militant trade unionism, 158
Militarism, 83, 161
Military power, 101, 121, 169, 244
Millennium of Darkness, 111
Mock order, 217
Money factor, 148
Money-oriented society, 127
Money-power, 135
Mongol rule of China, 194
Mongol rule, 94
Mongol warlord, 200
Mosque of Umar, 40-41
Mouthpiece organizations, 262
Mughal power, 95
Mughal rule, 95
Mughals, 118, 142
Muhammad Gharry, 119
Multicellular organisms, 73
Multiethnic society, 180
Multilateral society, 115
Multilateralism, 249
Muslim invasion of India, 194
Muslim liberalism, 116
Muslim orthodoxy, 114-116
Mynamati hills, 207
Mysticism, 28
Nationalism, 71, 104, 140, 239
Nawab of Oudh, 95
Naxalite movement, 154
Nazi era, 36
Nazi war machine, 244
Nehru, Jawaharlal, 164, 227
Neoplatonism, 88
Nepal border, 195
Niels Bohr, 65, 89, 97
Nomadic days, 263
Nomadic tribes, 16, 224
Non-aggression treaties, 244
Non-Aligned movement, 183
Non-Brahmin castes, 64
Nuclear power, 121

Old Testament, 45, 180
Operation Ajax, 186
Operation Eagle Claw, 187
Optimism, 176, 249
Organism, 73, 77
biological, 70, 123
human, 25
Origin of Species, 71

Pak-Afghan border, 257
Pakistan High Commissioner, 174
Pakistan Peoples' Party, 176
Palas of Bengal, 101
Peasant movement, 153
Peking University, 229
Political pragmatism, 104
Politics of Probabilities, 253
Polo, Marco, 91
Postmodernism, 86
Potsdam Treaty, 226
Power rivalry, 178
Power vacuum, 168-169
Pragmatism, 44, 133
Prambanan temple, 6
Price of Democracy, 133

Princess of Jodhpur, 95
Princeton University, 55, 90, 124
Prithviraj, 119-120
Prophet Muhammad, 39-40, 45
Protectionism, 147
Provident fund, 258, 260
Psychoanalysis of corrupt politicians, 139
Puja holidays, 96

Quit India movement, 153

Rajmahal hills, 13
Ramadan, 39, 47, 96
Ramakrishna Mission, 65, 129, 208-209
Ramakrishna Order, 124
Ramayana, 5, 17, 20, 63
Ranjit Singh, 167-168
Rationalism, 45
Re-industrialization, 158
Religious
  association, 28
  development, 95
  elements, 28
  liberalism, 93
  movements, 129
  war, 38, 105
Renaissance, 28, 47, 51, 124
Reserve forest, 48
Resettlement of refugees, 158
Romantic heroism, 243
Ruins of Angkor, 15
Russian Revolution Marxism, 71

Sage Ashtavakra, 106
Saraswati river system, 89
Saraswati river, 89-90
Sargon of Akkad, 87
Scheduled castes, 173
Scientific development, 46
Second Gulf War, 190
Second World War, 148, 153, 158, 161, 168, 182, 225, 233, 243, 253, 260
Secularism, 99-100, 148
Semitic religions, 44-45, 51, 180, 182
Sensual pleasure, commercialization of, 127
Serindian art, 91
Shah of Iran, 254
Shaivite schools of India, 21
Shillong Math and Mission, 208
Shunzhi Emperor of China, 200
Siem Reap River, 18-19
Sikhism, 129
Sino-Japanese war, 225
Sixth Dalai Lama, 199-200, 202
Social Democratic party, 163
Social organizations, 221, 241, 267
Social ostracism, 104
Social reforms, 255
Socialism, 82-83, 161, 163-164, 186, 210, 226, 230
Society of bees, 70, 267
Socio-intellectual movement, 100
Solomon's Temple, 33, 36, 180-181
South China, 14, 224
Soviet Union, 81, 162, 182, 203, 234, 243, 256
Special Services Group, 255
Spinoza, 54, 63, 86, 267
Splintering of parties, 148
Sri Ramakrishna, 64, 125-126
St Francis, 36, 49
State capitalism, 161
Sufi saints of Persia and India, 45
Sufi saints, 45-46, 95
Sufism, 95
Sultanate of Bahmani, 119
Sumatra, 14
Surgical operation, 26
Surplus manpower, 242
Sushruta Samhita, 25-26

Sweden, 114, 248-249
Tajik warlord, 257

Taoism, 105, 222
Tax
  concession, 260
  evasion, 251
  exemptions, 138
  havens, 259
Taxation, 265
Taxilla, 104, 256, 263
Temple-mosque, 107
Terrorism, 127, 144, 147, 169, 251, 256, 260
  global, 146
Theory of Relativity, 53, 58, 61, 78
Theravada Buddhism, 17, 22
Third Buddhist Council, 100
Tibetan border, 227
Tibetan Buddhism, 193
Tonle Sap Lake, 18-19
Total tax holiday, 138
Tower Museum, 37
Trade union movements, 242
Transborder accumulation, 249
Tribal days, 17
Trinity of Creation, 6

Ukraine, 243-244
UNESCO museum, 266
Unethical methods, 265
Unicellular organism, 55, 73
Union of Myanmar, 210
Unit Trust, 138, 145
Upanishads, 5, 17, 59, 64-65, 89-90, 124, 222

Valley of Kidron, 35
Vedanta philosophy, 88-89, 94-95
Vedanta, 4, 46, 54-55, 88, 107, 116, 174
Vietnam, 14, 19, 21, 234, 254-255
Violent regionalism, 83
Virgin Mary, 43
Vivekananda, 124-125, 128, 139
Vote machinery, 127
Votes, preferential, 84

Warring tribes, 210
Western Wall, 38, 41, 180-181
Wheeler, John, 55, 65, 89, 97, 124
World Trade Centre, 253

Xingjian Uighur Autonomous Region (XUAR), 228
Xinjiang Production and Construction Corps (XPCC), 228

Zhou dynasty, 221